2 5

The Springs of Adventure

The
Springs
of Adventure

WILFRID NOYCE

John Murray

FIFTY ALBEMARLE STREET

LONDON

*Πολλὰ τὰ δεινὰ κοὐδὲν ἀνθρώπου
δεινότερον πέλει*

Many things are strange
none stranger than man
SOPHOCLES

FOR

MICHAEL

Contents

Illustrations

❦ ❦ ❦ ❧ ❧ ❧

Illustrations

Illustrations

Preface

Some prefaces are informative, a necessary part of the story. I had thought that mine should be of that sort; but as I began to tie up ends, to wrap the parcel, as it were, in brown paper and string for a public, I realised that I could not add anything—or I must add too much. It was not till I came to compile a bibliography that I realised both how much I had quoted and how much remained to quote. Any writer, I think, who tries to survey, from whatever angle, the human adventure on and around this planet must be painfully conscious of both these factors in his work. And his first thought, as he writes his preface, will be of regret and apology for much that is excellent, much that would have just served his purpose, much that he has, let us face it, left out simply because it happened not to come his way.

His next feeling will be of gratitude to all those doers of deeds and writers of words who have eased his task, indeed have made it possible by giving an insight into their type of adventure. I have expressed that gratitude more specifically at the end of this book, before the bibliography. But I would here like to add a word of thanks, which is not so out of place as it may seem, to those numerous cheap editions which make some of the great stories accessible to others than the recondite reader; many of my adventures would never have come my way without them.

In preparing the text I have warmly to thank the House of Murray for its encouragement, advice and practical assistance throughout; Mrs D. Middleton, John Johnson and A. C. Pigou for critical and constructive suggestions; the Royal Geographical Society for advice and facilities; David Cox for suggestions incorporated in Chapter Nine;

Preface

Mrs Irving Bell for a gift of books on the Antarctic; the Godalming Branch of the Surrey County Library for researches undertaken on my behalf; and Mrs M. H. Ryder for proof-reading and an invaluable Index.

The pictures are not designed to instruct, but to amuse and to lighten the reading. They are impressions, simply, of action in some of the environments described. Here I have much to acknowledge, and to the details given in the list of illustrations would like to add my thanks for all the help I have received and the trouble so willingly taken.

WILFRID NOYCE

Godalming, 1958

The search for the springs

No man but a blockhead ever wrote except for money.
SAMUEL JOHNSON

What am I up to? And why, apart from Dr Johnson's admirable reason, am I trying to write this book about the impulses commonly grouped under the word 'adventurous'?

One day a friend, who was a mountaineer, after reading an article on 'Why I climb', threw down the paper in disgust exclaiming: 'What rubbish!' (The expression was stronger, but that will do.) 'I climb because I like it. Isn't that enough?' Of course it is, for most, and equally of course the great majority of climbers, divers, cavers and other suchlike cranks would give no more than that answer, if asked why they pursued their favourite madness. But the answer never really satisfied me; at least it left me with an uneasy sense that it was too easy. And slowly, last year, I began to realise why I must try to amplify and examine it on paper. I wonder if I can convey what I felt.

More than other music, I like listening to Mozart's, for the pleasure of it. And I worry no more than that about the delight I get from listening. But I also like having it explained to me, if anyone is willing to take the trouble. This is another side of me, the enquiring; and if that side exists in *me*, who am in general a most unenquiring person, how much more must it be present in many others among my fellows! It does most of us good to ask why, just sometimes; and at no time, perhaps, does it do more good than when we question what lies behind things that we ourselves have been doing for a long time without much thought. Like Monsieur Jourdain we wake up one day to the fact that we have been talking prose for forty years, and find the knowledge stimulating. If I had been climbing mountains since I was eight, and seldom really stopped to consider what I was doing or why I did it, it might be, I thought, that through this book I would solve some of my own queries by looking at those that face the balloonist, the flier, the Arctic explorer. And they, even if they disapproved of my book, might find some of their own solved by the mountaineers.

At this point I went off to a dictionary, to see if I could find a formula which would cover us all. I found this: '*Adventure:* an enterprise in which hazard or risk is incurred; a novel or unexpected incident.' I shut the dictionary. That covered a good deal too much; I must begin the pruning-down process straight away. Being held up by a gangster, an 'unexpected incident' if you like, ranks under that definition as an adventure. I must begin by asserting that all mine are self-chosen, thereby ruling out, incidentally, most war adventures. And then—do *all* adventures involve risk? I think not. And should not the word 'novel' go with the word 'enterprise'? Many people do daily jobs involving a certain risk, but these are not usually classed as adventures, and the motive is usually money. It looked as if I must do my own rearranging.

In the end I hacked out a definition of the sort of adventure I meant to consider. It ran something like this: 'A novel enterprise undertaken for its own sake.' That had at least the advantage of brevity; there was not so much of it to quarrel with. The word 'novel', some would say, ought to be changed to 'new', and in the bold days of my boyhood I would have agreed. But that, I think now, would be going too far. You will find that most of the exploits quoted in this book are 'first time done'—but by no means all. A thing can still be a novel adventure if others have done it before, and an adventure even if you yourself did it, in different circumstances at a different time. We change day by day; and sometimes look back on our earlier actions with a feeling close to amazement, as if we had been somebody else. To do the same thing again, therefore, can be a novel, exciting, adventurous enterprise.

> Never will
> My heart so beat again at sight
> Of any hill, although as fair
> And loftier . . .

Edward Thomas wrote, and it is true. To go back to the hills of childhood or the seas where once we sailed, this has a thrill about it equalled by no other. It is adventure, but adventure of a mellower brand, like an old wine to which a man returns when he is tired of the headier new vintages. Let us keep 'novel' therefore, and strike out 'new'.

What of 'for its own sake'? Here the men of science, the men of religion, the men of commerce, all of whom figure in these pages, may well raise angry eyebrows. Is a thing not adventurous if it is done in the name of scientific study, of missionary progress, of human prosperity? It certainly is. But I submit that if it is done with *nothing* but these in view, it will not be a through and through adventure in my sense. The Commonwealth Transantarctic Expedition went out, as any member of it will tell you, not just to map the polar plateau, find coal or measure the ice cap; but to cross a great continent *which had never been crossed before*. They hoped to realise Shackleton's dream, and Shackleton was not a scientist. In so far as this is its object, the expedition is an adventure first and a piece of scientific research second, if very importantly. I would like to, but dare not, go so far as the splendid paradox of G. K. Chesterton: 'I think the immense act has something about it human and excusable; and when I endeavour to analyse the reason for this feeling I find it to lie, not in the fact that the thing was big or bold or successful, but in the fact that the thing was perfectly useless to everybody, including the person who did it.'

What then of whaling, and those kindred occupations of a commercial kind which stand waiting their inclusion? *They*

3

were not 'perfectly useless'. No, but neither were those I have included 'perfectly commercial'. Who will forget Ahab, immortal captain of Melville's *Pequod*, who cried out 'What is it, what nameless, inscrutable, unearthly thing is it?' that drove him on in search of Moby Dick. Moby Dick killed Ahab and his crew besides; but there is something of the fierce hunt for its own sake even in modern whaling, with its explosives and mechanical butcheries. Adventure lurks here in a way strangely unconnected with commercial profit.[1]

Perhaps this is because part of the adventure is itself mechanical and even, in its broadest sense, intellectual. That is how I read the whale biologist Ommanney. But when I came up against pure intellectual adventure, divorced even from whales, I found that I must do one of the biggest of all my prunings. I could not allow it, though logically I should. 'Enterprise' in my definition rather implied physical enterprise, in which human bodies are involved. But I had to admit that intellectual adventure could be equally, if not more, arduous.

> Those Himalayas of the mind
> Are not so easily possessed:
> There's more than precipice and storm
> Between you and your Everest,

as Day Lewis has it. Therefore, logically, I ought to include them. But I am sorry, there just is not room. Galileo halting in amazement before the idea of earth's movement, Harvey at the circulation of the blood, Watt by the kettle or the Impressionists jubilant at the new visual world opened before them: all these, I will admit, were adventurers not moved primarily, if at all, by the prospect of fame or money, which they seldom got and regretted if they did, nor even by the thought of helping suffering humanity. They did what they did, in the teeth of fierce opposition, 'for its own sake'. They

[1] There are of course many other motives, as suggested later, and at the end of R. B. Robertson's *Of Whales and Men* his whaler's wife gives the curious one of sympathy between whaler and 'outcast' whale.

were adventurers, 'voyaging o'er strange seas of thought'—most often alone.

Still, I must cut them ruthlessly out, or I would be writing a History of Human Endeavour. I must confine myself to physical adventure, on land and sea or in the air. Like Browning's butterfly, I shall hover between all three, with 'Heaven above, sea under, but always earth in sight'. And I shall draw myself one other partly imaginary line. If I wrote of all adventure, even physical, I would have to start with the Egyptians or before. For reasons which I hope will slowly become apparent I take the end of the eighteenth and beginning of the nineteenth centuries as the time when the idea of adventure 'for its own sake' crystallised in the minds of men; when they began to stop regarding more material motives as a necessary justification. That does not mean that the great earlier names will not be mentioned; they go on living, in that very change of attitude which they helped to bring about. But I cannot spread my emphasis too far without the risk of losing it altogether.

❧ ☙   ❧ ☙   ❧ ☙

Already, it will be seen, I am pruning and pruning, fining down on 'Adventure' among all the multiple senses in which the poor word has been used or misused in the past. I wish there were a substitute; but there is none, which both means all that I want it to mean, and is also understandable at a glance. The best I can do is to cut out of my mind's eye all the wrong uses and forget most of the films whose titles have contained the word. That helps a little.

To assist myself I have adopted a novel arrangement of chapters. I have not taken flying, climbing, sailing, and so on, as separate sections and dealt with each. I have arranged chapters by the motives behind, which may be the same for a flier, for instance, as for a sailor. A. E. Clouston became a famous pilot, though he had wanted to be a sailor and had to

B

give it up because he was always sea-sick. Shackleton joined an Antarctic expedition in 1900, but at that time he might just as well have joined any other type of expedition, and made for himself a different name. And so on. But the motives which compelled, say, Shackleton and Wilson to the same adventure were largely different. It is by these motives that you will find the chapters arranged, the men divided.

This arrangement has other advantages. If I took each type of adventure separately I would feel some obligation to give a comprehensive view of it: a feat neither within my powers nor conducive to a manageable book. What I am trying to write is an essay on adventure, the thing seen through the eyes of an explorer of one type; an essay, not a history. And if ever I slip into the pontifical Noyce, laying down laws biological or historical, then for that I offer apology in advance. I do not mean to.

I have quoted widely, as I admit, but I have tried not to conjure up so many names that it is impossible to say anything about each, or put him or her as a person before the reader. When the latter must needs in any case flick from gliding to caving, ballooning to rock climbing, he has every right to be spared the ordeal of a dazzling galaxy of faces besides. In order to spare him, I thought it easiest to treat of people who are well known, as they need less wordy introduction. Unfortunately, however, the great are not always quotable, nor demonstrative of points that I want to bring out. Shackleton was as great a figure as Scott, perhaps greater, but he appears less here because he is less explicit in his writing. Despite my resolutions, therefore, some great names hardly appear at all; while others less known occupy their place. And I have been aware besides that one man does not prove a point, nor even establish a probability. Often I have had to strike a balance between expansion at the expense of clarity, and clarity at the expense of supporting evidence. A nice problem.

Time and again, in the course of writing, I have decided

that the whole thing was bunk and that the mountaineering friend was right. These things are done 'for the fun of it'. Why make further fuss? Surely my impulse to analyse and split into compartments, unusual (and therefore suspicious) as it is in me, was beside the point. For obviously, just as the same motive occurs in many very different people, so the same person can be moved by a positive assortment of motives, in differing proportions through the years. The thing is a jumble, and is it not best left as one?

But strangely, as I went on, I found that once I had accepted my artificial divisions, with their artificially general terms like 'escapist' and 'conqueror', it was surprising how many people fitted, with a bit of squeezing, into them; and that as one can accept the conventions of a stage in a theatre and pretend to see real life, so readers might be prepared for the time being to accept my conventions and then at the end forget them, standing back to see one side of life in a different aspect, but as a whole.

When I was a boy, I thought that if I toughened myself, slept out, climbed hard, and was out in all weathers, I could make of myself a human being impregnable in the face of 'nature'; be master of the relationship, as it were. There followed a good deal of frantic effort and unromantic frustration. Now I think differently. If I am careful, if I do things at the right time, I can perhaps establish a delicate balance at certain seasons. Not more. And what I do in them depends rather on what circumstance allows me than on how I act, provided that I act up to the best that in me is.

That, I think, is the experience of many of the adventurers in these pages, and I have curiously the same feeling as I present this book. At one time I might have thought that, given the leisure, I could treat the whole subject from all its angles. Now I know that the best I can do is to give you a certain approach to it, a balance of certain types which I label 'Livingstone' or 'Wilson' or 'Saint-Exupéry'; establish a certain contact with the theme, as one does with nature. And

7

then hope that when you have read the book (just as you did when you had climbed the mountain), you will sit back and close your eyes, and for a moment feel that something has been revealed, through the multiple experience of many people, which, for the pleasure of seeing it now, you are glad not to have seen before.

To get that something people go out and do strange things. To get a similar something from a book, we are going out to consider some of the men and women who do them. And the first I would ask you to look at is the man who does them for the paradoxical reason that they are unpleasant; the man who likes doing a thing because he does not like it; the man whose ancestor found satisfaction in wearing a hair-shirt next to his skin.

2

❧ ❧ ❧ ☙ ☙ ☙

The hair-shirt

The discipline of suffering—of great suffering, know ye not that it is only this discipline that has produced all the elevation of humanity?

NIETZSCHE

That new vision of the world won through hardship. . . .

SAINT-EXUPÉRY

'Polar exploration is at once the cleanest and most isolated way of having a bad time which has been devised.' With these words Apsley Cherry-Garrard starts his story of *The Worst Journey in the World*. And yet there are, at the time of writing, quite a number of people on the South Polar continent voluntarily exposing themselves to a bad time—not so bad, perhaps, as that of 1911–12, for science has been busy since then, but bad enough by most standards. To see why people choose these things, it is worth considering just how bad a chosen bad time can be.

There is an embarrassing wealth of examples, with polar exploration, as one would expect, well to the fore. Intense hardship was endured by the earliest expeditions; scurvy and poisoning racked the stomach, cold tore through the primitive sleeping bags, tents and clothing. A lot of this is passed over in silence, or pathetically easy to read between the lines. But by the time we come to Scott we find the most unendurable conditions endured, even accepted cheerfully by men like Bowers, and their horrors colourfully described. Here is the Winter Journey, undertaken by Wilson, Bowers and Cherry-Garrard through the Antarctic night to obtain embryos of the Emperor

9

penguin from Cape Crozier. A nightmare expedition of five weeks.

> The horror of the nineteen days it took us to travel from Cape Evans to Cape Crozier would have to be re-experienced to be appreciated; and anyone would be a fool who went again; it is not possible to describe it . . . It was the darkness that did it. I don't believe minus seventy temperatures would be bad in daylight, not comparatively bad, when you could see where you were going, where you were stepping, where the sledge straps were, the cooker, the primus, the food . . . could read a compass without striking three or four boxes to find one dry match; could read your watch to see if the blissful moment of getting out of your bag was come without groping in the snow all about; when it would not take you five minutes to lash up the door of the tent and five hours to get started.
>
> But in these days we were never less than four hours from the moment when Bill cried 'Time to get up' to the time when we got into our harness. It took two men to get one man into his harness, and was all they could do, for the canvas was frozen and our clothes were frozen until sometimes not even two men could bend them into the required shape.[1]

The temperature dropped to 77·5 degrees below zero (109½ degrees of frost). After terrible escapes and obstacles, they had got three eggs and managed to build an igloo. Then, first their tent was blown bodily away (it was recovered later by a miracle), then the igloo roof torn off, although it was held down by large snow blocks. They lay in the open, drifted over with snow, without a meal for over thirty-six hours. 'The journey had beggared our language: no words could express its horror.'[2]

How many instances jostle for record, of cold pain endured more or less voluntarily! Scott's southern, man-hauling journey from the *Discovery*, when Shackleton nearly died of scurvy; the privations of Campbell's party which spent a whole winter cut off in an igloo at Evans Cove. 'How

---

[1] Cherry-Garrard, *The Worst Journey in the World.*   [2] Ibid.

Campbell's party ever lived through what they did I don't know', Edward Evans (later Lord Mountevans) wrote after seeing the igloo. 'No cell prisoners ever had such discomforts.'[3] Or there was Admiral Byrd, over four months alone at a meteorological post in 1934, and sometimes too weak to eat. Once he found himself outside, unable to get in.

> There is something extravagantly insensate about an Antarctic blizzard at night. Its vindictiveness cannot be measured on an anemometer sheet. It is more than just wind: it is a solid wall of snow moving at gale force, pounding like surf. The whole malevolent rush is concentrated upon you as upon a personal enemy. In the senseless explosion of sound you are reduced to a crawling thing on the margin of a disintegrating world; you can't see, you can't hear, you can hardly move.[4]

Moving north to the Arctic we find, from the scurvy-ridden days onward, men in every uncomfortable attitude you could devise. The men of Nansen's period and before tend to be reticent. Moderns are more talkative. In 1930–1 Augustine Courtauld doomed himself to a winter's imprisonment on the Greenland Ice Cap. There was not enough food for two, and he had to wait till May before he could be rescued by Watkins. In his diary are entries like the following:

> *March 22.* . . . I cannot now raise the box, so I am completely buried. Paraffin has very nearly run out and things generally are pretty dismal . . .

> *April 5.* Now been here alone four months. No sign of relief. Only about a cupful of paraffin left and one or two candles. Have to lie in darkness almost all the time. Chocolate finished and tobacco almost . . .[5]

As for his would-be rescuers, they were agreed that the only moment in winter sledging that is 'any good' is supper-time. One of them, Martin Lindsay, wrote of a night on the Ice

---

[3] Lord Mountevans, *South with Scott.*

[4] R. E. Byrd, *Alone.* 'I really wanted to go for the experience's sake,' Byrd had said.

[5] J. M. Scott, *Portrait of an Ice Cap.*

Cap two years later: 'The second night was sheer unmitigated hell from start to finish. For ten hours we went through the worst kind of human misery.'[6]

The Poles are a calculated hazard because you know that blizzard and minus temperatures are to be your fairly monotonous meat. Mountains, sea and air are all more femininely variable. They can be kind, indeed there are days when it seems that they could never be otherwise. Then, suddenly, out of the blue, they strike. In 1953 a ten-day storm confined the Americans at a camp above 25,000 feet on K2, and Charles Houston wrote: 'Can such an ordeal be remotely conceived as "pleasure" or "sport"? Are we masochists to enjoy such a battering, such cold, such wind, lack of food, lack of sleep, lack of water?'[7]

The storms of Nanga Parbat caught the 1934 German expedition on the long ridge and drove them back, killing them off almost one by one as they descended. At sea, for centuries mariners have been shaken and smashed by the big seas of Cape Horn and the Magellan Straits. Or when they choose their peril, as now they do, lone sailors of the Atlantic (becoming fairly frequent these days) are kept for days sleepless and drenched. Like Gerbault, the first man to cross nonstop direct from east to west, they go 'tossing like a cork on the crest of the waves and fighting for life against hurricanes that buried my little boat under tons of green water and tore her sails to ribbons'.[8]

There is in all these forms of physical enterprise a certainty, accepted consciously, that you will have to suffer, and a possibility, to be discussed later, that you may have to die. Apart from which there is usually an acceptance of sheer physical strain. Joshua Slocum, the first man to sail alone round the world, fought four days of continuous storm as he came out of the Straits of Magellan. Gerbault spent seventeen and eighteen hours at the tiller, sometimes steering with his

[6] *Three got Through.* [7] *K2 The Savage Mountain.*
[8] *The Fight of the Firecrest.*

feet so that he could repair sails. African explorers like Mungo Park walked until they dropped from thirst, or Sven Hedin endured without water four days in the Takla Makan desert. Shackleton faced sixteen days almost without sleep in his small boat, the clothes which were drenched by day being frozen at night, on the last stage of his journey from the crushed *Endurance*. Or Hermann Buhl made, with the help only of drugs, his astonishing lone ascent of about 4,000 feet to the summit of Nanga Parbat.[9] Men know that they may have to face these things, when they go out.

❧ ❧   ❧ ❧   ❧ ❧

Why do they do it? Of course you can maintain that much of this hardship was endured in the cause of science. People measure ice caps, collect Emperor penguins' eggs, and even sit under the snow for months in order to add to the sum of the world's meteorological knowledge. But that seems to me only very partially the answer. I think that the reasons are many, and that one of them is simply that it is part of the human make-up to want to 'prove' yourself, to show yourself that you can do something you thought impossible, to wear a hair-shirt. Byrd was not primarily a scientist; Bowers was a naval officer, but he went on the penguins' egg journey. He was tough and enjoyed being tough, and if asked he would probably have said that he went 'for the fun of the thing'. But if you take it one further, you may conclude that his kind of controlled toughness stems out of the pleasure one gets from proving and hence mastering one's faculties. Moreover, by mastering and toughening himself so that he can extend his limits far beyond what he believed possible, a man has at the back of his mind also the feeling that he is on the way to

[9] Coming down: 'I was staggering like a drunkard, falling, crawling, standing, walking, falling again . . . then I remembered the Pervitin again. It was the only chance; its brief renewal of my strength might last long enough for me to get down to the tent.' *Nanga Parbat Pilgrimage*.

mastering the world. There will be 'nothing that he cannot do'.

Not everybody is taken that way. Most would prefer life at Claridge's to spending four months without changing their clothes. But the longing to travel far, using the road of self-mastery, is as natural, if you come to think of it, as the desire, which some have and some not, to dress well. If you possess a high-powered Jaguar you like to feel that you can control it with a touch; that there are no obstacles it cannot take—or at any rate that it can take far more than your neighbour's M.G. In the same way some of us like to feel that we are as much master of our own body and mind as we are of our tools.

To take two cases of this 'self-control' side of a man. The great explorer, H. M. Stanley, was a Welsh orphan named Rowlands who ran away from a St Asaph workhouse. Adopted by Henry Stanley and now a well-known journalist in America with big scoops to his credit, he was still shy and acutely sensitive to English gossip about his birth. Yet he was supremely confident that he would prove himself. Almost on the eve of his expedition to find Livingstone for the *New York Herald* (1871), he said to a friend:

> I mean, by attention to my business, by self-denial, by indefatigable energy, to become, by this very business, my own master and that of others . . . Pleasure cannot bind me, cannot lead me astray from the path I have chalked out. I am so much my own master, that I am master over my own passions . . . I have nothing to fall back upon but energy and much hopefulness.[10]

If anyone ever proved himself by this means, Stanley did. He seemed to delight in hardships which killed his two white companions, and compelled him to chain his native porters together by the neck, for fear they would run away. After disaster on disaster he reached Livingstone, of whom little

[10] Quoted by A. J. A. Symons in *H. M. Stanley*.

had been heard for years. On his second journey (1874–7) he lost his three companions through fever before he got down the Congo in canoes. And when, two years later, he returned upstream by steamer to found what later became the Belgian Congo, he had indeed conquered through pain. 'Sun, stream, crocodiles, cataracts, forests and mountains, he had conquered them all. His will had overruled everything, even the fevers so fatal to his comrades.'[11] Or so it seemed. He was master of himself, and seemingly that of his world.

Robert Falcon Scott stands out as another of the great self-provers: a man bound to figure largely in any book on adventure, but assumed by most to be a fairly straightforward character. He was not. Like many doers of great deeds, like his friend Edward Wilson and the American Lincoln Ellsworth, he started physically frail. That needed conquering, and by the time he led the Discovery expedition in 1900 he must have been as tough as anyone on the party. Here is the Southern journey, undertaken with scientific objectives but prolonged into self-mortification; a journey which laid out the young Shackleton with scurvy and ended with the two previous invalids dragging him home on the sledge.

> Reading between the lines, one perceives that this was nothing but a voluntary exile of three months' hard labour, in which extreme discomfort was the only relief to excessive toil, and toil the only mitigation of discomfort. It is this pitting of the last resources of human energy against stern circumstance that constitutes the 'fascination' of polar exploration.[12]

Spring sledging is like that; almost as bad as winter, and always the hauling, hauling, hauling, over surfaces that will not slide. He flogged himself physically. 'Even a blizzard had its silver lining' one of the polar party said, when he drove them on that extra hour of the evening before stopping.

But he had a bigger problem than physical weakness. I

---

[11] Ibid.   [12] G. Seaver, *Edward Wilson of the Antarctic.*

used to think of him as the tough, bluff sailor who took to command as a duck to water. He was not. Turn from biographies to a page of Cherry-Garrard:

> Scott was the strongest combination of a strong man in a strong body that I have ever known. And this because he was so weak! Naturally so peevish, highly strung, irritable, depressed and moody. Practically such a conquest of himself, such vitality, such push and determination, and withal in himself such personal and magnetic charm . . . His triumphs are many —but the Pole was not by any means the greatest of them. Surely the greatest was that he conquered his weaker self and became the strong leader whom we went to follow and came to love.[13]

It was because he had conquered himself that he stood out, even among the members of that expedition.

᠎᠎᠎

In Scott, as in many other explorers, there may be more than a streak of the ascetic—the Flagellant of the Middle Ages, for example. A man who goes up and down the country lashing himself must seem to the Rational Man to have no enjoyment in life other than that of not enjoying himself. Similarly, unless he sympathises with the motive of self-control behind, the Rational Man finds very odd this perverse habit that some people have of getting themselves to unpleasant places. Only one who accepts something of the ascetic position could tolerate polar exploration, or for that matter the rounding of the Horn in a sailing ship ('No land; no sun; no other ships; no peace' as Alan Villiers describes it) or three days sleepless in a small open boat. It is not rational.

The Flagellant was not, perhaps, rational, but he had something in him more compelling than reason. He was repenting for early luxury, for one thing, and though they do

---

[13] *The Worst Journey in the World.*

not put it quite like that, there is something of that idea in more modern wearers of the hair-shirt. 'Perhaps the comfort and luxury of early youth now asks for the counter-irritant of the plain life of a sailor with all its risks and adventure,' Gerbault said, about his own inexplicable urge to sail the Atlantic. And there is also a curious, almost scientific pleasure in seeing just how far one can stand a thing. It is nothing new, any more than is the fact that of all painful lashes the hardest to bear is separation from the beloved.

It was part of the discipline of the medieval ascetic to cut himself off from home and family. It is also part of the discipline of adventure. Renunciation of the world, its pleasures and ease; above all the intercourse of a wife, the soft delights of children. It has always been a painful business, and there are some heartrending cries from the bereaved. 'The act of orphanising my children, which now becomes painfully near, will be like tearing out my bowels, for they will all forget me,' Livingstone wrote in a letter in 1852. His was a sad family. It may be accepted, as R. Coupland wrote, that 'an explorer's life meant more to him than the break-up of the family', but the break-up was deeply painful for all that. From then on Livingstone had no family life; and when, ten years later, his wife came out to join him as the only way to achieve it, she was dead of disease in three months. However true it may be that he was happiest among Africans, his wife's death as the price of renunciation was a pill that even the savour of exploration could barely sweeten.

Another explorer, Fridjof Nansen of Norway, wrote: 'For the last time I left my home . . . Behind me lay all I held dear in life. And what before me? How many years would pass ere I should see it again?'[14] He was setting off in 1893, in the teeth of informed opposition, to prove that a ship properly built can ride up on the northern ice and not be crushed. From the ice-bound *Fram* he was to make a great journey on foot towards the North Pole.

[14] *Farthest North*, vol. I.

After he had left home, when he was cruising up the Norwegian coast, the sadness of the thing came upon him.

> Ah! those snug homes in the lee of the skerries awake a longing for life and warmth in the breast . . . It is a fine thing for a people to have a fair land, be it never so poor. Never did this seem clearer to me than now, when I was leaving it.[15]

'Both sexually and socially the polar explorer must make up his mind to be starved', as Cherry-Garrard put it, and to decide on starvation is no light matter. But once the decision is taken, as the passage from Nansen indicates, a quite new charm comes stealing in: the charm found in a deeper appreciation of the worth of what one is leaving, and therefore of the worthwhileness of what one is about to do. It is a pleasure all the keener for the bitter-sweetness of its taste, and one worth seeking out. A man leaves London for Greenland, and this is what he feels:

> I walked very slowly down Piccadilly, sniffing the air and savouring the spirit of wonderful London . . . To feel the very core of your beliefs and to appreciate your heritage in a way you have never done before, you must be alone in the streets of London at night, on the eve of a long absence abroad. I know of no keener emotion, for it is to me a very solemn and sacred moment—that prelude to departure.[16]

London means more to him than to many who have never left it.

For the flier, too, separation can be a bitter business, in a different way. He is not absent for so long; but during his absences even his heart must be as abstracted as a monk's. It is relevant that Saint-Exupéry the flier refers to monks, when reasoning of why a man enters aviation.

> The reason is hard to formulate. A novice taking orders could appreciate this ascension towards the essence of things, since his profession too is one of renunciation: he renounces the world; he renounces riches; he renounces the love of woman. And by renunciation he discovers his hidden god.[17]

[15] Ibid. [16] M. Lindsay, *Three got Through.*
[17] *Wind, Sand and Stars.*

That hidden god is so difficult for a wife to understand—and not unnaturally! Here is one, in a novel, who is to lose her husband in the sky:

> She thought of all a man must lay aside to conquer. 'So you don't like your home?'
> 'I do like my home.'
> But his wife knew that he was already on his way and even now his sturdy shoulders were pressing against the sky.
> 'I know how strong you are, but—do take care!'
> 'Of course I'll take care.'
> He shut the door behind him and, passing amongst the indistinguishable folk of the night, took the first step towards his conquests.[18]

Later, she knows within herself that he is dead in the storm, and goes to see his boss. But Rivière cannot comfort her, deeply though he feels,

> for action and individual happiness have no truck with each other; they are eternally at war. This woman, too, was championing a self-coherent world with its own rights and duties, that world where a lamp shines at nightfall on the table, flesh calls to mated flesh, a homely world of love and hopes and memories. She stood up for that happiness and was right.[19]

Yes, she had a right to him, but the adventure and the duty, the self-discipline of flying, had a right too. They won. So there is a sense of self-dedication about this business of parting, a solemnity in which the adventurers, while deploring its necessity, even seem to delight. The very poignancy of renunciation renders more exquisite the pleasure of achievement.

For the thought of achievement in untrodden fields is a delight that makes renunciation worth while. Here our course

[18] A. de Saint-Exupéry, *Night Flight*.   [19] Ibid.

separates from that taken by the Flagellants and their brother ascetics. An achievement; a great deed; a goal and object. It is worth it, for that. Nansen, still on his voyage north, looked at his crew and reflected:

> Why? To what end? . . . And here on board are men who are leaving wife and children behind them. How sad has been the separation—what longing, what yearning await them in the coming years! And it is not for profit they do it. For honour and glory then? These may be scant enough. It is the same thirst for achievement, the same craving to get beyond the limits of the known which inspired this people in the Saga times, that is stirring in them again today. In spite of all our toil for subsistence, in spite of all our 'peasant politics', sheer utilitarianism is perhaps not so dominant among us after all.[20]

It is this desire for the great enterprise which bends the will of many to suffer hardship, 'the pleasure that one so surprisingly gets from trying to do something that is difficult' (Martin Lindsay), and *because* it is difficult. It may be difficult and it may be dangerous, but it is a big new thing which you have proposed to yourself to do; a thing which you could not put into words or print without risking the ridiculous, and that is one reason why newspaper accounts of adventures often embarrass the adventurers. We can only say that in many people the desire to win through to something against obstacles and after hardship is a natural desire. The more obstacles the better, and of course when they are self-imposed they will seem the more absurd to those whose kink lies in a different direction. As the old dalesman, Will Ritson, said of the early rock climbers: 'What's makkin ye fellahs fash yer-sells seea mich aboot climming t'crags? Isn't t'fells big enough for ye?' He was right, of course. They are.

In the old days war provided much of the opportunity for achievement in a sporting way, and war is ridiculous enough, in all conscience. In a sense it still does, or did till 1945.

[20] *Farthest North*, vol. I.

1: Scott's hut, Cape Evans, as it was left by Shackleton's Ross party and photographed in 1956.

2

3

Richard Hillary, the young airman who would have been a brilliant writer if he had survived, reports himself as saying:

> I'm concerned with my own potentialities. I say that I am fighting this war because I believe that, in a war, one can swiftly develop one's faculties to a degree it would normally take half a life-time to achieve. And to do this you must be as free from outside interference as possible. That's why I'm in the Air Force.[21]

Fulfilling one's own potentialities; that means living one's utmost and using every faculty. Hillary came to see that war is not really the best way of doing this, because to succeed in fulfilling oneself positively on a negative basis must be impossible. It is true that many who had found life negative in peace-time, rejoiced in the reality of positive, collective effort during the last two wars; and equally true that others, the defeated particularly, received an impulse to fulfilment by self-proving, to make up for what they had lost. But in its most modern loathsomeness war has forfeited the possibility of even these limited goods coming out of it.

With most individuals there is a lot of straight pride about this pleasure of achievement. Here is Sir Richard Burton, the first Englishman to reach Mecca, in 1853. He performed the remarkable feat of disguising himself as a Moslem pilgrim and being accepted by his fellow pilgrims as one of themselves.

> There at last it lay, the bourn of my long and weary pilgrimage, realising the plans and hopes of many and many a year. . . . The view was strange, unique—and how few have looked upon the celebrated shrine! I may truly say that, of all the worshippers who clung weeping to the curtain (of the catafalque), or who pressed their beating hearts to the stone, none felt for the moment a deeper emotion than did the Haji from the far north . . . But, to confess humbling truth, theirs was the high feeling of religious enthusiasm, mine was the ecstasy of gratified pride.[22]

[21] *The Last Enemy.*   [22] *Pilgrimage to Al-Madinah and Meccah*, vol. II.

'he wonder of it will hold a man and make him forget even the cold
d pain.' 2: *Edward Wilson sketching on the Beardmore Glacier.*
Completing a picture in the hut, Cape Evans.

The same sentiment of 'pride in prowess', a very pardonable one, is expressed in connection with endeavours in many fields. Sir Francis Younghusband put it, rather naïvely perhaps, for Everest, after silencing the questioners by telling them to ask a University crew why it doesn't take a motor boat from Putney to Mortlake: 'Man means to *climb* Mount Everest—climb it on his own feet. That is the whole point. Only so does he get that pride in his prowess that is such a satisfaction to his soul.'[23] And Sir John Hunt, writing after the mountain had been climbed: 'To solve a problem which has long resisted the skill and persistence of others is an irresistible magnet in every sphere of human activity ... There is no height, no depth, that the spirit of man, guided by a higher spirit, cannot attain.'[24] If I cannot go on multiplying instances, I have given enough indication that for some there is an indefinable charm, selfish perhaps, in the achievement of a large and to the commonsense world quite useless feat, which is difficult and which has been done never or rarely before.

　　　🙟🙞　　🙟🙞　　🙟🙞

Two final lures occur to me. When people are together for long periods, in difficult situations, their best—as well as their worst—qualities come shining through. In calm civilisation it is easier to slip behind the mask. To find friends is not a major reason for getting into tight spots, and some people prefer getting into tight spots alone; but it may be a strong contributory one. In mountaineering that curious feeling of unity with another, which the rope gives and the sharing of a storm or difficulty, is worth having for its own sake; as in William Bell's verse:

> We do not care, although the storm blow colder,
> because the ranting breath will join us by
> a bond more strong and more elastic than

---

[23] *The Epic of Mount Everest.*　　　　[24] *The Ascent of Everest.*

the nylon rope that's coiled upon my shoulder,
and in the fellowship of peak and sky
enroll the cold and lonely mind of man.

That bond of the nylon rope is as strong, I think, as any fellowship of peak and sky. 'La corde fait de deux êtres un seul,' and the greater the difficulties, the more that is the case. As an instance, Alf Bridge, who had climbed rocks for years with Colin Kirkus, woke up suddenly in the middle of the night on which Colin's plane was shot down over Germany. He sensed that something was wrong, went for a long walk in the middle of the night and then wired Colin's parents. The rope was still there. He still felt the need to act when his leader fell.

It is the same on the biggest climbs, where the sheer formidable magnitude of the thing compels a team-work which later, as we shall see, becomes a pleasure. It is the same with underground exploration, which can be difficult, arduous and very dangerous. 'The team must work together as one man, and must consist of the best human material,' says the explorer of the great Trou du Glaz, if it is to succeed or even to survive. And it is the same with the sea, as any reader of Conrad or of *Two Years before the Mast* will acknowledge.

An attraction, therefore, of the struggle is that it is going to be a common one, and most men prefer struggling in company to a life of solitary ease. It is so much easier to be lonely in a civilised city than on the South Pole! For once again it is in polar exploration that the bond of hardship shows clearest. The Winter Journey of 1911 was a nightmare of five weeks, as we have seen. But it was undertaken by three friends.

In civilisation men are taken at their own valuation because there are so many ways of concealment, and there is so little time, perhaps even so little understanding. These two men, Wilson and Bowers, went through the Winter Journey and lived; later they went through the Polar Journey and died.

They were gold, pure, shining, unalloyed. Words cannot express how good their companionship was.[25]

Again:

I am not going to pretend that this was anything but a ghastly journey, made bearable and even pleasant to look back upon by the qualities of my two companions who have gone.[26]

The gold of companionship! It is strange to what extremes of difficulty and danger a man will go to find it.

The last lure of the hair-shirt is contained in the words of Saint-Exupéry quoted at the head of this chapter: 'That new vision of the world won through hardship'. He goes on: 'those trees, flowers, women, those treasures made fresh by the dew and colour of life which the dawn restores to us, this concert of little things that sustain us and constitute our compensation'.[27] Those who are plunged into physical difficulty and exhaustion, whether voluntarily or no, come back to look at the world with new eyes, seeing it shaded with rather the same colours as when they looked forward, when they renounced it to go out on their adventure. Only now they are seeing something never seen before, as well as the old under a new light. They have a different standard by which to appreciate, and that standard makes all the pain worth enduring.

With most this sensation of 'seeing something' comes when they return, stirred with the glory of what they have experienced. W. H. Murray, an exponent of this kind of vision, gets it 'at the close of a great climb' in Scotland, during which every faculty has been extended. But sometimes it is in the storm itself that the new quality reveals itself as 'a power, a balance and reserve that normally lie dormant' (G. Rébuffat) but which surge up in time of need and can so imprint themselves on the personality that they will never be forgotten. Take the Americans again, still at Camp VIII on

[25] *The Worst Journey in the World.*   [26] Ibid.
[27] *Wind, Sand and Stars.*

K2 and having made the discovery that one of them has developed thrombophlebitis and will have to be carried down.

> The deepest springs of character were tapped for our survival. The lack of oxygen at great altitudes may dull the mind and weaken the body, but there is an inner strength of spirit, a bigger power which emerges undiminished, even magnified, to bring a man through such an experience . . . perhaps it is this conquest, conquest of one's self through survival of such an ordeal, that brings a man back to frontiers again and again . . . By testing himself beyond endurance man learns to know himself.[28]

In whatever physiological terms it may be explained, that feeling has a root of reality which will remain, thank heaven, inexplicable.

We touch here very near to the religious motive, to be explored in later chapters. The point I would make now is that it is from strenuous effort verging on the extreme limits that men and women seem to acquire a new power in themselves which in its turn leads to some sort of 'total' view of things; as if exhaustion of their bodies freed their spirits from some clogging shackle of comfort and left them free to go wandering up. There, from the height attained, they had a view of this planet not easily granted to those who struggle perpetually here below; a view which they remembered, when they came back.

'By Endurance I conquer' was the Shackletons' family motto. What do I conquer? I conquer myself, it seems to say, and more than that, by glimpsing the springs of its being, I set out to conquer the world.

[28] *K2 The Savage Mountain.*

3

❧ ❧ ❧ ❧ ❧ ❧

Contrast and the cult of danger

The Power of Man is as his hopes;
In darkest night the cocks are crowing;
In the sea roaring and the wind blowing
Adventure—Man the Ropes.

JOHN MASEFIELD

These words hung in letters of gold over Watkins' Base hut in Greenland, 1930.[1] They reminded the expedition that, however bad a time one might be having on an ice-cap, somewhere 'the cocks are crowing'—a comforting thought. It is also comforting to think that some day one will again be listening to them.

The pleasure of contrast in life, as in all arduous adventure, is one of the most obvious and by itself passes without comment. 'No one', Livingstone exclaimed, 'can truly appreciate the charm of repose unless he has undergone severe exertion.' Everyone knows the pleasure of relaxed muscles after a vigorous sail or climb or game of tennis. To do those things simply for the pleasure of relaxing afterwards would be too like the case of the man who beat his head against a stone for the pleasure of leaving off. But the pleasure of contrast is bound to be a large component reason why one does them; one of those pleasures of the senses in which Keats indulged, when he put cayenne pepper on his tongue before tasting claret. And it will be contrast not only after the total effort but after each day, or each burst of activity: the contrast of a beautiful shell seen by the diver just after he has fought

[1] The plaque on which they are inscribed can be seen at the Royal Geographical Society.

a shark; the sight of a white town on the Andes after weeks confined to the Bolivian jungle; or the flowered alp which a mountaineer finds, after nights of blizzard.

No traveller can have put this pleasure more persuasively than Freya Stark:

> If I were asked the most agreeable thing in life, I should say it is the pleasure of contrast. One cannot imagine anyone but an angel sitting with a harp in Paradise for ever. The ordinary human being needs a change. This is the secret charm of the oasis, usually an indifferent patch of greenery made precious solely by surrounding sands . . . The beauty of an Alpine dawn lies half in the sleeping world below. A warm chair by the fire after a day with hounds, a shuttered room when the wind is tossing, belong to this category of pleasures. The Greek shepherd knew the joy of the safe pinewood when the storms tear the open seas . . .[2]

Her conclusion is very just, though I used to find it depressing when I was a boy, this idea that one had no right to enjoy things unless one had suffered for them beforehand. It seemed bad luck on the angels, that they should be condemned to eternal stagnation in a painless pool. I myself was appalled at the prospect, little realising how small was my hope of attaining that state of beatitude anyway. I would get very bored, I thought, not being used to pleasure unalloyed, and yet surely I ought not to be bored, if the angels could survive it? And on earth, well, I sometimes thought it would be nice to go on eating cream till one died, and still enjoy it.

But now—contrast is life, I accept that. And large chunks of life have to be accepted as unpleasant anyway. Without their unpleasantness, and the contrast of the pleasant ways, life would not be life.

Nansen had a relevant reflection, about two months before he left his boat, the *Fram*, stuck fast in the North Polar ice,

The Southern Gates of Arabia.

and launched out on foot with one companion—into he knew not what.

> Sometimes I delude myself with charming dreams of my return home after toil and victory, and then all is clear and bright. Then these are succeeded by thoughts of the uncertainty and deceptiveness of the future. . . .
>
> H'm! as if dissatisfaction, longing, suffering, were not the very basis of life. Without privation there would be no struggle, and without struggle no life—that is as certain as that two and two make four. And now the struggle is to begin, it is looming yonder in the north.[3]

And, one might add, without struggle there would be no 'home after toil and victory'—for that is a part of life too, and a wonderful part. Think of the depth of Shackleton's feeling when he returned from the great expedition which paved the way to the Pole and nearly reached it. 'None but those whose bed for months has been on snow and ice can realise the luxury of a real bunk, blankets and pillow in a snug little cabin.'[4] It is a joy worth experiencing for itself.

Most struggles are not so grim. Contrast usually gives a pleasure which lies as much in returning to the struggle as in escape from it. Gaston Rébuffat, the French guide, describes a man climbing very steep, difficult rock, using pegs (pitons). He has enjoyed the climbing but it is long, and he must spend the night out.

> At the end of the day the mountaineer looks for a ledge, lays down his sack, hammers in a piton and attaches himself to it. After the hard, acrobatic effort of the climb he is lost—like the poet—in contemplation; but to a greater degree than the poet he can be a part of the hills around. The man who bivouacs becomes one with the mountain.[5]

A man must bivouac, he claims, to get the full variety and

[3] *Farthest North*, vol. II.   [4] *The Heart of the Antarctic*, vol. II.
[5] *Starlight and Storm*.

contrast which mountains can give, and which a man who always sleeps in huts loses.

> We should refuse none of the thousand and one joys that the mountains offer us at every turn. We should brush nothing aside, set no restrictions. We should experience hunger and thirst, be able to go fast, but also know how to go slowly and to contemplate. Variety is the spice of life.[6]

This savouring of variety and contrast can become, in some people, a whole way of life. Happy is the man who enjoys both the civilised pleasures and the wilderness. Saint-Exupéry, who enjoyed the adventure of flying more fully and evocatively than most, 'was no rebel against Society, no voluntary exile shaking the dust of Europe off his feet. He went back to Paris on furlough and enjoyed the delicacies of life, especially the choice meals in which the gastronomes of his native city proverbially indulge.'[7]

Gino Watkins, who was leading his fourth Arctic expedition at twenty-five, seems in exactly the same way to have enjoyed the pleasures of London by contrast. Outwardly he looked the typical undergraduate who dislikes being seen taking things seriously.

> Some had never considered him otherwise than as an elegant and unserious young man, confident in his popularity among acquaintances or his charm of manner among strangers to ensure his enjoyment of the game of life.[8]

This apparent attitude was even one reason for his early success. Seeming to treat it all as a joke, 'always experimenting, always interested in everything and in himself in an amusedly critical way', he had the charm to attract others to his adventure. And these others felt that they could surely do as well or better than this 'unserious young man'; found that they could not, and tried all the harder. But what concerns us now is that he genuinely was amused by the sophisticated

[6] Ibid. [7] H. Peyre, *The Contemporary French Novel*.
[8] J. M. Scott, *Gino Watkins*.

scene as much as by the simple. Before setting out for the Arctic Air-Route expedition,

> Gino accepted nearly all his social invitations, and it was the height of the London season. He was loath to miss anything which might be amusing either at the time or in retrospect . . . Very often he went to dances, perhaps two or three in a single night. In the small hours of the morning he ran home—this running was his exercise—and four or five hours later he would be sitting in his room at the Royal Geographical Society, spruce and wide-awake, his mind entirely occupied with the work in hand.[9]

And on return, when many are disappointed and when his own companion, Spencer Chapman, wrote, 'In England, after the joy of the first long-looked-forward-to bath and the reunion with old friends, everything tended to fall flat,'[10] Watkins found a new joy.

> His family, his friends, London with its old associations and new buildings, its shops and theatres, its myriad sounds and clothes and faces which poured in and out of his life as he walked along the streets, all different, most of them forgotten in a moment but all somehow a part of the great flood of life which had carried him from childhood—these things, striking vividly in his mind against the white screen of the Arctic, fascinated and delighted him.[11]

Watkins was perhaps finding the balance which another traveller, Ella Maillart, hinted at about the same time in her *Turkestan Solo*.

> I shall pass months in a solitude as old as the hills. But then I shall be able to judge what crowds mean to me. With nothing but heaven over my sleeping body I shall learn what is a roof. Cooking over a fire of dung, I shall discover the true worth of wood.

That is a discovery deeper than the simple pleasure of contrast. For by going away, by making as it were the 'experi-

[9] Ibid. [10] F. Spencer Chapman, *Watkins' Last Expedition*.
[11] *Gino Watkins.*

ment in depth', in P. W. Martin's phrase, we come back to appreciate what is worthy and what worthless in civilised life; what fritters with superficial wideness and what gives a deep enjoyment.

Not everybody, of course, can live both lives like Watkins. The explorer may not like coming back. The one thing may have spoiled him for the other. Chapman found that he could not sleep for a week after returning to England; 'after living so long for one object, more or less, life suddenly becomes so terribly complicated'. It is amusing to compare the ends of two travel books about the same fine journey: Ella Maillart's *Forbidden Journey* and Peter Fleming's *News from Tartary*. After discussing future champagne and caviar dinners inter-mittently all the way from Peking to Sringagar, Fleming felt, nearing the latter point, that 'getting back meant less to her than to me, who had, paradoxically, at once more ties and more detachments: a greater capacity to enjoy a life to which at frequent intervals I feel myself a stranger, and at the same time more friends and facilities with which to enjoy it'.[12] Ella Maillart, in spite or perhaps because of that appreciative faculty of which she had written earlier, felt very flat.

> In the dining room at the hotel we amused ourselves like true savages, while prim couples, bare-backed and massive-chested, manifested open disapproval of our shabby clothes, untidy hair and buccaneer-black faces which no topee had ever shaded.
>
> But our amusement soon wore thin. It was too depressing to be so near that world, all dressed up as though it was going to act in a comedy. After our months and months of anticipation it was almost without pleasure that we clinked our champagne glasses.[13]

That restlessness of the traveller in society, plunging him or her back into escape from it after he has summed it up unfavourably, we shall look at later.

꿩 꿩   꿩 꿩   꿩 꿩

[12] *News from Tartary.*   [13] *Forbidden Journey.*

The springs of adventure

I often wonder where it began, this idea of enjoying the alternation of civilised and primitive. Essentially, I suppose, it existed always. One thinks of the medieval baron leaping joyfully from flagon and hogshead into battle, and equally joyfully back again; while Sir Francis Drake seems to have got a peculiar satisfaction out of leaving a bowling green to thrash the Spaniards. But the adventurers of those days were less conscientiously vocal than they are now, while life ran on with fuller flow, worrying less about dividing itself into neat channels, in and out of which a man could be aware of stepping.

Conscious thought about these matters dates from more recent times; many a path which our ancestors pursued instinctively, we have to stop and think about. The Industrial Revolution, following on the grimly stirring times of the Napoleonic wars, has something to answer for here too. For the division between the practical and operative on one side, and the directive and theoretical on the other, was deepening. The latter, being mainly also the rich, needed something. In this country their 'outlet valve' is perhaps most noticeable in mountaineering.

Mountaineering had been born of science; in the early days, as C. F. Meade puts it, no respectable climber would climb a peak 'without at least boiling a thermometer on reaching the top'. During the nineteenth century however it came to be practised with no other end in view than that of getting to the top. This seemed to many practical people very odd.

Many minor reasons can be given in an effort to explain how it was that a few hundred lawyers, doctors, scientists, clergymen and merchants were willing to leave their well-servanted homes for the ragged bivouacs under the colder if more inspiring panoply of the Alpine stars. The most usual explanation is that the Victorian mountaineers were over-fed with wealth, ease and luxury; they had, for one reason or another, to get away from it all. They were in a manner of speaking the real

Ivory Tower gentlemen for at least a few weeks every year. Alternatively, they were in some way best known to themselves salving their consciences in the Alps, finding something in the mountain world that might redress the balance of the factory world in which, even if they worked twelve hours a day, they worked under circumstances vastly different from those of their less fortunate employees.

This physical, Marxist explanation is correct so far as it goes. The material advances of the Victorian years, it is true, not only gave men the craving for hard physical exercise under the sky, but also enabled them to reach the Alps with an ease never before known. Yet when one considers the physical factors which gave birth to this new sport, the most astonishing thing is that the Victorians were tough enough to do what they did.[14]

There were other reasons too, as we shall see, religious and scientific. But on the physical plane, and with no reservations needed, the Victorians (the same being true to varying degrees in other countries) did go out partly to redress a balance which too great physical ease seemed to be upsetting. As to why they were tough, it was probably because they trained themselves to be. Watkins going for long runs at Cambridge has his ancestor in Leslie Stephen doing marathon walks there on Sundays. Arrived near their Mecca the pioneers lived hard and lodged in primitive conditions. (Of fleas: 'I have them', one pioneer put it). Often they either slept out under their peak or did the whole climb from the valley, starting the night before, after a good dinner. And they had a much longer season than most can afford nowadays. No wonder they were tough.

The mountaineers carried this business of experiencing the rough yet kindly touch of Nature one logical step further than most of their contemporaries. This was very right, for they felt the artificiality of the picnic at the end of the carriage-drive; they knew not only the limitless suggestions but also the limitations of Box Hill and Hindhead and the other physically lesser

[14] R. W. Clark, 'Half of their Lives', *Cornhill Magazine,* Summer 1952.

mountains of the world. They realised that to regain what their age had lost they had to give genuine hostages to fortune; they had, at some time in the process, really to stand alone and battered by the gale with only a fair chance of getting home alive. Nothing less would do.[15]

Toughness—in contrast with ease of living and the hot-house of civilized life. Simplicity—in contrast with the Victorianly furnished mansion. A complete rest from intellectual effort. Leslie Stephen maintained that he could never read a serious book in the Alps, and described the rise and fall of a pair of hob-nailed boots as the most soothing of motions. In all these things a standard was formulated and a new depth of pleasure discovered, for which we are still grateful. For we have seen how, out of this pleasure, there is born an appraisement of those things with which the freer life is contrasted. If man could never step back from his day-to-day confinement, if he were for ever shut in the room, how miserably poor and straitened that room would become!

❧ ❧   ❧ ❧   ❧ ❧

Love of contrast and the acceptance of danger are forms of the 'physical exertion' motif in adventure. Neither these two nor the 'self-proving' motive of the last chapter have much to do with pleasure; usually they have a good deal to do with its opposite, but are ideas accepted and even welcomed as means to a greater good. Danger by itself I had not at first meant to include. Nobody, I thought, except the enthusiasts who roll themselves over the Niagara in barrels, would do a thing just because it was dangerous. But reading and further thought convinced me that, while there may be few at the Niagara end of the scale, there are a great many who would not do a thing unless it had some danger to it, and still more for whom the slight sniff or spice of danger adds zest to the gentlest donkey-ride or punt outing.

[15] Ibid.

Rather at the Niagara end of the scale come feats like flying under the Severn Bridge—feats such as are described weekly in the Sunday papers. Usually they are done without much conscious thought; a dangerous thing is the most obvious challenge to manliness. Often there is the opportunity of showing off, and it is noticeably the male rather than the female who indulges in this pleasure. Daredevils seem very seldom to be women; but from the sea-elephant upwards, or downwards, males have fought before their chosen, not only to vanquish a rival but to demonstrate to all comers their high virility.

Sometimes, however, it is more complicated even at this level. When Richard Hillary flew under the Severn Bridge during the last war, he felt he must do it because somebody else had done it. But his friend Peter Pease said:

> 'Richard, from now on a lot of people are going to fly under that bridge. From a flying point of view it proves nothing: it's extremely stupid. From a personal point of view it can only be of value if you don't tell anybody about it.'
>
> He was right, of course.
>
> To fly under the bridge now simply to come back and say that I had done so would be sheer exhibitionism. It would prove nothing. Yet I knew I would fly under it. I had to for my own satisfaction, just as many years before I had had to stand on a twenty-five-foot board above a swimming pool until I had dived off.[16]

He did it, with inches to spare, and said nothing. The initial impulse was of bravado, or sheer courage. Then he did it from a motive akin to that discussed in the last chapter, to prove to himself that he *could* do it (the reason suggested by Peter Pease). He did it also, I think, like the other fliers, because it was part of the total experience of flying. He would have missed something, without it; just as the rock climber may feel that he must do everything in the scale, even a dangerous solo ascent, not because he wants to but because he might, if

[16] *The Last Enemy.*

he did not, miss something in the gamut of emotions—perhaps something that would have suited him exactly.

Somewhere near this experience come some of the earlier flying feats, like Lindbergh's air circus parachute jumps. In the early twenties, 'if flying was considered dangerous, wing walking and parachute jumping was considered suicidal'. Lindbergh, in those days 'Daredevil Lindbergh', describes the state of 'exhilarated calmness' before his first jump.

> I would have no pay in money for hurling my body into space. There would be no crowd to watch and applaud my landing [there were later]. Nor was there any scientific objective to be gained. No, there was a deeper reason for wanting to jump, a desire I could not explain. It was the quality that led me into aviation in the first place, when safer and more profitable occupations were at hand, and against the advice of most of my friends. It was a love of the air and sky and flying, the lure of adventure, the appreciation of beauty. It lay beyond the descriptive words of men—where immortality is touched through danger, where life meets death on equal plane; where man is more than man, and existence both supreme and valueless at the same instant.[17]

Later, when he came to be the first man to fly from New York to Paris, he flew with all the precautions, but it was still a risky business. The fate of his rivals in the field showed that. But risk was part of the job, hence of enjoyment.

> Of course there's danger; but a certain amount of danger is essential to the quality of life. I don't believe in taking foolish chances; but nothing can be accomplished without taking any chance at all.
>
> I believe the risks I take are justified by the sheer love of the life I lead. Yes, just being in the air on a flight across the ocean to Paris, warrants the hazard of an ice field below.[18]

Thus the 'total experience' is worth the danger (as with Hillary), which is itself accepted as part of the 'total experience'. That feeling of course, is far from being confined to

[17] *The Spirit of St Louis.*   [18] Ibid.

4: '*And what remains of all I see and ʃ if I let go?*'

5

6

flying. I shall choose, to make this point, a few words, Germanic in their enthusiasm and straightforwardness of purpose, from the Austrian diver Hans Hass. A pioneer in the years before the last war, he worked out a system of maskless hunting with the harpoon which at the time was considered first impossible (he was once nearly arrested for 'poisoning' fish), then unbelievably dangerous. Needless to say that charge was denied; and the danger admitted he claimed to be 'worth it.'

I became very conscious of how completely anyone who defies danger in any form is at the mercy of chance.

But ought one really to draw a conclusion from this? Should one expose oneself the less to danger and to chance? A life spent in constant anxiety over losing it would be no life at all. It would not be worth a single day really lived. We must be thankful to fate for every single moment, but must not turn one step aside from the path we have entered on.[19]

To return to flying: Lindbergh's words would have been echoed, had he been a writing man, by another and perhaps greater contemporary airman, Wiley Post; a character as zestful for the joys of flying as any there has ever been, a body so vigorous that he could, in remarkably brisk record time, fly round the world with only one eye and one sound ear. Such was the spirit abroad in that golden age of flying. Just outside it, I think, is the remark of the test pilot quoted by Admiral Byrd, who said of his job: 'I like it because I take up planes that have never been flown. Half the excitement is not knowing what is going to happen.' For some people that may be so. For most, even then, it was a doubtful inducement. Byrd himself, one of the most adventurous men of modern times, is of a similar opinion to Lindbergh's, but with more emphasis on the practical advantage:

I have always believed that no matter how hazardous an endeavour may be, it is justified when the end sought is human knowledge and augmented progress. Where would we be today

[19] *Diving to Adventure.*

D

The splendid perfection of the shark.'
. . . waving sea whips and circling fish.' Diver with a sting ray.

if there had not been pioneers in the past who launched out into the unknown? [20]

He flew in a way to justify his theory; making the first flight to the North Pole in 1926; crossing the Atlantic and crash-landing in the sea off France very soon after Lindbergh's flight; then in 1929 establishing the base of Little America just above the Bay of Whales on the Antarctic Continent and from it flying over the South Pole; five years later wintering alone at a meteorological post far south of that base as part of a second scientific expedition. He was a spectacular flier and he wrote persuasively *In defence of spectacular flights*.

Despite the scientific justification, however, and his own very careful preparations, Byrd found himself, when lecturing, rebuked by wives for putting ideas into their husbands' heads. And looking at his own career he admits amusedly (this was in 1929): 'An Arctic flier who has responsibilities feels more like a selfish sinner than an explorer going forth to conquer.' 'Wicked and thoughtless', the good ladies exclaimed, and Byrd had a hard time combating them. Wicked perhaps, he admits, but thoughtless no, because in this game all risks are weighed and none taken unnecessarily.

For—and here is the rub—adventure can be undertaken, danger accepted, from a sense of responsibility. The responsibility may be simply to the community, when the work done is going to be of importance to it, now or in the future. Happy the organiser who *knows* in himself, as Byrd did, that an undertaking apparently perilous is worth the risk. Or responsibility can be directly to an organisation, as the mountain guide's is to the *Corps des guides*. The single airman who volunteers for a service may be happier still (if less of an adventurer); for he has the pleasing sensation of duty done and the world, represented for the moment by André Gide, at his back:

Is it not in aviation that man's courage is most admirably and usefully displayed? What would otherwise be rashness ceases

[20] *Skyward.*

to be so when practised in the cause of a service. The pilot, who is risking his life all the time, has some right to smile at the idea of 'courage' which we commonly build up.[21]

Gide must have approved specially of the combined courage and sense of responsibility of test pilots, which I think wholly admirable, whatever my private opinion of the usefulness of flying. I admire greatly the spirit of, say, the test pilot A. E. Clouston before the last war, flying to great height and getting iced up on purpose so that the effect of icing could be studied—with unpleasant consequences. Later he flew into wire in order to further the cause of barrage balloons:

> Each time the length of wire was increased until it started cutting so deeply into the main spar that the tests were really dangerous. We had learned that the last few yards of wire had a habit of whipping in a complete circle round the wing before finally dragging free. If an explosive charge were attached to the end of the wire, it would . . . blow the aircraft to pieces. This, however, the scientists were prepared to take for granted without practical demonstration.[22]

This was a voluntary running of risks accepted with a sense of responsibility.

We are at this point about half-way between the Niagara rollers and the mildly-stimulated-by-thrills. We are in the realm of risk accepted when necessary with the eyes open, but minimised when possible. Some pioneers are very anxious to establish the distinction between necessary and unnecessary risk, converting it into a distinction between difficulty and danger. Even when they do things which seem to their contemporaries suicidal, they insist that if you are trained, these are no more than normal difficulties. Thus Captain Voss, one of the very earliest to sail round the world in a small boat, maintained that he was even safer than in a large ship:

> The cruises which I have made in small vessels not infrequently have been denounced as foolhardy undertakings. However,

[21] Preface to *Night Flight*.   [22] *The Dangerous Skies*.

39

when I have given a short explanation such doubters would become silent. They soon understood that there is still much to be learned about breaking waves, and that there is no better way to study the safety of ocean travel than these solitary cruises on which all kinds of weather and sea dangers are met with and fought.

Then, I ask, why should not a seaman like myself who loves the ocean and likes to sail on it, devote his time to this study? The more so as I for one feel perfectly convinced in my own mind that I am safe in my small vessel of which I have complete control, far safer indeed than thousands who race across the briny deep in big greyhounds and have to entrust their lives to the care of others! [23]

This is illogical, of course, and like much of Voss a queer mixture of brag, solid knowledge and modesty. Going on to emphasise that unlike Captain Slocum (who also considered himself very safe) he was almost never without a mate, he forgets that he has already committed statements like 'A good shipmaster never reflects on danger until he be right near it,' and described a mighty narrow escape in a typhoon which could have been avoided. It is significant, or at least interesting, that Voss and Slocum were both finally lost at sea.

The same distinction, however, is made by the mountain guide Rébuffat when he writes: 'The guide loves difficulty but abhors danger, which is a very different thing.' And in a rather curious passage about the 1,900-foot sheer north wall of the Cima Grande di Lavaredo:

When I had asked him . . . 'How is it possible to climb a continuously overhanging wall for 720 feet?' he had replied 'You'll see.' And now that we had reached the top of the yellow slabs he said to me amusedly:

'If you drop a stone, not only will it not hit the wall, it will

[23] *The Venturesome Voyages of Captain Voss.* The same is true of an apparently dangerous sport like caving. 'If the physical strains were greater than on the mountains the dangers were usually less, depending to a greater extent on our own actions, and gradually diminishing with the growth of experience.' P. Chevalier, *Subterranean Climbers.*

bounce on the scree slope more than sixty feet away from the bottom of the face.'

And it was quite true, for I tried it! I was surprised that it should not for one second occur to him to think: 'If we fall, we'll do the same as the stone.' He knew as much, but such a morbid idea did not even enter his head. That is why I enjoyed being with him, for we were not daredevils or madcaps. We did not like being afraid, we loved life as we loved our jobs.' [24]

I think he means that this looks like danger, but you need not think it is dangerous for the experts though it would be for the inexperienced. He personally and Soldà (the leader) do not like danger, for its own sake, but they are happy here, because they are confident in their technique.

There is truth in this view, but it must be taken with a pinch of salt. The greatest guides have been known to fall.

꿩 ꥤ   꿩 ꥤ   꿩 ꥤ

Cima Grande and the Eiger North Face had long defeated the so-called 'danger merchants' between the wars, much decried by contemporary British climbers. Dangerous things were often done, admittedly, but I think we failed to under-stand how and why, just as we failed in politics to appreciate the depth of bitterness in defeat (or near defeat, as in the case of the Italians). We did not recognise a new approach to danger. The Germans had failed to fulfil themselves, in one sense, through war. Therefore they sought to make up by fulfilling themselves, after defeat, in another. The remark of a young man on the eve of his death on a difficult climb is well known: 'We Germans have nothing more to lose.' But more significant to me is the considered reasoning of Paul Bauer, leader of the great Kangchenjunga expeditions of 1929 and 1931:

In those joyless days we needed some means of proving that he who was dauntless and undeterred, he who was prepared to

[24] *Starlight and Storm.*

make the greatest sacrifices, and he alone, could aspire to the highest attainments. Defiantly resisting the spirit of that time, we had to show again and again what these virtues could achieve in spite of the heaviest odds.[25]

These expeditions were masterpieces of organisation. They had about as tough a time as anybody has ever had in the Himalaya, sometimes having to burrow into the great north-east ridge of the mountain because there was nowhere to put a tent. To the participants they proved something more than just that there was 'nothing more to lose'; even if they were not quite sure what.

The frustration of defeat and a misunderstanding of Nietzsche, 'prophet of the *Herrenvolk*', certainly drove some to desperately bold and disastrous attempts, notably in the Alps. But I think it is evident that danger was not sought just for itself, as the accusation ran. 'This new type of climber,' C. F. Meade wrote in 1940, 'proud of his skill in the use of hammers, pegs, rope-rings, balustrades, stirrups, slings and pulleys, finds a new source of joy in a mystical worship of danger as an end in itself, so that he considers even the most foolish feat praiseworthy, as long as courage, skill and endurance are displayed in performing it.' This seems to me plain misunderstanding. Might not any non-climber just as reasonably accuse the Everest man, with his oxygen, pegs, snap-rings, rope and duralumin ladders, of a 'mystical worship of danger'—since what other object can he have in wanting to get to the top? I believe that for the Germans danger was incidental to the general and perfectly understandable desire to prove oneself as good as the next man. For this they needed to go one better; there were a limited number of safe places on which one better could be gone, and they passed to the dangerous ones.

So far as technique goes, many of them were simply ahead of their time. They fell off, largely because they were not yet skilful enough at hammering their pegs into overhanging

[25] *Himalayan Quest.*

42

rock, at hitching themselves up on stirrups or at descending when they got stuck. British climbers, hardened now to the use of 'hammers, pegs, rope-rings' and the like, have since 1945 done more severe climbs than were dreamed of by assailants of the north faces between the wars. Therefore some of the pages of Meade and others are read with a smile by the newest generation; for the danger cult of one man may be considered the perfectly safe way of his skilful successor. The question: What is justifiable danger? remains unanswered; or rather to be answered by each generation according to its own judgement and in the light of its improved technique.

The answer of Gino Watkins is of interest and would be approved, I think, by Voss and Rébuffat. Watkins lost his life at twenty-five, kayaking alone in a Greenland fjord. He was hunting seal and his companions had tried to persuade him to be accompanied.

> He did not go out hunting in his kayak until he had become as skilful a performer as the Eskimos. Now he was far the best hunter of the expedition, for the others were more apt to scare the seals. The presence of a companion increased his safety, but it reduced the chances of successful hunting; and so, when he needed seals, as he did now, he went alone to look for them.[26]

But with due respect to Watkins, as to Voss and Rébuffat, there are unavoidable dangers awaiting even the expert climber or sailor or explorer, as real as any in flying. The distinction between danger for the expert and for the novice should be made, if only to warn the novice for his own good, but it cannot be pushed too far.

Where then can we place courage? Display of courage for its own sake (the Severn Bridge type) is held by the more thoughtful to be waste of time. When Dr Alain Bombard sailed across the Atlantic on a raft, he faced appalling risks.

[26] *Gino Watkins.*

But he did it for the purpose of scientific and philanthropic experiment.

> A human life should only be risked in such an experiment as mine if some useful purpose is being served. If there are any young people who think they see a short cut to fame in setting off in a raft for America or elsewhere, I beg them to reflect or come and see me first.[27]

And Saint-Exupéry the flier is even more openly scornful of courage for its own sake. After describing a fellow pilot forced down in the Andes, walking for five days and four nights, frostbitten, cutting his boots open to take his swelling feet, crossing ice cols at 15,000 feet in temperatures twenty degrees below zero, he continues:

> There is a tendency to class such men with toreadors and gamblers. People extol their contempt for death. But I would not give a fig for anyone's contempt for death. If its roots are not sunk deep in an acceptance of responsibility this contempt for death is a sign of an impoverished soul or of youthful extravagance.[28]

Courage divorced and alone is not a great quality. Courage linked with a sense of responsibility is. It takes more true courage for a girl wittingly to choose to spend her life looking after sick parents, a traveller to forgo travel in order to finance a family, than it did for Hillary to fly under the Severn Bridge.

I think it was that sort of greater courage that Ann Davison meant to find, when she forced herself to sail the Atlantic in order to find some guiding quality in life. (She was the first woman to sail it east-west, in 1953.) It was a curious way to do it, as she bluntly admitted. 'Most people come by it naturally, but I had to sail across thousands of miles of ocean to find out that courage is the key to living.' That depends on the sort of courage; but if she followed up her definition of it as the will 'to face every day of your life and

---

[27] *The Bombard Story.*   [28] *Wind, Sand and Stars.*

every humdrum trivial little detail of it, and realise that you don't amount to much'[29] she will have come nearer the mark than the most audacious daredevil. Let us therefore leave animal courage to the mercy of Saint-Exupéry, giving it the *coup de grâce* with a reference in a letter written to André Gide:

> I understand now why Plato (or Aristotle?) puts courage the lowest of the virtues. It is not made up of very fine feelings: a bit of anger, a bit of vanity, a lot more obstinacy and a common or garden sporting pleasure. Especially the sublimation of physical strength . . . No, I shall never admire a man who is only courageous.

ঙ ঙ   ঙ ঙ   ঙ ঙ

We conclude that danger for its own sake is seldom sought. When it is, it is the means of exhibiting 'courage'; the companion to difficulty sought by men desperate after defeat; an opportunity for self-proving or showing off. Usually it is accepted as necessary in some responsible tasks and as faintly inevitable in certain adventures, but controlled as far as possible by skill. Apart from real serious danger, however, everybody knows that the feel or spice of risk gives an added zip to any adventure, even the mildest. It can be described in the much misused word 'thrill'. As small boys delight in those evil swooping contraptions which leave your stomach behind on top of Bertram Mills' Circus, so the test pilot gleans thrills from his swoops towards earth. Neville Duke paints the picture:

> One of the thrills of flying is to take up the Hunter to over 40,000 feet, up into the clear, deep, sapphire blue. Down below, you can see the earth, far away—it is best to pick clear days for vertical dives in the Hunter. Now . . . at full throttle you half-roll over and pull through. The nose of the Hunter is pointing straight down at the earth; and you are hanging

[29] *My Ship is so Small.*

forward in the straps, feeling as though you may slip out of them and fall forward at any moment. Now you are really beginning to move. The indicated speed begins to build up and so does the Mach number. Soon you are going straight down at the earth at supersonic speed. You can see the earth rushing up at you. The needle on the altimeter is whirling madly round, reeling off thousands of feet as you go down, straight as an arrow. It's a wonderful thrill.[30]

That is not everybody's meat; but then neither is the climber's sensation, as he stands safely on a ledge and enjoys his own little thrill contemplating the drop.

> In this short span
>   between my finger tips on the smooth edge
>   and these tense feet cramped to the crystal ledge
> I hold the life of man . . .
>   For what is there in all the world for me
>   but what I know and see?
> And what remains of all I see and know
>   if I let go?[31]

Again, some but not all would share Hans Hass's thrill under the Red Sea.

> I often had the feeling that every muscle in my body was enjoying itself on its own initiative . . . And all my impressions gathered a special strength from the fact I was entering forbidden ground. I was never allowed to forget that a shark might be waiting behind the next rock. I could never so lose myself in the beauty of a view as to forget to keep a sharp look-out.[32]

[30] *Test Pilot.*

[31] G. Winthrop Young, 'The Cragsman', *Collected Poems.*

[32] *Under the Red Sea.* Hass goes on with the words: 'The diver's greatest danger lies within himself: it is the sudden onset of fear. So long as one keeps calm and encounters further hazards with full realisation of all the dangers inherent in them, everything is all right. But it is fatal to allow oneself to be disconcerted.' This does not mean that it is wrong to be frightened. Chapter Two of F. S. Chapman's *Living Dangerously* stresses that point. 'Beware of the man who says he's never frightened.' The man who gets things done is the man who anticipates and controls his fear.

The point that I would make here, and my last point, is that these three thrills, each peculiar to an adventure, have a semblance of danger much greater than the reality, which is here virtually under control. The more experienced one is, the less likely one will be 'to allow oneself to be disconcerted', in Hass's phrase, and so the less present the danger, though the thrill remains. This thrill is sought for its quality as a crisp seasoning is sought for a dish. It can have a quickening effect on the whole personality; stimulating the senses and goading nerves jaded by soft living into an activity undreamed of at home.

'He has a heart who knows fear, but he overcomes fear who sees the precipice, yet is undaunted.' So Nietzsche wrote, in the person of Zarathustra. Danger can be valuable to enterprise if fear is controlled, not ignored. And to the man who overcomes his fear and thereby moderates danger, the greatest things are possible. No less than the hair-shirt, the prick of peril stimulates us into the farthest places, and keeps us keyed to them when we arrive.[33]

[33] It will be noticed that there are no specific war dangers here. This is because they are seldom self-chosen, and when they are, as in the French Resistance during the last war, the motives are very mixed: patriotism, bitterness for killed relatives and the like mingle with the spirit of pure daring. Just sometimes the thing seems to be done almost for its own adventurous sake. There is an element of this in F. Spencer Chapman's *The Jungle is Neutral*, and also, returning to the Maquis, in books like Peter Churchill's *Of their own Choice*. The very title shows something of the spirit in which these works of sabotage were undertaken. But war motives form a vast subject of their own, with which I have tried to meddle as little as possible.

4

The anatomy of pleasure

I · MOTION · SKILL · HEALTH

Oh, the wild joys of living! The leaping from rock up to rock,
The strong rending of boughs from the fir-tree, the cool silver shock
Of the plunge in the pool's living water, the hunt of the bear,
And the sultriness showing the lion is couched in his lair.
And the meal, the rich dates yellowed over with gold dust divine,
And the locust-flesh steeped in the pitcher, the full draught of wine,
And the sleep in the dried river channel where bulrushes tell
That the water was wont to go warbling so softly and well.
How good is man's life, the mere living! How fit to employ
All the heart and the soul and the senses for ever in joy.

ROBERT BROWNING

Physical pleasure in these days advertises itself so loudly that little seems needed to supplement the posters. Not only are we advised, beyond all hope of resistance, to eat well, to drink well and to improve our bodily state by soaps, unguents, scents, toothpastes, spring mattresses and other commodities, but also, more germanely to our theme, bronzed damsels of the hoardings invite us to ski, surf-ride, hike, cycle, swim and skate—in short to 'be fit and enjoy life'. It may be said without fear of contradiction that our age recognises the importance of the physical pleasures, including those that involve bodily movement.

The said damsels (they must be sisters), when they are seen swooping ecstatically on ski down some vertical slope, imply by the modest suggestion of lessons at the bottom of the poster that their skill is to be learned. 'Lessons are fun,' they say, and are sometimes blunt enough to add: 'Only fifteen guineas a course.' They usually imply also that you, after that course, will be swooping with their own perfect agility. But they are right, bless them, on two counts. First, the animal pleasure of doing certain things skilfully is worth having; it also (as they omit to mention) may lead on to bigger adventure beyond. Secondly, in almost every case of 'pleasure in motion' there is a skill behind to be learned, obstacles to be overcome, and that learning and overcoming are themselves part of the pleasure. Everybody has had the experience of watching a champion lawn tennis player, admiring the fluid wonder of his strokes, and then, with depressing results, going away to try them himself. Or a superlative rock climber is seen gliding effortlessly up an overhang on which, when it is your turn, you fail to get off the ground. There seems a magic about the thing, apparently out of reach of ordinary mortals.

About the very highest standards of performance there is, I believe, a magic, quite indefinable. Some have it, some have not. But in more ordinary flights the Open Sesame lies usually in practice and the acquiring of a technique, which are themselves pleasures. A book like *Mountain Craft* (by G. Winthrop Young) is one long account of how to win that mountaineering skill which makes big or difficult climbs look easy. Take an expert 'rope', the author says, on steep rock or ice: each man doing different things, each apparently unconscious of the other, yet the whole machine moving in ultimate rhythm up the mountain. 'Style is the mastery of rhythmic movement.' This rhythm becomes obvious by contrast if the climb is tried by the inexperienced; for everything has to be learned, in stages, the hard way.

To become a good individual climber, we have had to train our limbs and discipline our nerves until movement has become masterful, confident and easy. To become good mountaineers, we have had to educate our judgement by experience, without lessening our spirit of enterprise. In our association with others on a rope, we must contribute, in addition, our share to a common pool of good temper, of unselfishness and of the discretion which deepens resource and makes for a reserve of safety.[1]

There are climbers, as there are initiates in every sport, who seem to have an annoying natural ability for doing the right thing straight away without all this learning; as if they had had a pre-birth view of it. I am thinking of men like John Streetly and Joe Brown. But we must hope that they are exceptions which prove a general rule: that learning is a hard business, whether you scrape your shins in rock chimneys or spend week-ends capsizing small boats on Southampton Water. And you usually enjoy your education, whichever it is.

In this business of skills it seems to me impossible to draw a line between the pleasure experienced in the 'mechanical', that which demands a machine, and the 'physical' in which the human body is the instrument. You can distinguish *motive*, as I shall try to do in Chapter 11, where we look at those who go adventuring primarily because they are interested in mechanical contrivance. But for the *pleasure*, I think it is of the same essential quality, however outwardly different, whether you are handling a Hawker Hunter at 43,000 feet or swinging an ice-axe at 10,000. In each case you have the sensation of being master (for the moment) of a skill, and the purely physical joy of smooth motion. '*Il lui faut un outil*', Saint-Exupéry says of man, and that is true. But whether the tool be an aqualung, a human body, balloon, glider, ice-axe, ski or sledge, seems to me of less importance than the truth that in each of these activities there is a delight in technique and movement similar to that experienced in the others.

'What of driving a car?' you say. 'Taking a Jaguar up to Snowdonia in three and a half hours? Or any sport, tennis, football, skiing?' Quite true, there is an overlap here. Why not? Speed, skill, nerve, smoothness, they are all here too and all have to be learned, usually the hard way. They all look easy when near-perfection has been achieved. Skiing, as one

[1] *Mountain Craft.*

example, has a foot in both camps. It is, first of all, superlatively a thing of skill and pleasure in control. Taken purely on a beaten *piste* it is, as Arnold Lunn has said, a splendid sport but a sport, no more. Taken over untrodden snow, on glacier and névé, mountain summit and hollow, it is something bigger: a satisfying sensation and also, in the wider sense, an adventure. To ski roped down a new glacier—a feat I have admired and will never be competent to achieve—must be as good a physical adventure as one can hope to have.

Let us admit then that our type of adventure and sport (in the usual sense) have much in common. Even the danger is common; and it is probably easier to break a leg at soccer or ice-hockey than gliding or caving. Let us claim that what 'adventure' has over sport is the sense of bigger things and the zest of the unknown; and now, conscience-free, go nearer to examine just what those pleasures are that may attract the novice.

Of all the pleasures in pure motion those of the balloonist, the glider and the undersea diver must be among the purest. These people may be escaping, yes, into a fluid world in which dream and reality become one. But their prime joy is going to be the plain simple pleasure of the thing, and of the skill demanded. Take diving. J. Y. Cousteau, early champion of the aqualung, approached it in a spirit of scientific enquiry. He hoped to (and did) revolutionise diving; and his book has a crisp scientific tang throughout. Science, you would say, takes first place. But no. Pressed between the pages and peeping out all the time is the original desire, the desire to have the physical joy which would be given by masterful motion through an uncharted element. His first few pages tingle with excitement.

To halt and hang attached to nothing, no lines or air pipe to the surface, was a dream. At night I had often had visions of flying by extending my arms as wings. Now I flew without wings.[2]

[2] *The Silent World.*

The springs of adventure

The dream of flight! The sheer joy of achieving, in another element, what Leonardo planned and what can never, in the air, be realised.

Other divers are more specific about the pleasure they get from this new freedom of movement. I have the feeling that we are now in the golden age of this type of diving; for it is still a comparatively recent discovery, to be sung lyrically, and not yet at the mercy of machine or commerce. It is a pleasure that stems, of course, from simple swimming. In the last century the poet Paul Valéry, heir to Byron in being a strong swimmer, was writing in his journal: 'To plunge into water, to move one's whole body from head to toe, in its wild and graceful beauty, to twist about in its pure depths, this is for me a delight only comparable to love.' But the delight is intensified if the swimmer can literally bury himself in his water, can feel a magnification of his body as it moves, elongated, in an unaccustomed way through a familiar element. I am no diver; but one of the pleasures of enthusiasm for one type of adventure is that it leaves me with a very enjoyable armchair appreciation of the others. Passages like the following give it to me.

> If I wanted to make an upward leap of five metres, I simply gave myself a little push up and there I was. If I wanted to descend ten metres, I simply bent forward and glided down like a bird. I never got so near to a third dimensional life as I did in this wreck, where every ladder and door provoked comparison with those of a normal vessel. No bird, however cleverly it might wing its way through the rigging, could surpass me. For in my case gravity did not count at all. I could glide in whatever way and in whatever direction I chose, and I could with equal ease remain perfectly motionless in space.[3]

That is Hans Hass, and there is an unwitting echo of Valéry's, 'My body becomes the direct instrument of my mind, the author of its ideas.' More introspective is Philippe Diolé, but he also can give a simple sensation.

[3] *Under the Red Sea.*

I continue to go down, slipping over rays of sunlight half strangled by shadow. A silky silence broken by the rhythm of my breathing: a comic gurgling, like pipe bubbles, accompanies my exploration of this endless blue silk.

I roll over on my side for the pleasure of lying on a bed made of water. At the same time I bask in my loneliness: the sea surface seems far away. Someone overhead is throwing pearls into the sea. No, I am wrong, these pearls are born of my breath.[4]

There can be few sensations more enjoyable than these; and they explain why, in the warmer waters of the Mediterranean, girls and boys are now taught aqualung diving as they used to be taught swimming; why whole families take the day out, not by but *in* the sea, among the fishes; why a new and satisfying sport has established itself, in the wake of adventure.

Ballooning gives a pleasure in pure motion more closely associated with the 'machine'. But the machine is a very unmechanical one; here and in gliding it interferes far less with enjoyment than does the aeroplane, in calm weather perhaps less than the small boat. It is sad that ballooning as a sport went out, more or less, with the advent of the aeroplane. It must have been a most pleasurable adventure but doomed, I suppose, in the more crowded England. Ropes trailing across the fields and ballast thrown out on to suburbs would not be popular nowadays. Besides, those who had been keen balloonists lost the art when they went over to aviation.

But the old was the enjoyable. Between about 1890 and 1910 vigorous balloon clubs flourished, competitions and races were organised, thrills were had by all. Frank Hedges Butler, founder and first President of the Aero Club, ballooned over the Channel in 1905 and once took a trip down to Brighton by moonlight, descending in a private garden to ask the way. There is a pleasing picture, hard to visualise nowadays, of the sleepy owner rubbing his eyes at the

[4] *The Undersea Adventure.*

strangers sitting on top of the elm tree. An even more evocative account of a flight appears in a charming chapter of C. F. Meade's *Approach to the Hills* (a rather queer approach this). Meade records a sixteen-hour journey from Paris to Basle. Part of it does *not* make me anxious to balloon: headlong falls, the experience of being blown off course and not knowing where one is, frantic throwing of precious ballast overboard. But the sensation of moving noiseless above the clouds —or rather what he calls 'the ecstasy of immobility, for the roles of the traveller and scenery are transposed; to the traveller in a balloon the sensation of immobility is absolute, while the landscape floats noiselessly past,'—*that* I can appreciate, as I appreciate the soundless glide which made early airships a pleasurable adventure as well as a commercial proposition.

I appreciate no less the sensations of the gliding enthusiast, all the keener perhaps because his motion is undisputed as he swoops and soars at will, undisturbed by noise or machine. Even a first flight can give the impression that man is divine.

> Never before or since have I experienced such a sensation of perfect flight. We climbed from 400 to 2,000 feet in a few minutes, wafted through a veil of liquid gold towards the west. Once we passed close to another craft, from which the pilot gave us a great shout of greeting. So might two gods have called to each other from their kingdoms.[5]

Gliding demands a skill in the judgement of wind speeds and hot air currents which brings it as a sport half way to flying. And if it is argued that it is the less of an adventure, because no new ground is covered and no new speeds attained, then I would say that in these respects no adventure is now much better off. We have only (at present) this planet to play with; we can only fly faster and faster round it, sail in smaller and smaller boats on variations of known routes, dig out smaller and smaller unknown corners of its surface. Taking it that in these things it is the spirit that counts, I would add that a

[5] Terence Horsley, *Soaring Flight.*

man who flies a glider over the Alps from Grenoble to Italy, as has been done recently, is as adventurous as most.

The pleasures of the machine have of course the difference that control of the machine is substituted for control of the muscles; or rather, not substituted but added to, for if you count glider and small boat as machines, to handle these well muscle and nerve need to be finely adjusted. Gerbault used to go into training before long sails. To some people this 'sedentary' type of sensation is not so satisfying as that in which the body moves to its own rhythm, each muscle singing out that so it was destined from eternity that it should move. I have that feeling myself. In a small boat I am always wanting to get out and stretch my legs. However I have no doubt that the real sailor can properly claim the best of both worlds, since the running of a ship large or small demands co-ordinated physical effort but *also* nervous control of the 'machine', these combining sometimes to produce intense pleasure.

> You steer the gallant little vessel as she reels off her eight knots an hour before the steady breeze, rolling and heaving gently as the great green seas pass under her, sometimes playfully dropping a bucketful of salt water over the bulwark . . .[6]

> One of those rare glorious experiences that lift you right out of the commonplace (though God knows there is little of the commonplace about being at sea single-handed) on to Olympian heights of delight. The wind had backed right round to the north-east, and *Felicity Ann* was flying before it, her boom way out and lifting, tugging at the mainsheet as if she was alive and impatient of restraint.[7]

So Ann Davison wrote of the Atlantic, and indicated also another of the pleasures of control—that of feeling your steed move under you like a living thing.

Flying is the most mechanical of the pleasures ranged before us, and the physical activity enthusiasts will bemoan

[6] E. F. Knight, *The Cruise of the 'Falcon'*. This remarkable voyage over the Atlantic took place in 1880; two crew, two passengers (useless) and one boy.

[7] *My Ship is so Small*.

55

that it is possible to be a first-class flier weighing eighteen stone and incapable of much more movement than is required to lift a beer mug to the lips. Much has been written of the physical delights of flying. Personally I have an affection for those who are speechless with enjoyment or express it as briefly as Amelia Earhart, when she flew the Atlantic, accompanied, in 1928 and said, simply, 'I enjoyed every minute of it and would do it again.' She did it again, next time alone; and of a later flight said, very sensibly: 'I want to do this flight because I want to.' But I need something a bit more explicit than that. Here are two expressions, separated by almost fifty years of flying. The first is Frank Hedges Butler, in a Journal of 1908, after he had just flown four and a half minutes (with Wilbur Wright)—one of the first Englishmen to fly.

> Like a bird in a cage, yes! I have flown! To look back seems like a dream . . . One asks what it feels like to fly; the answer is, there is no sensation whatever: it is as if man has always flown. To give an idea, it is like gliding over sparkling water where you can see no bottom. A perfect feeling of security and stability; turning the corners and tipping the wings is like skating on the outside edge.

And here is a test pilot of the 1950's:

> For me there is no greater satisfaction than sitting in the cockpit of the Hunter, beautiful in design and construction, representing the thought of so many people, and feeling it respond to the slightest movement of your fingers. . . . You have the sky to play in—a great limitless expanse.[8]

The test pilot, like the sailor, finds a major pleasure in the touch of the instrument. With flying it looks as if this pleasure, in the future, will more and more outweigh the physical. The bigger and more powerful aeroplanes become, the less physical contact there is bound to be with the air (or lack of it) surrounding, and the less direct physical effort demanded.

[8] Neville Duke, *Test Pilot*.

This goes, of course, with added emphasis, for anything that is likely to happen in space.

❧ ❧   ❧ ❧   ❧ ❧

Of all the purely physical adventures mountaineering gives perhaps the widest range of pleasure. Here we are right away from the machine; the main difficulty now is to distinguish the pure pleasures of climbing rock or ice from the bigger joy that comes from the total experience of mountains.

> The joy of climbing is easier for us all to understand [than the joy of mountains]. It is the joy of physical self-expression, the joy of the long innings, the hard rally or the close finish, united to that finer pleasure, the cumulative joy of good combined play.[9]

Back to games again! The 'joy of physical self-expression' on rocks has become nowadays so much part and parcel of the climbers' reason for climbing, that there are numbers who seldom bother to go on from the cliff to the top of the mountain; while low outcrops and the gritstone edges are frequented at week-ends by many who have no interest in bigger mountaineering at all. And why not? This is a sport, like any other, and a sport which can both give extraordinary satisfaction (if one can only get up that overhang or round that corner!) and be delightful to watch.

But to return to the sensations. Climbing is peculiar in that what seems delectable to the climber can seem the very reverse to the majority of his fellows. It is a question partly of liking that sort of thing, partly of experience. Here, in his own particular heaven, is an expert on a difficult rock climb which he is trying to do at high speed: the North Face of the Dru above Chamonix.

> We found ourselves climbing with ease and pleasure. Our movements were linked in smooth rhythm, like water flowing

[9] G. Winthrop Young, *On High Hills*.

from a spring. All skills have this effect on a well-trained body . . . Thus the whole climb was pure joy, for, while superficially watching over the actual ascent, the spirit had leisure to wander happily. It was an exquisite afternoon; no incident marred the day.[10]

That is a Frenchman speaking. The British tend to be less vocal about the sensual pleasure which there undoubtedly is in moving gracefully up steep rock; but here is Dorothy Pilley Richards on the first ascent of the well-known Holly-tree Wall in Snowdonia (1918):

Soon we were beside him, back in a rapture again. To have just the holds you need on the first ascent of such a wall, no more and no less, gives every step the flavour of a victory . . . In the bay we sat down to relish the moment. Everyone who has enjoyed a first ascent will understand our sublime content.[11]

This content can be so 'sublime', indeed, that there seems no need to look further. Even the mountains in the background are forgotten.

If mountaineering, as I have indicated, merges at one end into sport, at the other it becomes lost in wider exploration, of col and valley, glacier and desert. In this greater exploring the physical pleasure of a particular type of movement cannot be so concentrated as in the last examples quoted. Climbers who take to exploration usually have to sacrifice the highest standard of specialised technical performance on rocks, and the pleasures therewith associated. The purely physical delights of wider exploration are not usually such as to attract a novice by themselves; aesthetic, scientific and many other motives supply the initial impulse, the pleasures being incidental. In the first place, the technique itself is vast but ill-defined. What is it that puts a Shackleton or a Watkins, a Livingstone or a Stanley above their fellows, apart from determination? You cannot say that they mastered one

[10] G. Rébuffat, *Starlight and Storm.*   [11] *Climbing Days.*

technique completely; only that they had a number of techniques, plus the indefinable something, ahead of anyone else. The pleasures are equally ill-defined, besides being incidental, and as varied as those of everyday life. They may range from gliding down unexplored rivers with Sven Hedin to walking briskly through a jungle, which can be very like walking anywhere else. Some like walking, some do not. Livingstone did, and therefore exclaimed in his Journal:

> The mere animal pleasure of travelling in a wild unexplored country is very great. When on lands of a couple of thousand feet, brisk exercise imparts elasticity to the muscles, fresh and healthy blood circulates through the brain, the mind works well, the eye is clear, the step is firm, and a day's exertion always makes the evening's repose thoroughly enjoyable.

Peter Fleming even found himself 'feeling good' and exhilarated when wading up a river in the Brazilian hothouse.[12] But that must be unusual, and perhaps goes to prove that it is the sense of novelty that makes one feel good, rather than the particular movements one happens to be performing at the time.

Much of the story of polar exploration would go to support that theory, for there is still less direct pleasure here. Satisfaction, yes, there is that; a grim pleasure, if you like to style it so, to be had in pulling a polar sledge against odds. And Bowers, for instance, was always happy on skis. But he is a difficult person to judge by, as he was also always happy in a tight spot, and the happiness of getting a hard job done is very different from the pleasure found in doing it. Few would go to the Poles for the latter; the former is one of the strongest incentives, as we have seen. Physical pleasures there are (apart from the visual one of the scenery)—the downhill ski run after heartbreak hauling, the *élan* of a well driven dog

[12] See *Brazilian Adventure*.

59

team (or nowadays Snocat), sometimes the collective rhythm of a manhaul. But these take a bit of finding.

❧ ❧   ❧ ❧   ❧ ❧

I am conscious of cruising, among the pleasures of motion, upon the calmer waters of this book. They are closely linked, to my mind, with the pleasure of fitness, or health. Without fitness (a word I dislike for its suggestion of inevitable gymnasia, but it must be used) the climber or diver could not enjoy his skill; and conversely, much adventure brings health in its train. When it ceases to do so, it is usually time to stop, as Livingstone's last years of tormenting dysentery show.[13]

The pleasures of health with its attendant sensations form another set not peculiar to adventure. Anybody may be healthy. These pleasures are the only ones agreed upon by all the characters in Lowes Dickinson's *The Meaning of Good* to be without question *good*. They stem from physical sensations: the bathe of a healthy, tingling body in the sea at sunset, the long skate over miles of virgin ice, the sunshine that browns the tramper of the valleys. All these are good, though as he points out that type of enjoyment is both complex (the aesthetic pleasure of the scenery comes in, which we shall consider shortly) and precarious. 'The water which quenches our thirst also drowns; the fire which warms and comforts also burns . . . Nature not only ministers to our bodies, she torments and destroys them.'[14] A *purely* physical pleasure he defines as something like a cold bath when one is hot. About others which are more venturesome he is doubtful, since there is in them a sense of short-lived precariousness. But that precariousness I find to be the very tonic which braces the explorer and adds to his sense of well-being.

It is hard to define, this type of health. It comes, I think,

[13] At his 'peak period' he could boast of having drunk water 'putrid with rhinoceros' urine and buffalo dung', and of being none the worse.

[14] *The Meaning of Good.*

partly from the simple, physical exertion demanded of the explorer, the diver or the climber; partly and still more from the awareness of doing something unusual in unusual surroundings. With many people this acts magically; they feel themselves far better, physically, than if they had stayed in their supposedly healthier homes. 'A merry heat doeth good like medicine' (Livingstone) may be said even in equatorial Africa, given the right conditions, and the remark would have been echoed by the 'Medicine Woman', Evelyn Cheesman, who spent years in some of the unhealthiest islands in the world, collecting insects, and enjoyed it. In Malekula, the worst island among the New Hebrides for climate and savages, she spent a year of perfect health; and such was her energy that she once, in New Guinea, managed to collect 744 moths between 7 p.m. and one o'clock the following morning.

Everybody knows the doctor's prescription of 'a change of climate'. The adventure prescription simply carries this one logical stage further. A change of climate, yes. The tropics, for instance, after Britain. Then a change of occupation as well, and since 90 per cent of us are engaged on routine or fairly sedentary jobs, that means something unusual and even exciting. This well-being which comes from the varied zip of venturing is not one of the goods catered for by Lowes Dickinson, concerned as he is with purely physical sensations which are *always* good by their own nature. But it is no less real for that. To return to the worthy Captain Slocum: that great seaman might have sailed innumerable hours up and down the coast of Boston; but he would not then have written, as he did after his lone journey:

> I had even gained flesh, and actually weighed a pound more than when I sailed from Boston. As for ageing, why, the dial of my life was turned back till my friends all said, 'Slocum is young again'. And so I was, at least ten years younger than when I felled the first tree for the construction of the *Spray*.[15]

Nor, had he not really felt it, would Livingstone himself have

[15] *Sailing alone around the World.*

written of travel in Africa, in another part of the well-known passage already quoted:

> The body is soon well knit; the muscles of the limbs grow hard and seem to have no fat. The countenance is bronzed and there is no dyspepsia. Africa is a most wonderful country for appetite, and it is only when one gloats over marrow bones or elephant feet that indigestion is possible.

There are many cases, too many for more than a brief selection, of men and women physically frail in youth but stimulated to health by the very idea of their adventure. We have seen Scott toughening himself away from seedy boyhood, and Edward Wilson, who, when he first went to the Antarctic, still bore the scars of tuberculosis on his lungs. Frank Smythe was invalided out of the R.A.F. in the twenties; but his early pursuit of hills led him to train to be a climber, in the Alps and at home, with such success that he became one of the outstanding Himalayan mountaineers of his generation. Lincoln Ellsworth, the American Antarctic flier, was not only weak as a boy but timid, and known as 'Fraidy' by his small sister four years younger than himself. Freya Stark, as a young invalid woman, was forced to diet on raw eggs but 'found I was able to walk as long as I did not eat'. Finally, a recent example, Hermann Buhl, the Austrian climber, toughened himself with an almost monomaniac passion after a weakly boyhood until he had done all the hardest Alpine routes, each with a bit extra, and climbed alone up Nanga Parbat in 1953, spending the night out without tent or sleeping bag at 26,000 feet. This was perhaps the biggest single *tour de force* in the history of mountaineering.

But the person I am going to examine in a little more detail is not so well known as these. She is for all that an even more remarkable case of the effect of travel and excitement on the health, and she resembles Freya Stark in her liking for nice hats. Her name is Isabella Bird and she was born in 1831. At home in the Island of Mull 'she seldom rose before noon and wore a brace to ease the pain of her diseased spine'. She was very small, and this misshapen spine made her subject to nervous depression and insomnia. When her mother died her sister, Henrietta, stayed on at home, but as for Isabella 'the physique which was to withstand the icy winds of the Persian uplands, the enervating heat of Malaya, the drenching rains of Hawaii, broke down at the mere contemplation of actually living in the Island of Mull . . . the constant backache, the insomnia and nervous fears to which she was a martyr grew worse and worse, and a complete collapse seemed inevitable'.[16] The doctor ordered travel, and off she went.

Fortunately she wrote, not only books but affectionate letters to her sister (like Freya Stark later), who seems to have been exactly the right *alter ego*, receptive and stay at home and not likely to come out and live the same life herself. When she did propose joining her, Isabella found plenty of good reasons why it was not a good idea. For if you share these things, to whom can you impart them with that delightful sense that it is you doing them and not they?

She started with Hawaii, felt better and began to do some climbing there. Thence to the Rocky Mountains, where on her first mountain ride she was thrilled to be thrown from her horse, which shied at a grizzly. She lived the tough life of a ranch with men, and climbed Long's Peak (14,000 ft), stimulated by the wolves howling round camp at night. In Malaya she forded the Perak River, half-submerged on an elephant; then in 1878, finding herself on the point of marriage and unable to face the prospect of being an 'invalid wife', she packed her boxes for Japan, where she lived among the hairy Ainu of Hokkaido. Out there she had 'the appetite of a tiger and the stomach of an ostrich'. At seventy, back in England, she ordered a tricycle for exercise, but was off to Morocco 'for a rest' before she could use it, and there rode

[16] Dorothy Middleton, 'A Lady's Life in the Rocky Mountains', *Cornhill Magazine*, Winter 1952–1953.

thirty miles a day on a horse so high that she had to mount by ladder. When she was on her deathbed, at seventy-three, her trunks stood packed for China. 'She died as she had lived, in flight from life's humdrum routines, under a hired roof, with her luggage corded and labelled for a strange port on the other side of the world.'[17]

Isabella Bird would not come in Lowes Dickinson's category of those who are stimulated by *purely* physical sensation. But she sums up for me the health-bringing zest to be had from doing strange, undreamed-of things in strange places; the cure lay in the simple fact of being away from home and a person in her own right, not a Henrietta. It would be a worthy study to go on from here, and examine just how many invalids, men and women, have had their lives transformed by the little known parts and pursuits of the world. They would make an encouraging list. And how gratifying for the parents of sickly children to think that their daughters might do what Isabella Bird had done, their sons grow up with the body of a Scott or a Wilson, an Ellsworth or a Hermann Buhl!

[17] Ibid. I am indebted to Mrs Middleton for much information.

5

The anatomy of pleasure

II · ALONE AND WITH FRIENDS · THE SCENE

Comrade, look not on the west:
'Twill have the heart out of your breast.
'Twill take your thoughts and sink them far,
Leagues beyond the sunset bar.

A. E. HOUSMAN

Some pleasures come from inside us, from what we do and feel. Others present themselves, unasked, to sight and sense. When we were small we climbed the hill 'for the view'; and still, above or below earth, the scenes that meet our eyes form the happiest fountain of hope and memory. For their sake, even, we choose our adventure.

Some are born to explore the scene surrounding in the company of friends. Others, the lone wolves, prefer going it on their own. We have already seen comradeship as a support against disaster, as the one feature of unpleasant times that made them bearable. But it would be perverse to choose to have a bad time because somebody else will be having it too. There is a more positive and simpler pleasure, that of doing a thing you like in company, of acquiring a 'collective rhythm'. This is the team work, in a bigger context, which makes a good soccer side delightful either to watch or to play in.

To find companionship and to lose personal loneliness and responsibility men go to sea. 'The strong bond of the sea and also the fellowship of the craft', in Conrad's phrase, is the more real because of the unsociable expanse around. Even the bluntest feel it.

They all worked. That crew of Liverpool hard cases had in them the right stuff. It's my experience they always have. It is the sea that gives it,—the vastness, the loneliness surrounding their dark stolid souls.[1]

A ship like the *Cutty Sark*, last of the great clippers, became under its best captain, Woodget, 'a happy abode of hard-working mariners in half-deck and forecastle'.[2] That spirit was born of necessity, true, in the first place, as *Moby Dick* and many a book testify, but in a good ship it is sought for its own sake also, because it gives pleasure.

It is pleasant to do most things in company, and not only the obviously co-operative things like mountaineering. Surprising, too, what a sense of good company there is even among those who seem to be heading off alone. The sailor depends upon the friendly co-operation of his boatmakers and lighthouses; the diver and underground explorer must have their crews above to help them, the airman his ground staff below. To balance his apparent solitude in the air the latter feels an especial need of the co-operative. Saint-Exupéry exclaims:

> Happiness! It is useless to seek it elsewhere than in this warmth of human relations. Our sordid interests imprison us within their walls. Only a comrade can grasp us by the hand and haul us free.
>
> And these human relations must be created. One must go through an apprenticeship to learn the job. Games and risk are a help here. When we exchange manly handshakes, compete in races, join together to save one of us who is in trouble, cry aloud for help in the hour of danger—only then do we learn that we are not alone on earth.[3]

And it was Saint-Exupéry who said, of love: 'Love is not looking into each other's eyes, but looking together in the same direction.'

Enough of the goods of companionship in adventure, for

[1] Joseph Conrad, *Youth*.   [2] Alan Villiers, *The Cutty Sark*.
[3] *Wind, Sand and Stars*.

it must be obvious how stimulating they are, even when we have to be for stretches alone. Solitude as a *motive* is not so easy. Indeed in some parts of America wanting to do things alone is deemed a dangerous kink. Your family has you psychoanalysed, unless you are quick enough to escape to Europe. Sometimes solitude is just a second best to the ideal companionship. Peter Fleming has travelled far and often alone; he wrote after his solo journey to disturbed Manchuria and China in 1933: 'Occasionally you find the ideal companion. . . . But the ideal companion is rare, and in default of him it is better to make a long journey alone. One's company in a strange world.'[4] With others, however, going alone represents a real need. They just do things better when nobody else is about, and enjoy their own company. 'I have always loved solitude,' says André Migot, lone explorer of Tibet and the Southern latitudes.[5] 'I am now alone, absolutely alone,' exclaims Alain Gerbault, escaping with satisfaction from New York on his world cruise.[6] Then there is Hermann Buhl, the climber, who seemed to rise to special heights of mountaineering prowess and audacity when alone, and Lindbergh, congratulating himself on the advantages of lone flying:

> What advantages there are in flying alone! . . . By flying alone I've gained in range, in time, in flexibility: and above all I've gained in freedom. I haven't had to keep a crew member acquainted with my plans. My movements weren't restricted to someone else's temperament, health, or knowledge. My decisions aren't weighted by responsibility for another's life. . . . I've not been enmeshed in petty quarrelling and heavy organisational problems.[7]

Some people then, odd as they may be thought by the majority, approach the central experience better alone; not only because they function better like that, but also, in some cases, because with no companion to dilute their intimacy,

---

[4] *One's Company.*   [5] *The Lonely South.*
[6] *In Quest of the Sun.*   [7] *The Spirit of St Louis.*

they feel closer to the Nature surrounding them. Not everyone would admit to that, but more feel it than would admit. I have had this sensation of intimacy often on mountains. Climbing alone is a practice often condemned and not to be indulged light-heartedly or for long periods at a time. The risks are there: even the sprained ankle, say the criers of woe, can be fatal. But the rewards are there, too. The man who has lain alone at sunset on a peak, or felt the 'fierce joy' of its lonely rock buttresses under his fingers—that man has lived deeply, for a while, and returns with a queer feeling of inexplicably deeper living to the everyday round. My example of the 'deepening' process and its effect is not taken from mountaineering, but from a profoundly wise man, William James, who once passed the night alone on Mt Marcey.

> I spent a good deal of it in the woods, where the streaming moonlight lit up things in a magical checkered play. . . . The intense significance of some sort of the whole scene, if only one could *tell* the significance; the intense inhuman remoteness of its inner life, and yet the intense *appeal* of it; its everlasting freshness and its immemorial antiquity and decay. . . . I can't find a single word for that significance, and I don't know what it was significant of, so there it remains, a mere boulder of impression. Doubtless in more ways than one, though, things in the Edinburgh lectures will be traceable to it.[8]

All I shall remark, for the moment, is that the experience could only have come to him when alone, noting that like many such it was impossible to put into words, and that it was to have its effect, to 'come out' afterwards. The only quality that the active explorer or climber can add to such experience is the tingle of a sensation of being alone in a faintly dangerous Nature. Nerves are taut, the personality receptive. But if the sensation of danger is too strong, then the quiet necessary to the experience disappears.

[8] Letter to his wife, quoted by P. W. Martin in *The Experiment in Depth*. The Edinburgh lectures are best known as *The Varieties of Religious Experience*.

7: 'And in the fellowship of peak and
enrol the cold and lonely mind of m

A long spell of solitude is tough meat, and unsafe for some natures. The flier returns to his airfield, the explorer comes upon villages, the sledger rejoins his companions, unless he is one of those very few souls, like Byrd and Courtauld, who can stand months alone at a meteorological post. Courtauld, after some three months alone and with more to come, confided to his diary that 'If I ever get back to the Base nothing will induce me to go on the Ice Cap again.'[9] Perhaps as lonely as any is the lone sailor, who has chosen this experience and cannot know what it will be like. Ann Davison wrote of her Atlantic crossing:

> It is an experience few of us are ever called upon to undergo and one which few of us would voluntarily choose. It is almost unimaginable, because solitude is normally something that can be broken at will. Even being on one's own in undeveloped country, popularly supposed to epitomise loneliness, is not true solitude, for one is surrounded by trees and bushes and grass and animals, all part of the substance of one's own living. But the sea is an alien element; one cannot live in it or on it for long. . . .
>
> For years I had been constructing an armour of self-sufficiency, deluding myself it was strong enough to resist any onslaughts of physical or spiritual loneliness. People—why I could take them or leave them alone. But . . . my independence was by no means as complete as I had believed.[10]

To live alone for long, and to go on getting something out of it, one needs perhaps a strong sense of mysticism, like that of Madame David-Neel, who lived as a Buddhist lama in Tibet, some of the time alone. It is relevant that this French-woman, who probably penetrated the mysterious land more deeply than any European, was possessed by the urge to live there long before she saw it, and even before the momentous meeting with the Dalai Lama (1911). But her motive is so mingled with the religious quest into Buddhism, that we

[9] J. M. Scott, *Portrait of an Ice Cap.*
[10] Ann Davison, *My Ship is so Small.*

As lonely as any is the lone sailor.' Ann Davison setting off from Plymouth to cross the Atlantic.

cannot honestly class Tibet's attractions for her as those of physical adventure, under my present definition. She was, primarily, a determined seeker in the spiritual realm of Buddhist teaching, to which the 'mystics and magicians' delightfully crowding her pages are almost incidental. Incidental too, in the long run, was the physical boldness which she had to show, first to get into the country, then to be accepted by it. And finally she was fascinated, as others were, by the landscape. I know that my own too brief glimpse of the land, rolling brown and grey into an enchanted silver distance, made me feel that outward charm must have something at least to do with its magnetism. Among those endless recesses anything could happen to the solitary pilgrim.

But I am straying from my purpose, which was to remark that Madame David-Neel had the strength of fibre to be alone. For most of us, built of flimsier material, solitude means contact, for a short time only, with the common pool of natural things, a strange glimpse at moments into their meaning, and a greater certainty of ourselves. That is a good worth seeking. But we are sociable animals in the main; and it is unfair to keep the animal too long from its fellows.

※ ※   ※ ※   ※ ※

For each the scene, explored alone or in company, is different and compellingly attractive, each to its own type of personality. How many people do choose their type of adventure because of its scenery and environment it would, of course, be absurdly impossible to compute, since these are inextricably mixed up with what one does in them. But certain it is that a dusty picture of clipper or ice-cap or cloudy peak hung on a classroom wall has set many a boy dreaming a dream from which he only escapes with death. 'A child leaning from a railway carriage window looking towards the dawn, while mother and nurse slept . . . And as the child gazes there appears something that is not of the Earth as the child knows it, something wonderful, something nearer Heaven.'[11] The child looking at that peak, Frank Smythe, died with the plans for a new mountain expedition in his head.

What draws different people to different scenery? We seem to be made each with a different germ which reacts electrically when confronted with a certain scene. I am indifferently moved by sight of the grey sea; but a fine mountain does something to me inside. Often the thing is 'in the blood', the result of a father's teaching and example; in that case the son is more unlikely than anyone to know 'why he does it'. Imagine Yann, the *Pêcheur d'Islande*, explaining what it is about the northern seas that takes him there year after year to fish, when there are more profitable and less dangerous trades at home! Certainly the beauty of the sea, its changeful wonder and the greens and greys and blues that are for ever chasing across its surface, form a great part of the fascination it lays on some men, whether they know it or not. This draws them, with little hope of material reward, to its service.

> The call of the sea is a strong one. The blue waves and whistling breezes have a never ending charm to him who has spent a life in their company. And though it has been much toil and little gain it does not make an iota of difference.

That is the tough Captain Voss in his *Venturesome Voyages*, and the sort of way of putting it that a landsman can understand. But perhaps only the poets can really express what it is in this sea that draws us. Masefield is much quoted but has the essential charm in him:

> . . . the wheel's kick and the wind's song and the white sail's shaking
> And a grey mist on the sea's face and a grey dawn breaking.

[11] F. S. Smythe, *Climbs and Ski Runs*.

I must go down to the sea again, for the call of the running tide
Is a wild call and a clear call that may not be denied;
And all I ask is a windy day with the white clouds flying,
And the flung spray and the blown spume, and the sea-gulls
    crying.

In France Valéry with his:

> Une fraîcheur, de la mer exhalée,
> Me rend mon âme. . . . O puissance salée,
> Courons à l'onde, en rejaillir vivant!

And, for the undersea wanderers, Heredia's fine sonnet that
begins:

> Le soleil sous la mer, mystérieuse aurore,
> Eclaire la forêt des coraux abyssins
> Qui mêle, aux profondeurs de ses tièdes bassins,
> La bête épanouie et la vivante flore. . . .

Or Heine in Germany, of the North Sea:

> Ein seltsam Gerausch, ein Flüstern and Pfeifen,
> Ein Lachen und Murmeln, Seufzen und Sausen,
> Dazwischen ein wiegenliedheimliches Singen—
> Mir war, als hört'ich verschollne Sagen,
> Uralte, liebliche Märchen.

Or hear it ringing out from the prose of Herman Melville and
Joseph Conrad. It needs no other advertisement.

Eric Shipton spoke of these 'intangible' attractions of
country:

> Some men appear to derive a strong philosophical satisfaction
> from dragging a sledge across miles of Arctic snow, or from
> mere existence in strange conditions. Many people have an
> intangible though profound feeling for certain types of
> country, and can be completely content doing any job which
> takes them into such places. Presumably such a feeling for
> mountain country is the principal reason for climbing.[12]

Add to this that the satisfaction of dragging a sledge is by
no means the only one acknowledged by polar explorers. A

[12] *Upon that Mountain.*

man like Edward Wilson was attracted both by the science and even more by the sheer beauty of the Antarctic forms and colours, which he painted superlatively. (Illustrations 2 and 3, facing p. 21.) Here is a pen picture:

> Now and again one hears a penguin cry out in the stillness near at hand or far away, and then perhaps he appears in his dress tail coat and white waistcoat suddenly upon an ice-floe from the water, and catching sight of the ship runs curiously towards her, crying out in his amazement as he comes from time to time, but only intensifying the wonderful stillness and beauty of the whole fairylike scene as the golden glaring sun in the South just touches the horizon and begins again to rise gradually without ever having set at all. We have now broad daylight night and day, but the beauty of the day with its lovely blues and greens amongst the bergs and ice-floes is eclipsed altogether by the marvellous beauty of the midnight, when white ice becomes deepest purple and golden rose and the sky is lemon green without a cloud. No scene in the whole world was ever more beautiful than a clear midnight in the pack.[13]

Not everyone who goes out has Wilson's eye, and none his artistry. But to many this beauty and environment become a call not to be resisted; the wonder of it will hold a man and make him forget even the cold and pain. And now, thanks to colour photography, a book like *North Ice* seen in a bookshop might change a boy's life.

As for Shipton's mountains, they have come to be generally accepted as one of the types of country for which people have that 'intangible feeling'. The story of how they gradually ceased to be the 'Uniformity of Barrenness' of Dr Johnson is a long one, not to be attempted here. The twin forces of science and sentiment broke the spell and led the nineteenth century towards the 'Playground of Europe'. What is of interest here is that once mountains had been accepted as beautiful on the wave of romanticism, the pioneers used their

[13] Quoted by G. Seaver in *Edward Wilson of the Antarctic*.

beauty as cover; they justified their unconventional ascents by long descriptions of all the aesthetic charms of sunrise and sunset on the snows. Only look at the tremendous, conscious striving after the right epithet which afflicted everybody, both the professional aesthete like Ruskin and the 'hard-boiled' scientist. As an instance, if you glance through a list of Victorian comparisons made in the hope of showing what peaks look like, you will find them compared to all these: man, woman, lion, pyramid, up-ended ship, ship's prow, queen, giant, sugar loaf, palace, Titan, Achilles—and many more.[14] This striving was partly a direct outcome of the novelty of the whole game. With some, as I have said, it joined science as a justification for mountaineering; with Ruskin and others it turned into a justification for opposition to climbing, on the grounds that it defiled the sanctuary of beauty. Hence Ruskin's famous likening of climbers to children, who set up soaped poles in a garden and then slide down them with shrieks of delight.

The Ruskinian view wilted after Leslie Stephen's witty rejoinder that only the mountaineer had the right to judge how true it was, since only he tasted *all* the delights of mountains and could judiciously compare them. Since those days they have continued to attract the aesthete as well as the explorer and technical enthusiast. They have their poetry and their art. We think quite naturally of their forms as beautiful, and even enchanting, in the variety of rock ruggedness and swirling snow crest, and we do not now even trouble much to say so. It is sad, but true, that good things once accepted lose the keen edge of their value. And so, perhaps, it will be with the hills.

Some types of scenery have the surprising power of exercising their charm even before people have set eyes on them. Deserts, for instance. The great Swedish explorer Sven Hedin seems to have felt this magnetism of the Takla Makan

[14] See Chapter II of *Escape to Switzerland* by G. R. de Beer for the evolution of metaphor.

Desert in Central Asia. On the first of his three crossings he nearly died for want of water; and his reasons for crossing have not the weight usual with most of his scientific journeys. Tibet I have already mentioned, and its appeal to Madame David-Neel. For the Swede too it had a charm outside his science, an irrelevant appeal. His two attempts to enter in disguise were perhaps the least scientific of his expeditions. In each case, after a difficult and uncomfortable passage, he was politely escorted back to the frontier.

All deserts fascinate. It has been said of them that you either like or dislike them violently. If you like them—then your fate is sealed. It was certainly a feel for the desert, for what he calls 'the spiritual loveliness which came upon us by the way', which overtook Lawrence in Arabia, and made his job the more worth doing. Lawrence's war-time adviser about things Arabian, Gertrude Bell, fell inescapably before the magic of it on her first visit. Here is an early letter:

> Oh, the desert round Teheran! Miles and miles of it with nothing, *nothing* growing; ringed in bleak bare mountains snow crowned and furrowed with the deep courses of torrents. I never knew what desert was till I came here; it is a very wonderful thing to see; and suddenly in the middle of it all, out of nothing, out of a little cold water, springs up a garden. Such a garden! trees, fountains, tanks, roses and a house in it, the houses which we heard of in fairy tales when we were little. . . .[15]

She died in 1926; and the charm of her writing about the desert passed into the pages of Freya Stark.

Others who succumb to other distant places often seem strangely prepared beforehand, as if they knew that they were waiting. What was it that made Mary Kingsley, going out to West Africa in 1893 to finish her father's anthropological work and collect fish ('a hunter of beetles, fish and fetishes'), fall before its spell—a spell which many do not find there?

[15] *Letters.*

The springs of adventure

The charm of West Africa you never excape from. It gives you pleasure to fall under it when you are out there, but when you are back it gives you pain by calling you. . . . You hear the sound of the wind talking in the hard palm-leaves, the thump of tom-toms, the cry of the parrots passing over the mangrove swamps at evening . . . and you want to go back to the coast that is calling you and saying, as the African says to the soul of his dying friend, 'Come back, this is your home.' [16]

Incidentally, it must have taken her more courage to stay in England, championing the cause of Africans and traders, after confessing 'my ability to be more comfortable there than in England', than it would have to return to the Ogowe, with all its dangers of cannibals and disease and wild beasts.

🕊 🕊   🕊 🕊   🕊 🕊

Myriads of men and women from earliest times and from the records of Herodotus onward have known the physical magic of these far lands and (to them) new environment. But what of the air and the undersea and underground, all realms properly explored only in the last fifty odd years? The ecstasy of the flying sensation has called forth a corresponding aesthetic ecstasy of enthusiasm for the great expanses of the sky:

We have found a new freedom, a new ocean. For thousands of years we have crawled or run on the earth, or paddled across the seas, and all the while there had been this great ocean just over our heads in which we sail with joy. The longing for the sea: the call of the sea, one has heard of that, and that was the natural adventure in the past. But now it is a longing for the air, to go up. The air is more marvellous than any sea, it holds more beauty, more joy than any Pacific swell or South Sea lagoon.[17]

Dangerous comparisons! No sailor would allow those ones

[16] Quoted by W. Holmes in *Seven Adventurous Women*.
[17] From David Garnett's *A Rabbit in the Air*.

to pass; but they demonstrate at least that there is a similar charm about the two elements, which men who have experienced it cannot escape. 'I know of nothing, nothing in the world, equal to the wonder of nightfall in the air' (Saint-Exupéry). And above the air, in the stratosphere, that beauty is not lessened. 'The beauty of the sky (nine miles up) is the most poignant thing we have seen: it is sombre, dark blue or violet, almost black,' Professor Piccard wrote. For him, I believe, the sheer loveliness of it was part of the total charm.

The seamen can retort, of course, that they have the benefit both of the sea *and* sky, of the 'windy day and the white clouds flying' as well as of the 'flung spray'. And now they have the undersea also. The undersea explorers, a comparatively new breed if we do not count the early apparatus, will remark that they enjoy a variety of colour and movement unknown in any other form of adventure. First there is the variety of beautiful forms in fish; the 'splendid perfection' of the shark, for one, has had poems (he appears in Heredia's sonnet) and books written in its honour.[18] Then there are the colours. 'No painter could reproduce the luminosity of the blending colours. There is no expression for the colour, no words to describe it.'[19] And the sense of dramatic movement, 'where a lunar light revealed waving sea whips and circling fish', as William Beebe, inventor of the bathysphere and a formidable name in diving, saw it. Finally the shells and coral, which moved a tough pearl diver, making his first dive in a suit years ago, to devote his life to this new world.

I stood on the bottom completely bewildered at the sight which greeted me. What I had taken for a sandy bottom was a fantastic coral formation. It was a fairy-tale landscape, a new world, which I had only surmised from my glimpses

[18] See *Lords of the Sharks* by Franco Prosperi, as well as the books of Hans Hass.
[19] Mitchell Hedges, explorer and pioneer of shark hunting. From *Battling with Sea Monsters*.

through the water glass. I was so overawed that I d‹
my whole future life to this coral kingdom.[20]

The sea is wide and its wonders are for all to see.
body, it is remarked by the authors of *Man and the Und‹
World*, can nowadays go down and enjoy them. F
patient, and for those in search of a really *recherché* satis‹
there is a rather similar charm to be found in the
colour and light found in a great cave. The graceful fall of the
stalactite and the compelling upsurge of the stalagmite, the
'topaz light' and the 'gleam of diamonds on a bed of gold'
are there to be admired, however prosaic the scientists like
Casteret may, and do, assure us that their origins are. To me
it is faintly disappointing, if necessary, to learn that a rock I
have been admiring is of Pleistocene period, or that a flower
must be called *Lloydia*. They are beautiful, and that is what
matters.

In all earth's mysterious places there is this diverse beauty
to charm the eye of all its diverse beholders. *Chacun à son goût*.
Heaven knows how the taste of each is acquired; and thank
heaven we are all different.

[20] Victor Berge, *Danger is my Life*.

6

❦ ❦ ❦ ❧ ❧ ❧

Escape simple

La chair est triste, hélas! et j'ai lu tous les livres
Fuir, là-bas fuir! Je sens que les oiseaux sont ivres
D'être parmi l'écume inconnue et les cieux. . . .

Je partirai! Steamer balançant ta mâture
Lève l'ancre pour une exotique nature.
Un Ennui, desolé par les cruels espoirs,
Croit encore à l'adieu suprême des mouchoirs!

STÉPHANE MALLARMÉ

The more anyone reads the story of others' adventures or contemplates his own, the more he must be struck with the frequency of the escape motive, and I mean escape in no derogatory sense. Mallarmé's escape may have been a literary exercise rather than a practical proposition, but it represents a very real desire. Escape is different from the craving for contrast. Those Alpine pioneers of the Victorian era were not bored with their money making, their donning or their parish visiting. The escapists would have been; and while there is a strong escapist streak in all of us, it will probably come out strongest in those who add to their vigorous 'Wanderlust' a deep dissatisfaction with their jobs. It is surprising how many people take to an adventurous life quite simply because they are fed up with the office, the factory, the class room—and then go on from there.

Happy is the man who can turn his escape into a new job. And this very often happens. One of the most amusing books of Antarctic travel that I know is F. D. Ommanney's *South Latitude*. The author was a lecturer in zoology.

The springs of adventure

The beginning of every new session of the college . . . gave me a dreadful feeling of inevitability, of the circularity of life. It was like going round and round on the Inner Circle and fetching up endlessly and regularly at the same station. So in June 1929 I applied for a vacancy on the scientific staff of the *Discovery II* expedition . . . They said 'We've given you a pretty dirty job.' I did not care. My First M.B. class could assemble without me.[1]

The job was the scientific inspection of the carcasses of whales, and out of it came a profession and a good book. The scientist is lucky in being (usually) absorbed in his job; luckier often than the whaler himself, for many people escape into whaling and then:

'You like this?' he [a young Norwegian whaler] said. 'How you like to do it every day? Not so much damn fun eh? When I go home to Norway I say, Olafsen! You are a bloddy fool. This is the last time you go south. But here I am again. Ja! Every year'.[2]

Or the other Norwegian:

He had been to the University of Oslo but got tired of learning and went whaling instead. Then he got tired of that and went to work on a sheep farm in the Argentine, working eighteen hours a day at shearing time. Then he got tired of that and went whaling again and worked twelve hours a day all the time. Now he was tiring of that and wondering what to do next.[3]

The escape hole itself can be boring, and yet binding too with a bigger fascination. Moreover the second passage gives the clue to one component factor in escape—restlessness. Americans seem very prone to that disease, men like Lincoln Ellsworth in the same story. The first man to fly across the

[1] *South Latitude.*

[2] Ibid. See also R. B. Robertson's *Of Whales and Men* for the motive of escape into whaling, and the other motives which make men pursue that occupation.

[3] Ibid.

Antarctic Continent, from Graham Land to the Ross Sea
(1935), he returned in Discovery II. 'He never sat still for
long, and if he settled himself with a newspaper or a book,
he would be up again in a minute or two to begin his
wanderings anew. It was perhaps this restlessness that urged
him forth across the Poles and sent him up in aeroplanes over
waste and lonely places.'[4] Ellsworth himself finishes his
autobiography (*Beyond Horizons*) almost sadly: 'I find myself
restless, unhappy in spirit, trying to grasp some settled peace
wherein I can be content. There is more for me to do. I am
a strong and vigorous man with years of strong life ahead of
me. My whole training has been wrong for sedentary existence. . . .' He would have had a fellow sufferer from the
itch, twenty years later, in Sir Edmund Hillary. I well
remember, on Everest in 1953, the 'Battle against Boredom'
which used to be waged. It was sometimes won by exertion
and exhaustion: some of Ed's times for peaks and marches
were startling, the marches through Nepal being known as
'desperation marches' or just 'desperations'. Generally restlessness is a symptom of a deep uncertainty about oneself
and one's purpose, and generally it results in a frittering
away of time and personality. Adventure and beauty can
harness it to a strong central impulse which holds the personality and makes of the most restless men the most effective
men of action—while they last.

The Norwegian's predicament gives a clue also to why
many young men in 1939 welcomed war. The 'long-haired
boys' of Oxford described by Richard Hillary were restless,
over-talkative, quite uncertain what to do when they went
down. In their joining up there was usually a second motive
added to the obvious desire for self-fulfilment:

> For myself I was glad for purely selfish reasons. The war
> solved all problems of a career, and promised a chance of self-
> realisation that would normally take years to achieve. As a
> fighter pilot I hoped for a concentration of amusement, fear

[4] *South Latitude.*

and exaltation which it would be impossible to experience in any other form of existence.[5]

War was, for some, quite simply an escape from the difficulty of making up one's mind. Exaltation the airman *did* get, at first at any rate. ('I was released, filled with a feeling of power, of exaltation': Hillary of his first Spitfire solo. 'Frankly, I was terrifically excited and elated': Duke of his first fight.) Later Hillary found his true springs of action, rather different from those of adventure, to lie in the community which is the sweet fruit of bitter war, and which enables men and women to pull through it, despite the suffering and the heartbreak. Then he was killed.

Away from war-time, escape is usually the plain common impulse to leap up from desk or counter and out, into the world. Already in 1883 we find the future Arctic explorer Nansen, then a biologist, writing to his father after hearing of Nordenskjöld's successful Greenland expedition:

> I feel a sneaking longing to break loose every time I hear of such adventures—a longing for further experiences, for travel— and such thoughts bring a restlessness which is often hard to subdue, and troubles me a good deal before it finally calms down. However, the best remedy for it is work, and I apply it, as a rule with good results.

And at about the same time a London barrister, E. F. Knight, was watching a beautiful yacht anchored at Greenwich.

> I was more than usually thirsting after changes from city life— and lo! already there was an autumnal beauty in the sky; it would soon be too late—a summer wasted; all these glorious months of sunshine and breeze,—winter was near.[6]

In five minutes he and his friends had decided to buy an 18-ton yacht and sail across the Atlantic, to South America and back. 'All our discontent vanished like a smoke, and a most joyous enthusiasm succeeded it.'

That discontent and that enthusiasm are a recurrent

[5] *The Last Enemy.*   [6] *The Cruise of the 'Falcon'.*

theme of adventure books, making it very difficult to date them. In almost the same terms, some forty-five years later, I find an office man, a Bolivian diplomat and a cinematographer plotting to throw up everything and to make an amateur journey through the Bolivian jungle.

> When a man yields to the urge of Ishmael, the voice of Sarah is raised at tea-parties; for there is more heart burning over one sheep that escapes, than over the ninety and nine that catch the eight-fifteen to town every morning. . . . Nevertheless . . . Ishmael was stirred in each of us, making us dream of camp fires in a place where the richest man on earth could not find us if he wished.[7]

The party was as inexperienced as might have been expected. Sailing up the River Paraguay to the starting point they were told by an Australian host: 'If you weren't my guests, I'd say you were the biggest bloody fools in South America.' Luckily they were joined by Alexander Siemel, 'Tiger Man', an escaper of a different sort, a Russian who had fallen in love with his best friend's wife and cleared off into the jungle to be rid of his own emotions. They suffered intense discomfort, including thirst and tiny insects that keep a man awake for days, before reaching the slopes of the Andes. But they were satisfied. They had *done* something, and something utterly out of their everyday experience.

It was this same very simple urge to clear out that struck Alain Gerbault at Stanislas College, Paris. 'There, shut between high walls, longing to escape, to see the world, dreaming of adventure, I spent the unhappiest years of my life. . . . After the war I could neither work in a city nor lead the dull life of a business man. I wanted freedom, open air, adventure.'[8] So he bought a boat and sailed away alone in that. Finally, a last example out of many, Edmund Hillary again, on seeing two men who had just climbed Mt Cook.

[7] Julian Duguid, *Green Hell.*   [8] *The Fight of the Firecrest.*

The springs of adventure

I retreated to a corner of the lounge filled with a sense of futility at the dull, mundane nature of my existence. Those chaps, now, were really getting a bit of excitement out of life. I decided then and there to take up mountaineering. To-morrow I'd climb something! [9]

≈ ≈   ≈ ≈   ≈ ≈

The obverse of the desire to escape is the routine which prompts that desire. Nobody has painted its binding quality more deftly than Saint-Exupéry. The fact is, he seems to say, *people don't know they're stuck*, so fast are the ties. As a young airman, the night before his first flight with the old French Aéropostale, he walked about lighted Toulouse, a 'warrior in danger' standing aside from 'men's festivities'. Then, next morning, in the bus that drove him to the airfield, he listened to the office clerks talking.

I heard them talking to one another in murmurs and whispers. They talked about illness, money, shabby domestic cares. Their talk painted the walls of the dismal prison in which these men had locked themselves up. And suddenly I had a vision of the face of destiny.

Old bureaucrat, my comrade, it is not you who are to blame. No one ever helped you to escape. You, like a termite, built your peace by blocking up with cement every chink and cranny through which the light might pierce. You rolled yourself up into a ball in your genteel security, in routine, in stifling conventions of provincial life, raising a modest rampart against the winds and the tides and the stars. You have chosen not to be perturbed by great problems, having trouble enough to forget your own fate as a man. You are not the dweller upon an errant planet and do not ask yourself questions to which there are no answers. You are a petty bourgeois of Toulouse. Nobody grasped you by the shoulder while there was still time. Now the clay of which you were shaped has dried and hardened, and naught in you will ever awaken the sleeping musician, the

[9] *High Adventure.*

84

9: '*Tossing like a cork on the crest of the waves.*' The '*Joseph Con.*
on her world cruise.

poet, the astronomer that possibly inhabited you in the beginning.[10]

This sounds unkind to the clerks, especially after what I have said, and repeat, of courage. It may take more courage to lead the life of routine, and to give it a purpose and shape, than to go out adventuring beyond the seven seas. As Peter Fleming put it, wittily pooh-poohing the glamour of exploration:

> So it requires far less courage to be an explorer than to be a chartered accountant. The courage which enables you to face the prospect of sitting on a high stool in a smoky town adding up figures over a period of years is definitely higher, as well as a more useful sort of courage than any which the explorer may be called on to display.[11]

But he puts his finger on Saint-Exupéry's point when, having defended the young men of today as being by nature no less adventurous than formerly, he says that it is from lack of time or money, and from a sense of duty, that they take to the bowler hat instead of the topee. Then, as the years go by, the chance is gone. 'They don't have the chance and they have wisely given up hoping for the chance. In many cases, indeed, they have schooled themselves with almost too complete success to eschew the coloured dreams of boyhood. By quite forgoing those dreams, they have all but forgotten that they ever had them.' I think that is how Saint-Exupéry meant it, not the unkind way. He is sympathetic with, but sad at, the man who, *while* leading that life, loses sight utterly of the things round the corner. The miracle is that so many, in the myriad jobs of office, industry and commerce, somehow do manage to attain and hold the explorer's vision; whether through books, or from brief glimpses in the occasional plunge outside.

These men rotate the wheels of the world. If they all flew, or explored, or sailed the oceans, those wheels would stop.

[10] *Wind, Sand and Stars.* [11] *Brazilian Adventure.*

The Amazon jungle. '. . . the mystery of its vast unexplored wilds.'

We are grateful to them; and especially are we grateful
when they remember, with us, that the world has mysteries
as well as wheels.

🐿 🐿 🐿

Escape is a word of diverse meaning, covering 'a brief recup-
eration from battle training or waiting two hours in a queue
for a pound of hake', G. R. de Beer puts it. The book in
which he wrote that is called *Escape to Switzerland*, for in
Switzerland, with its wild scenery and sport, the routine-
tied have long been wont to make the maximum escape
possible in the shortest period. But now, in these after-war
days, the word escape can also cover a real physical running-
away from difficulties—into adventure. One of the extraordinary recent stories of a sea voyage is that of Frank and
Ann Davison. Everything seemed to have gone against them:
an aerodrome in 1939, a gravel-quarrying project, a small
holding, a geese-and-goats farm on Loch Lomond. To get
away they bought, after the war, a 70-foot fishing vessel
and everything went wrong with that. They had almost to
rebuild it, but in doing so landed themselves heavily in
debt. The ship, mortgaged, was about to come up for auction.
They decided to escape England, quite literally, across the
Atlantic, and they escaped. In the appalling voyage everything went wrong again, and Frank lost his life. The point
here is that they escaped, partly because it seemed an
obvious way out of financial and other difficulties, but partly
also because disappointments had put them out of tune with
the civilisation they hoped to be escaping. A vain hope.

Six months of civilisation. Six months of the frightful bond
man has imposed upon himself in the name of progress. The
island years had raised an insuperable barrier between us and
our urbanised fellow men, but whereas we could to some
extent appreciate their aims and attainments, having once
been on their side of the fence, they had no glimmer as to what

we were after, and obviously found us too brawny in outlook to be comfortable companions.[12]

So they escaped, in a small boat. The sequel to the tragedy was the quest for courage which took Ann Davison right across the Atlantic, this time alone.

The Davisons' *mal de vingtième siècle* is in line with the desire of many men and women to 'get away from it all', not only from routine but from the whole complexity of civilised life, as well as from 'the lies, the truths, and pain'. Undersea diving seems to me a perfect form of temporary escape, because the diver, wandering peacefully through a new element, enjoys a smooth mastery such as he can never achieve in 'real' life. I was, therefore, delighted when I found an aqualung diver writing:

> I have travelled to another world in which 'action is sister to the dream'. I have swept away in the heart of the sea, at a depth of several fathoms, all my anxieties as a man. Worries of the moment, scientific curiosity, metaphysical doubts have all been hurled into the sea and I do not regret any of them.
>
> Like many others I do not feel in perfect harmony with our age and the solitude of diving lulls and stays a deep-rooted dissatisfaction. Down below, where dreams and action move silently forward through the dense waters, side by side, man feels for a moment in tune with life.[13]

But like some others, J. Y. Cousteau for example, he goes on to justify the simple escape by the scientific and commercial advantages to which it will lead.

> We are surrounded by so much steel, rubber and electric wire that we should not sneeze at the chance of making direct contact with a natural element essential to life—the sea. It would be a great victory over the machine if we were able to dispense with the increasingly complicated mechanisation of our day and prove that we could get, at less expense, all that we needed from natural elements, animal and vegetable life.[14]

[12] *Last Voyage.*   [13] P. Diolé, *The Undersea Adventure.*
[14] Ibid.

The springs of adventure

I part company here. We are all bound to the wheel of science, explorers and climbers with the rest. Even Himalayan wanderers must needs scrape up scientific results to justify their grant from the Everest Foundation. But it seems to me that the real value of an escape lies in escaping, in 'regarding your profession with a lordly unconcern', as Diolé was doing a moment ago. Now, as if waking to the truth that what he has said may be taken down against him, he sets himself to marry escape to commerce, hoping that the union will make the former respectable. There is a danger here, that you may lose the best of both. It seems more satisfactory, if you feel that way, to be impenitent and impolite about the whole thing, like H. W. Tilman returning to England after the Second World War with plans for a new Himalayan journey already in his head:

> So loud and all-prevalent was the din raised by the planners of the new world that it was hardly possible for me to avoid absorbing something of the spirit of the times, so that I did feel some slight uneasiness at attempting to do once more what I wanted to do as opposed to what the mandarins might expect me to do. But I argued as Falstaff did about stealing, it was my vocation, 'and 'tis no sin for a man to labour in his vocation'. But an expedition at such a time! I could find no one who was either brazen enough to turn his back on the promised land or who was not indispensable to a planned economy.[15]

Tilman struck his own balance, and went off with two Swiss to try and climb Rakaposhi. It is a balance which each individual finds for himself. A lot of nonsense has at various times been talked about the immorality of escapers—very often by those who would like to escape but cannot. 'They are shirking their responsibilities,' these cry. 'When the Nation is crying out for lawyers, teachers, doctors, mechanics . . . And they escape into an unreal world!' The question of a man's profession is really beside the point. Would he be allowed to clear out if he ran football pools but not if he

[15] *Two Mountains and a River.*

was a dentist? As for unreality, surely it, like usefulness, is in the eye of the beholder. It is true, and that is about all one can say, that some people choose to weigh their balance on the side of adventure, find that it is not real for them 'full-time' and then seem to drift, between escape and everyday. But it is equally true that many are in the position of Saint-Exupéry's clerks, who have for so long chosen not to see the great day dawning that they do not realise it is there.

A man who always knew that he was escaping, yet considered the escape worth the risk, was Eric Shipton of Everest. In 1934, with Tilman, he was planning to visit Garhwal and make the first entry into the apparently inaccessible basin of Nanda Devi. It was the sort of problem to delight Shipton, and he is engagingly frank about his conscience.

> Then the thought occurred to me, 'Why not spend the rest of my life doing this sort of thing?' . . . It was a disturbing idea, one which caused me much heartsearching and many sleepless nights. . . .
>
> I do not know how long I fought the temptation. I certainly suffered qualms of conscience, but they were due more to the mere prospect of such exquisite self-indulgence than to fear of the consequences of abandoning the search for an assured future, provision for old age and other worthy ambitions. I had always rather deplored the notion that one must sacrifice the active years of one's life to the dignity and comfort of old age. Also the less conservative of my monitors assured me that things had a way of panning out so long as one knew what one wanted. So the decision was taken, albeit with a faint heart.[16]

That is a man taking off and knowing whither, more or less. As example of the man making off into adventure that is unreal, justifying the outcriers, we may take John Hornby. A Harrovian unable to tolerate his Nantwich home, 'cricket, and horses and hunting', he made his life in northern

[16] *Upon that Mountain.*

Canada and became a legend even among the tough trappers. He could run 100 miles in twenty-four hours and go barefoot and bareheaded in winter. But he did not fit into their life. 'He had no commercial or scientific ambitions, no will-o'-the wisp dream of gold or fur. His past was not notably disreputable.' [17] He just drifted, therefore, often over difficult country, with 'a rifle, a fishnet and a bag of flour'. Even his ascetic or masochistic spirit, shared with the travellers of Chapter 2, had in his case no aim beyond its own 'positive value', and perhaps a sort of blissful agony to be suffering in the country he loved.

He served in the 1914–18 War, was wounded and decorated and returned, across the Great Bear Lake, 'a desperate man running away from civilisation, looking like death, making the tremendous trip in a little boat no better than a broken-down packing case', as one who saw him put it.

His expedition with Bullock in 1924–5, involving an Arctic winter in a cave and a 535-mile journey in 107 days, was 'a feat of endurance perhaps, an act of folly certainly, but not a notable journey by any rudimentary standard of judgement or skill'. There was no plan worthy of the name about it. However, Hornby still hankered after one more trip. In 1926, in England, he persuaded Edgar Christian, then sixteen years old, to come out with him. Joined by Harold Adlaird they went north. The story of how they wintered, too late for the caribou migrations on which they had relied for food, and died one by one, is heroic and futile. [18] What matters here is that Hornby, the 'tragically light-hearted' purposeless rolling stone who had got them into this mess, killed himself in his efforts to save the others by hunting.

The aimless philosophy (or lack of it) of escape had

[17] G. Whalley, 'In the Land of Feast and Famine', *The Cornhill*, Spring 1957. To this article I am indebted for my information.

[18] *Unflinching*, by Edgar Christian. (The diaries.)

worked adequately when he was alone. It did not do so with others.

If it did not work with Hornby in the sense of giving him a positive purpose, it did strangely work in the case of the Latvian who writes under the name of Fred Rebell. He had greater cause for despair: a broken marriage and no home, disappointment in love, Australia on the dole in 1931.

> There seemed to be only one way out, for me: the way which many were taking every day in those times: the leap from the Gap (the cliffs at the mouth of Sydney Harbour). . . . This would be the end of one born so obviously a misfit in life. But even as I stood there about to take the plunge, a notion crossed my mind . . .[19]

The notion was that, if he destroyed his body, his soul would still be tortured. So back he went to the Sydney Public Library to read about the Hereafter. Having done that, and decided to emigrate, he could not get a visa. He, therefore, remembering his jilting and determined to prove himself in those qualities which the beloved must have found deficient (there is a mixture of motives here), went back to the Library and read up sailing. On December 31, 1931, he set out from Sydney for America in an 18-foot open boat. But the manner in which he arrived, and the religious experiences which made the whole thing, for him, mean something, belong elsewhere.

What a diverse collection the escapers are! And what a revaluation they need to do, if they are to decide which for them is real, the refuge or the bonds escaped; which should demand their first loyalty! Yet they continue to go out, and the heart to be sore, as it has been ever since Ulysses left Ithaca. To those who stay behind it seems that they go with joy upon their faces. 'She might snare him,' the wife of the airman thinks, 'in a fragile net of music, love and flowers,

[19] *Escape to the Sea.*

but, at each departure, he would break forth without, it seemed to her, the least regret.' [20] Each time, he escaped her.

⁂

This leads me to a last point about the business of 'reality'. Many who go out from the crowded routine claim that they escape into reality, not from it. That is the justification of a longing, it may be said. But it is true that some people 'find themselves' and become real people in solitude, as they never could in society. The explorer Stanley 'found himself' by being alone, on the horrible 350-mile journey from Bagamoyo to Unanyembe, *en route* to find Livingstone in Tanganyika. We have seen what he hoped from this journey. But he could not know that the death of his companions, swamp and disease, even the need to use a dog whip to keep his porters going—all these would have an exhilarating effect, as if he had escaped life's complications into a simplicity with which he could deal effectively.

> This self-dependence, which might have demoralised a weaker nature, worked very otherwise with him. It produced 'a delightful tranquillity' in his soul to be free of European trammels; not to care what governments stood or fell, what the news of courts and cities was. To be independent of criticism, safe from the possibility of ridicule, and free to grapple with events; to be not only his own master but also the master of others; this life, despite the heat, malaria and various trials of Africa, suited Stanley. He grew and hardened.[21]

Stanley went on to be both a great explorer and a great commercial coloniser. Others, feeling perhaps that their positions and their realities are more assailable, turn to the new set of values for defence. Frank Smythe, who devoted

---

[20] *Night Flight.* C. J. W. Simpson, at the end of *North Ice*, remarks the paradox that those who have the happiest homes often seem to feel most the need to leave them.

[21] A. J. A. Symons, *H. M. Stanley.*

his life to climbing and photographing and writing about hills, tried to make them mean, at the 'mental' level, a *return* to reality. 'They bring (man) face to face with realities and in doing so inculcate a valuable lesson in the association of simplicity and happiness.' [22] The first statement simplifies things into a *cliché* and I do not believe means very much. Realities can be faced just as well in a Dublin dock or London street as on the top of Kamet. The second, of course, contains its truth and is repeated in almost the same terms by very many. [23] The modern spontaneous return to the country and the sea is a recognition of the benefits of a return to natural things. The problem which Smythe, with his simple explanation, does not solve, which perhaps nobody can solve, is how the mass of men is to adjust the plain reality which it perceives, at present, on holiday, with that other life, of city and factory, which must be admitted to be as real and as exacting as hill or sea. You cannot just run away, and not many can make mountains their life. A multitude, therefore, lead a double life, yearning from the office stool after the heathery rock under the fingers, the little tent on green turf and the salt touch of big seas. There is a danger of these 'realities' turning into uncomfortable will o' the wisps.

Let us agree that reality is overwritten, perhaps over-dramatised, and leave the last word with Peter Fleming: 'No one can say with certainty, "I found reality at such a place and such a time"; but there are days and circumstances in which, when one looks back on them, it seems as if reality was not so far away as usual.' As for the word itself, 'Too many leader-writers, too many shaggy women overheard in small restaurants, too many of the starker authors have sapped the word's vitality. It should be

---

[22] *The Spirit of the Hills*. And see all Chapter XXI.

[23] For instance, C. J. W. Simpson, introducing *North Ice*, his book on the 1952 Greenland expedition, elaborates 'a directness and simplicity of outlook which is rare in the busy Western world'.

subjected as seldom as possible to the strain of a public appearance.'

🙖 🙔   🙖 🙔   🙖 🙔

We fly out of routine, into the hills. And the strange thing, the final twist to the story, is that the very element to which escape is made can have an anemone-like quality which absorbs a man's powers. At the same time it instils a consciousness that it does so, together with, often, a strange yearning to get *back*, to escape from escape as it were. A young and well-known mountaineer, who has given years to climbing and to teaching how to climb, wrote in a letter: 'Increasingly I feel that the whole business of climbing is perverted, irresponsible and immoral: but, unfortunately, I still like it. What a waste of time and money and life. Aesthetic experience as easily gained otherwise too.' [24] In the air, we all know of men like A. E. Clouston, who refused high-powered jobs which they would like to do, because they must be *in* the air; and for that charm, of flying, no money or responsibility could be compensation. But the greatest claimant is the sea, for it demands most. Even marrying a woman killed Yann, the Breton mariner of *Pêcheur d'Islande*, who had vowed that he was betrothed only to the sea. When he went out again, leaving his bride, the sea claimed him.

The story is symbolic. How many have tried to escape back again in different ways, some of them like Billy in Masefield's *Hell's Pavement*:

When I'm discharged in Liverpool 'n' draws my bit of pay,
I won't come to sea no more

he says—but back he comes, his bit of pay spent, his only safety on the grey sea. Or, to come back where we started this chapter, listen with Ommanney to the runaway students,

[24] Devotees of a sport can have rather the same feeling. A few days before being killed in the Mille Miglia (1957) the Marquis of Portago concluded that 'racing is a vice and, as such, extremely hard to give up'.

94

shop assistants and the rest who are all potential Billies. They chat as they near home after a whaling season.

I know, when I hear them talking in this simple and ingenuous way about giving up the sea and about launching out on to seas far more perilous than the Southern Ocean, that they will all sail again, or nearly all—if not in this ship then in some other. When they pay off, their hard-earned cash, necessarily saved at sea because there is no way of spending it, will soon all be gone 'having a good time', whatever that may mean. And when the good time is over, it will be so much easier to slip round to the shipping-master's office and sign on again— if not in this ship then in some other. The call of the sea is all my eye—it is the impossibility of escape. The sea is terribly possessive.

'D'you know a quick way of making money, sir?'

'No, son. I don't.'

'How would it be if I bought a coffee stall?' . . .

'I've got ambitions you know, sir. I'm going to attend evening classes when I get home.'

But the sea is terribly possessive.[25]

And it is hard to escape from an escape.

[25] *South Latitude.*

7

Escape becomes lodestone

Who has known heights and depths shall not again
   Know peace—not as the calm heart knows
Low ivied walls, a garden close,
   The old enchantment of a rose.
And though he tread the humble ways of men
   He shall not speak the common tongue again.

In the twilight of Himalayan June I sit below a mountain in Nepal. It is now nearly a year since we first knew that we were coming to try to climb this peak of some 23,000 feet: nearly a year of thought and care and preparation culminating in a six weeks' struggle with the toughest snow and ice problem any of us have faced. Why have we done it? And how has this great beetling tower come to loom so large in our lives?

Among all the 'escapists' whom we have been considering, there are some who link the desire to get away with a complementary fixation of mind about the places to which they *want* to get away. They are like—or should I say we are like, for there is a great company of lesser escapists—children who turn from the complications of a school or world which they cannot understand, to focus their eyes on some large object more easily comprehensible. If they could only climb or fly or sail that,[1] then they would in some mysterious way catch up with their neighbours who excel in all the everyday virtues. The large object is simple, easy to keep the eyes on: the Niger, the Nile, Everest, the Pole, the seven seas. Since

---

[1] 'If I could navigate a ship across the ocean on my own, it might be that I would be well on the way to learning how to live.' Ann Davison, in *My Ship is so Small*.

mountains are the largest single objects on earth's surface, and since they culminate in a point on which ambitions, hopes, aspirations can very easily be deposited, they have become, since the last century, especially liable to be dreamed about by hungry humans.

The trouble with dreams is that they tend to get in the way of other necessary things in life. Perhaps, I think as I sit waiting for the last dusk to be swallowed in night, perhaps my mind wandered in those months of teaching before we came out. Perhaps I sat dreaming of the great shape and singing the name (after I had found out how to pronounce it) of Machapuchare, when I should have been attacking the pile of French proses in the corner; for I taught French, and ought to be teaching it now. But the habit of thinking this way about hills is hard to break; it has been the same with me ever since Snowdon and Tryfan kept popping up above my school desk to comfort me, and later, during those Army days in war-time India, when the thought of a twenty-three thousander made summer almost endurable. Besides, my cousin and boyhood hero, Colin Kirkus, did he not dream too, in a Liverpool office? He was perhaps the best known rock climber in Wales between the wars; and he dreamed of a new route that he might find among the cliffs at each weekend. Then, when the weekend came, off he would go, sometimes walking or cycling to Snowdon if he had not the railway fare. The world would never have called or made of Colin a super-successful man of business; but he found success incidentally, in the only way he wanted it, quietly on the steeper sides of British hills, and once in the Himalaya. He came near to finding it on Everest, which to him, as to many climbers, was the ultimate lodestone.

As I sit on and it becomes too dark to write, for dusk does not give you much time out here, I determine to look more closely at some of the lodestone seekers of earlier date, to see whether they give any help to my wonderings.

🦅 🦅   🦅 🦅   🦅 🦅

The springs of adventure

Of those whom I had read or knew, and who had had a very strong yearning after a particular goal in the world, it seemed to me that about half came into what I could call the 'escapist group'. With the others, usually the more extroverted, ambition was in line with their general life and in keeping with their career. When Robert Peary reached the North Pole in 1909 after twenty years of effort it was the crowning point of his career as a naval officer, and in fact he was promoted to rear-admiral not long afterwards. True, the promotion was clouded with controversy; for another man, Dr F. A. Cook, claimed to have reached the Pole already and publicly disputed Peary's findings. But that is another story, and almost incidental to the feeling of America about him. Now Peary was as ardent as any man could be for the Pole's attainment. When he reached it he wrote in his diary:

> The Pole at last! The prize of three centuries. My dream and goal for twenty years. Mine at last! It seems all so simple and commonplace. [The last feeling is recorded also by Hillary on top of Everest.]

He even said that the Pole had become so much a part of him that he considered himself no more than the instrument for its attainment. At the same time he did not *escape* to it. For the Pole itself, as he regarded it, could become instrumental to the plans of his own wider life.

For my 'escapists' I am going to take the cases of three men of a different sort; men in whom an overwhelming desire to find some particular thing swamped all other desires and made them meaningless. Like a magnet it drew them and for it they abandoned routine and home, civilised life and friends. In each case (the last almost certainly) the goal killed its seeker.

What the Pole was to be to Peary the Niger became, and more, to the Scotsman Mungo Park. He escaped first from the confinement of his family manse, then from the routine life of a doctor. How he picked up his passion for the unexplored Niger is hard to see: another case of inexplicable attraction. For ten years, until it killed him in 1805, it dominated his thoughts.

The first journey (1795–7), during which he was the first white man to set eyes on the river, makes the healthier reading. He was alone, and he resembled Stanley in being at his easiest when alone or with a handful of men whom he could ruthlessly command. The journey is a strange story of privation and capture by the Moors, escape, exhaustion, a thirst so overpowering that he swooned and thought he was dead. But he reached the Niger, determined its course and inspected its upper reaches; then he almost succumbed to fever on the way back.

I want to distinguish between the official and the personal motives for both Park's journeys. Officially he went in the name of geography for the Africa Association, and of commerce for England. Personally he went, as it seems to me, because this great uncharted river charmed him more than anything else in the world. By 1804 he was a respectable married doctor in Peebles with a family and a career. But he was determined to go again. The second journey holds the reader in fascinated horror. The party of thirty-eight soldiers, five shipwrights and two officers, which he led, started only six weeks before the rains (he never says why) and ran straight into fever. Park was courageous and ruthless. The living he pushed on, the dying he left with a loaded revolver. Three soldiers, one of them crazy, Lt Martyn and Park prepared to embark on the Niger and follow its course to the southern sea. Before embarking he wrote to Lord Camden:

> ... I shall set sail to the east with the fixed resolution to discover the termination of the Niger or perish in the attempt. ... My dear friend Mr Anderson and likewise Mr Scott are both dead, but though all the Europeans who are with me should die, and though I were myself half dead, I would still persevere; and if

99

I could not succeed in the object of my journey, I would at least die on the Niger.[2]

He did die, on the Niger. In November of 1805 his party was ambushed and himself drowned trying to escape.

The case of another Scot, David Livingstone, is more complicated. I would be the last to venture a short biography of him; but he seems to me relevant to our present purpose. He started life as a missionary. 'If he had pursued to the end the vocation he chose in his youth he would have won a high place, no doubt, in the roll of heroic missionaries.'[3] But he did not. He became, in the admiring eyes of a biographer, 'an explorer, a missionary, but also a geographer, a scientist and a humanitarian statesman'.[4] In the eyes of the very critical, that is myself, he remains one who shared both the escape and the lodestone with the other protagonists of this chapter.

Consider his life. He began looking north on his very first mission in South Africa. On the bigger journey of 1851–2 his unfortunate wife bore her fifth child 'whilst the party was still in motion'. Then she was sent home. Livingstone pushed up north and spent with Africans those great wander years of 1853–6, during which he crossed the breadth of Africa. He came back and was lionised—but quarrelled with the London Missionary Society which had sent him in the first place and felt, understandably, that he had neglected missions. When he started on his last journey in 1866 it was ostensibly to further the campaign against slave traders. 'The Nile sources are valuable to me only as a means of enabling me to open my mouth with power among men,' he wrote. But they had other charm.

The part played by him in getting the slave traffic

[2] *Travels of Mungo Park.* I cannot understand the Everyman editor's admiration for Park. There is an inhumanity and *idée fixe* about the Journal which are frightening. But the man's courage seems to have tamed a number of those who have written about him, from Sir Joseph Banks onward.

[3] R. Coupland, *Livingstone's Last Journey.*

[4] J. Simmons, *Livingstone and Africa.* Note the order.

stopped is hard to define. To his countrymen he was a symbol of the fight. Certainly he compromised with the traders, and even lived with them for a time in a way surprisingly at variance with his intentions. That was partly the force of circumstances; even Samuel White Baker compromised, in order to be allowed to move at all. Still, it seems almost ironical that the trade, stopped so soon after Livingstone's death and to his glory, was stopped largely through the efforts of a much less known man—John Kirk. With the Nile, however, Livingstone could not compromise. The idea of finding its sources and early course lured him on, a *fata morgana*, through the dreary years between 1866 and 1873. Somewhere, just around the corner, they must be. When found by Stanley he would not return with him because 'he must finish his work first'—in other words 'determine for all whether his "dream" were true or false'.[5] He even convinced himself that this was his duty. On February 18, 1872, he wrote in his Journal: 'My judgement said "All your friends will wish you to make a complete work of the exploration of the Nile before you retire." ' By that time he was racked with chronic dysentery and once went eight days without eating, yet 'the idea of yielding to it, of admitting that he was attempting something beyond his strength and going back, seems never to have crossed his mind'.[6] And Simmons, almost unwillingly, writes: 'From the bare records of the closing weeks of his life, it seems that the problem had come to dominate his mind. The very last words he wrote were concerned with the name of a river.' [7]

[5] R. Coupland, *Livingstone's Last Journey.*

[6] Ibid. Only those who visit the African waters can understand Livingstone's mixed passions. L. van der Post writes: 'I could understand as I had never done before how Livingstone could be both such a God-drunk and lake-intoxicated person. Having looked that wide land full in the face and seen those waters in their great frame of mountains and incalculable sky, it is not hard to realise how a search for them could easily be identified with a search for God.' *Venture to the Interior.*

[7] J. Simmons, *Livingstone and Africa.*

Is that the sickness of a man working only to stop slav
traders? He wandered on, trailing circles on the map, per
forming prodigies of endurance, denying a father to hi
children and humbly believing it all to be the divine will–
until he died, the problem no nearer to solution. Indeed, a
the last, he was looking in the wrong place.

Livingstone an escapist? From what, pray? From England
for one thing. 'He was a born leader of men, but of blac
men, not of white,' Coupland has written. From the ties of
family. From the routine life of a missionary—but *not* from
a religious conception of his work. And whither did he escape
Into the magic of Africa, towards a goal that seemed th
more attractively compelling the more remote it became, fo
that is a quality of the will o' the wisp. Towards the Nile
A very great explorer, yes, but besides that? I wonder.

The last of my three is Colonel P. H. Fawcett, still
figure of mystery though over thirty years have passed sinc
he disappeared. Him I can treat more briefly, partly becaus
the only real authority for his life and work is his own book
Exploration Fawcett, edited by his son, partly because th
main purpose of his last nineteen years is in outline ver
clear.

First of all it should be said that, while not of the statur
of the other two, he was a very genuine explorer, not
stunter, with good scientific work to his credit. He was
Founder's Medallist of the Royal Geographical Society. Th
idea of South America had attracted him already; as we hav
seen, types of country can attract people even before the
know them. He was asked in 1906 if he would take on
boundary delimitation in Bolivia.

Would I? Here was the chance I had been waiting for—th
chance to escape from the monotonous life of an artiller
officer in home stations . . .

Naturally I accepted the offer. The romantic history of th
Spanish and Portuguese conquests, and the mystery of its vas
unexplored wilds, made the lure of South America irresistibl

to me. There were my wife and son to consider, and another child was on the way; but Destiny intended me to go, so there could be no other answer![8]

But as he went on, becoming to an ever greater degree fascinated by his exploration, the idea of a hidden city in the jungle of Matto Grosso took possession of him completely. By the time he was preparing his last expedition (1924–5), he was almost diseased, obsessed with it. There is pathetic sadness in the end of this part of the book, as if he knew that his dream *must* come true, the dream on which he had spent years of life, or else . . .

If the journey is not successful my work in South America ends in failure, for I can never do any more. I must inevitably be discredited as a visionary, and branded as one who had only personal enrichment in view. Who will ever understand that I want no glory from it—no money for myself? . . My wife and children have been sacrificed for it, and denied many of the benefits that they would have enjoyed had I remained in the ordinary walks of life. . . . Of our twenty-four years of married life only ten have been spent together.[9]

The gaunt figure became more silent, more apparently odd.

Ever since his return to England late in 1921 my father's impatience to start off on his last trip was tearing at him with ever-increasing force. From reticent he became almost surly.[10]

But the plan materialised. Fawcett disappeared, with his son Jack and another white companion, into the jungle of his desire. His last words, written to his wife, are reminiscent of Mungo Park. 'You need have no fear of any failure.' Possibly the Indians killed him. Possibly he found his city. Probably nobody will ever know for sure what happened, despite the search expeditions. In any case, it is not the end but the journey that matters.

🐦 🐦   🐦 🐦   🐦 🐦

[8] *Exploration Fawcett.*   [9] Ibid.   [10] Ibid.

A rather different type from these, but one whose name occurs to me irresistibly when I think of them, is a woman, the Lady Hester Stanhope, at one time styled 'Queen of the Lebanon'. She is different partly because her desire to leave England, and the aim of her ambitions in the East, were curiously mixed with her desire for power, the physical need to dominate others.

'The last of the eighteenth-century eccentrics, the first of the nineteenth-century pioneers' was a niece of William Pitt, for whom, after a stormy youth with an eccentric father, she kept house. She left England chiefly to escape the inferior social position to which she would be reduced after his death in 1806. From England she moved east, then east again, and later renounced British citizenship altogether. But the escape turned itself strangely into a mad wandering with a mad purpose. At Brusa, where she was trailing her twenty-two-year-old lover and her doctor behind, she first heard of North's failure to reach Palmyra, the fabulous desert city of Zenobia. It became her ambition to be crowned 'Queen of the East' there, and so she was, after overcoming all the obstacles of a difficult and dangerous journey. It was a moving ceremony, but one which she took more seriously than the other participants. She styled herself 'Queen of the Arabs' and nobody contradicted her, since she paid well for the title.

Poor Lady Hester! The mirages flickered one after the other before her eyes. A voluntary outcast from England, she could not return where now 'she would be ignored as a fading old spinster with a tarnished reputation'.[11] The last mirage was the least possible of attainment. She was to make a triumphal entry into Jerusalem, to be crowned queen there too. She ended her life a broken old woman shut up in her house under the Lebanese hills, yet to the last so imperious and so intimidating to the boldest emir that in wartime her courts were crowded with refugees. There they were safe.

[11] Joan Haslip, *Lady Hester Stanhope*.

The years pass, but the desires remain. Through the twentieth century life becomes more complicated, the pattern of fiddling pieces more difficult to fit together. Men begin to despair of ever fitting it together at all. More insistently the great simple objects of the world seem to beckon to them at office windows. More pressingly the problems of desk or uniform push them out, towards something they know they can understand and think they can achieve.

Sports multiply, and the great mountains become accessible, while the expanses of the ocean yield to ever smaller boats.[12] Motives entwine themselves beyond hope of disentanglement.

What of the lodestone of John Caldwell, who had a bride in Australia after the last war and found himself demobilised in America, with no prospect of getting to her by the routine methods? He escaped those and sailed a small boat 8,500 miles across the Pacific, was wrecked but arrived. He knew almost nothing of sailing before he started, read *How to Sail* in harbour and capsized on the way out; but 'somewhere was the ultimate of faith that all would come right in its time'.[13] His goal was his wife, and he reached her. It could be called a miracle.

There are so many more. The mountaineers have appeared already in these pages, and I have not gone on pressing upon them a doubtful title. But there is one figure which sticks out. I do not mean that George Mallory, a name inevitable in any story of adventure, was an escapist in any of the common derogatory senses. But he was a man who, before Everest, seemed to come together as a person only in action, on mountains. As writer, teacher ('He couldn't keep order,' was Sir Frank Fletcher's dry comment) and soldier he seems to have been still incomplete. Then came the first

[12] The smallest that I know is the canoe of Captain Romer, in which he paddled across the South Atlantic, taking three months over the journey and arriving 'encrusted in dried salt'.

[13] *Desperate Voyage.*

The springs of adventure

Everest expedition of 1921. The spearhead of the reconnaissance, he found what seemed the only route. In 1922 a great
attempt was made. But before 1924 he had a new job in
which he was deeply interested, and his family was increas-
ing. When invited he hesitated. But the tug of Everest had
become almost in imagination a duty. He might write, as he
did, that something would be lost when that lonely summit
was reached; but he could not hold back from trying to
reach it. He showed supremely at his best on the mountain,
drawn to it as by a charm, claiming it as a prize. On
April 19, 1924, he was writing to his wife: 'The conquest
[there is a good deal of 'conquest' in these letters] of the
mountain is the great thing, and the whole plan is mine
and my part will be a sufficiently interesting one and will
give me, perhaps, the best chance of all of getting to the
top. . . . It is almost unthinkable with this plan that *I* shan't
get to the top; I can't see myself coming down defeated.'

Ironic words for one doomed never to come down at all.
In the last letter, on May 27: 'Six days to the top from this
camp!' Here is an amusing touch of an assumption that it is
his mountain, that *he* is going to climb it, which is curiously
at variance with the modest character recorded in Pye's
biography [14] and by conversation with friends. The idea of
Everest, his lodestone, had grown into his life to exclude
other goals. There have been many successful schoolmasters;
there has never been a man whose name is linked more
closely with one great place or object. For that association it
would perhaps be worth any failure.

The adventures of war form a vast subject of their own
and are very seldom 'of their own choice'—apart from
escapes, and these are a stern choice indeed. But these
escapes are normally made with the sole object of getting
back to one's own lines, and I include there the remarkable
escapes of F. S. Chapman in Malaya, when his own lines
were no more than himself. Having escaped he went on

[14] David Pye, *George Leigh Mallory*.

killing Japanese. But the escapes which were not made with that one end in view might properly be claimed in this chapter, because they must be made with some very attractive goal in view.

Two examples. One early morning of 1942 an Italian prisoner of war in the Kenya P.O.W. Camp 354 stood looking at the distant Mount Kenya. He determined to climb the mountain, then come back and give himself up. The story is well known. 'To get out into the deluge of life' and to try the impossible, to escape and climb a mountain, these were the ideals, the more ardently cherished the more ridiculous they might appear to others.

> I enjoyed in imagination hearing this sort of thing: 'Have you ever heard of such madness? To risk catching a bullet in the ribs for the fun of dying of cold up there, or of being mauled by wild beasts.' At which the sentimental one would add: 'And all three married and two of them have children too!' The very clever one would remark: 'I can understand escaping with the purpose of reaching Mogadisco or the neutral territory of Portuguese East Africa. Impossible? I quite agree, but at least one would live in the hopes of regaining one's liberty, not the fixed programme of going back into the camp in the certainty of being punished at that.' [15]

Felice Benuzzi and his two companions experienced fantastic difficulties in making crampons and ice-axes out of tins, patching together other equipment, escaping, carrying heavy loads for nine days to the foot of the mountain (the modern traveller with porters does it in one, but besides their other difficulties they had no map). They reconnoitred, then attempted, Batian, the higher summit. One of them fell ill; but the *idée fixe* had got them, and his companions left him to wait while they tried a subsidiary 16,000-foot point called Lenana.

> He knew that after Lenana we should have to march back practically without food. His condition could not improve and

[15] *No Picnic on Mount Kenya.*

he had only to wait, and to wait is one of the most horrible things on earth as every prisoner knows.[16]

He waited until they could start back, really starving now and suffering, to give themselves up at the end of it.

They got nothing out of this, except punishment. Nothing but memory. Back in camp they could romance at ease. 'The dream you dream shall live in your memory,' says the wind, 'a delight that will never stale. It will be your inspiration in the bitter years to come.' That was the comfort of Kenya; and that is what a dream does, a dream to which men escape gladly.

My other wartime escaper, Heinrich Harrer, had also a lodestone before him; but in his case it changed. An Austrian interned in India in 1939, he had the idea, when he escaped, of getting across Tibet to the Japanese lines in Burma or China. Like Benuzzi, who licked his lips over 'the first coffee in freedom', he enjoyed that liberty which only the imprisoned can know. 'This was the first time in my life that I really understood what it meant to be free. We enjoyed this glorious feeling . . .' [17] But also, as a mountaineer, he rejoiced in the thought of the Himalaya and Tibet. 'Up here we had the Himalayas right in front of us. How attractive to a mountaineer was the thought of winning through to Tibet over the passes.' [18] As he went on, through hunger and cold, danger of capture and discomfort of every kind, it was the idea of reaching Lhasa, the Holy City, which drove every other objective out of his mind and that of his companion, Peter Aufschnaiter.

The war had ended before they reached what had become the ultimate goal.

It was January 15, 1946, when we set out on our last march . . . We turned a corner and saw, gleaming in the distance, the golden roofs of the Potala, the winter residence of the Dalai

---

[16] *No Picnic on Mount Kenya.*   [17] *Seven Years in Tibet.*
[18] Ibid.

Lama and the most famous landmark of Lhasa. This moment compensated us for much. We felt inclined to go down on our knees like the pilgrims and touch the ground with our foreheads.[19]

Arrived, they had to overcome obstacles that had defeated Sven Hedin and stretched Madame David-Neel; for very few foreigners, other than officials, have been allowed to stay in Tibet. They did finally, as all know, become 'officials of the Tibetan Government', and Harrer the confidant of the Dalai Lama himself. When the latter fled the communist invasion Harrer went with him, and returned to Germany, distressed at the fate of Tibet. 'Part of my being is indissolubly linked with that dear country.' Aufschnaiter has remained in Nepal, yearning always towards that roof of the world to which he came by chance. It holds him, so that for its sake he will give up everything he has, everything that he might be at home.

More people than we usually suspect do things out of the ordinary with little idea, to begin with, other than that of fleeing the rut or the prison camp, real and spiritual. But as they go some single goal takes possession of their mind, a thing simple and big and worth while, a great wood which contrasts splendidly with the trees in which they have been lost. Towards this they make their way, sometimes furtively in weekend snatches as if trying not to be seen, sometimes boldly in defiance, sometimes only gradually losing themselves in the sublime idea ahead, not aware that they are neglecting home or work or the opportunity of everyday. Sometimes, if they do realise that, they look upon themselves as Maries who have chosen the good, against the Marthas who absorb themselves fruitlessly in the trivial round.

[19] Ibid.

The springs of adventure

I believe that there is a streak of madness in these men and women whose eyes are fixed upon the stars. They are quite right, the criers of woe and the protectors of Martha. In a world having the majority of its population under-fed and in constant danger of war, there are other things to be done than to dream dreams of an escape towards some glorious and useless goal. Yes, there is a streak of madness about them. But it has descended from the stars on which they fix their eyes. It is a divine madness.

8

❧ ❧ ❧ ❧ ❧ ❧

Fame and money

Die That ist alles, nichts der Ruhm.

GOETHE

Some set out to explore
earth's limit, and little they recked if
Never their feet came near it
outgrowing the need for glory.

C. DAY LEWIS

Fame and money. Why together? Because they are both
outward, visible and material rewards for anything that one
does, and because, in seeking them, a man aims at something
other than the satisfaction of his most private impulses.
Moreover, fame very often means money, while money
always confers upon its possessor a certain degree of fame.
As Monsieur Jourdain's music master remarked, it is not
much use praising with empty hands.

There is fame and fame. Milton, when he wrote 'Fame
is the spur that the clear spirit doth raise . . .', would not
have had in mind a headline in the Sunday papers. In the
field of adventure, the Royal Geographical Society's Gold
Medal or the Britannia Trophy are rewards with which any
man might be pleased, since they mean the discerning
approval of his own particular group, the people best
qualified to judge his performance. Nobody would say that
a Gold Medal is an object striven for by itself. The thought
of one might conceivably quicken the muscles, and it is very
nice when it comes. But what it stands for, the approbation
of fellow experts, is obviously a good for which explorers in
any field will strive, and whose importance is shown up in

cases like the North Pole controversy between Peary and Cook. There is another sort of fame, presumably that which Goethe had in mind, since he was himself not averse to the praises of the discerning: the public fame which is akin to notoriety. Now among those who go off and do strange things there is a wide variety of feeling towards this kind. A few do things in order to gain it; others use it in order to do the things; a great number regard it as an unpleasant necessity; a few are shocked and run miles to avoid it.

Those who go out frankly in order to cull reputation can be conveniently called the stunters. I mean the word in no harsh sense, for why not? It does nobody any harm, and interesting feats are sometimes performed. To take an example or two from the last century, thus showing that the game is not as new as we sometimes think. Mademoiselle Henriette d'Angeville is well known for her ascent of Mont Blanc (in 1838). Not so much is known of her character and reasons. She was a 'romantic woman longing for glory and excitement; a thwarted maiden lady in her forties, eager to become a society lion, possibly jealous of well-known women, George Sand for one. . . . She had a strange craving for publicity; she wanted glory as a mountaineer, as a writer— a fact evidenced by her elaborate planning of her famous Album, which was never published. She sat for her portrait in mountaineering dress, had it engraved and widely circulated'.[1] Besides other ambitions, she thought of going to the bottom of the Channel in a diving bell and going up in a balloon—both unusual activities for a lady of gentle breeding.

In those happy days it was not so difficult to find something novel and exciting. Nowadays a more recherché adventure is needed. 'You can lay the foundations of a brief but glorious career on the Music Hall by being the First Girl Mother to Swim Twice Round The Isle of Man; and anyone who successfully undertakes to drive a well-known make of car along the Great Wall of China in reverse will hardly

[1] Claire-Eliane Engel, *Alpine Journal*, Vol. LIV, No. 266.

fail of his reward,' Peter Fleming maintains. But in the 1830's it was enough simply to be a woman climbing Mont Blanc; and even in the 1890's it was sufficient to ride a bicycle round the world. This was done (1896–8) by John Foster Fraser and three companions. A book was written.

> We took this trip round the world on bicycles because we were more or less conceited, liked to be talked about and see our names in the newspapers.[2]

Fraser goes on to apologise for not having broken even a leg to make it more exciting.

In the very idea of a book you see the money motif entering, for it generally creeps sooner or later into the fame kink. Two years later Captain J. C. Voss, already an expert seaman, had the idea of his world cruise in a small boat put to him by a Canadian journalist, Mr Luxton.

> 'There is five thousand dollars in it, out of which you will receive two thousand five hundred if we cross the three oceans, and apart from that I shall publish an illustrated book, if we complete the voyage, and you shall have half of what we make out of it.'
>
> 'Do I understand, Mr Luxton,' I said, 'that you intend to go yourself on the cruise you are speaking about?'
>
> 'I certainly do,' was the reply. 'How otherwise could I publish a book?'[3]

There is a modern tang about that. In this case Voss rigged out the *Tilikum*, an old Indian canoe, but Luxton, who had no sea experience at all, endured only the first part of the journey. Voss finished round the world and wrote the book himself.

Voss was a tough roving seaman not averse to money— he had taken part already in a wild Pacific treasure hunt. A traveller who met him twelve years later in Tokyo commented: 'The influence of that band of hero-worshippers

---

[2] John Foster Fraser, *Round the World on a Wheel*.
[3] *The Venturesome Voyages of Captain Voss*.

which gathered round Voss . . . was not very good for him.
I fear we spoilt him.' Therein lies the greatest danger to
stunter and solid adventurer alike. How can a man be expected to bear the burden of publicity, to which adventure
is by its very nature unsuited? Either he will go to seed like
Voss, or he must find it a considerable nuisance.

The modern seafaring eccentric suffers publicity to a
degree that would have astonished Voss and Slocum. (The
latter, in 1896, was inconvenienced by a bellman in
Australia, but little more.) When Bombard wanted to cross
the Atlantic on what was little more than an inflated raft
with a sail, he ran the whole gauntlet. Both for the purpose
of the voyage, which was to prove to the world that shipwrecked sailors could live off the sea, and to ensure funds, it
was desirable that the public should know about it. But when
it came to the point things were different.

> This wave of publicity was unfortunate as far as our departure
> was concerned. Certainly the press has a right to keep the public
> informed, and quite often it is not so much a sober account of
> the facts as the human anecdote which interests the great mass
> of readers. But the whole spirit of the expedition was falsified in
> the eyes of a number of people and discredited in the minds of
> others. The departure had to be made 'sensational', so everyone
> lost sight of the reasons for our preliminary canter in the
> Mediterranean: the testing of equipment and crew. . . . We
> were presented as the stars of a dramatic situation. This false
> picture given by the press was particularly dangerous in view
> of the fact that we were setting out to challenge generally
> accepted principles and the dictates of common sense.[4]

This sort of publicity may be one minor reason why so many
explorers go out in the teeth of opposition to their theories.

There are really two points of note in the passage quoted.
First the sheer inconvenience of modern limelight, for Bombard was plagued and pestered throughout in a manner
which made Slocum's voyage look like an incognito joy ride.

[4] *The Bombard Story.*

There are shining exceptions among the newspapers, but it must be said that many instances could be given of such inconvenience, the most dramatic being those of the airmen. Airfields are specific and, therefore, good assembly points. The airman must come down to them. There is no escape. Before his Atlantic flight, at Roosevelt airfield, Lindbergh found himself seriously worried for his propeller, and still more for his mother, who came over because of the disturbing newspaper stories. 'The tabloid press . . . didn't care how much they hurt her feelings or frightened her about my flight, so long as they got their pictures and their stories.' [5] And when the airman descends, as descend he must, there are fresh hazards to face. Lindbergh's reception in Europe was the biggest ever given to a flier (absurdly big, compared with the comparatively little fuss made of Alcock and Brown after the first Atlantic crossing eight years before). But it was dangerous. At Le Bourget:

> I heard the crack of wood behind me when someone leaned too heavily against a fairing strip. Then a second strip snapped and a third, and there was a sound of tearing fabric. That meant souvenir hunters were going wild. Carried bodily out, I was afraid that I would be dropped under the feet of those milling, cheering people; and that after sitting in a cockpit-fixed position for close to thirty-four hours, my muscles would be too stiff to struggle up again. [6]

In the end he escaped when a gallant journalist put on his flying helmet and attracted the crowd's pursuit.

In a sense the breakers of records asked for it, since they, and certainly the men who made their aircraft, must have expected some glory from the exploit, for the 'promotion of aviation.' Everest climbers are, I think, more genuinely surprised when limelight which is quite unsought fixes them; I remember Ed Hillary's face when he heard that he was to be knighted. 'You go and have a good time on a mountain

---

[5] *The Spirit of St Louis.*　　　　　[6] Ibid.

and then this happens to you!' But Everest climbers escape the worst experiences of the early aviators (and there is only one Everest). Charles Kingsford-Smith, the first man across the Pacific in 1928, was surrounded by a crowd of 300,000 at Sydney. Amy Johnson, on landing at Port Darwin after her flight to Australia,

> was caught up in such a torrent of publicity as few people have had to endure before or since. Australia went hoarse with excitement. She was deluged with gifts and congratulations, among them a telegram from the King and Queen. The *Daily Mail* collected £10,000 to buy her a new aeroplane, and all the newspapers around the globe blazoned their praise of 'Our Amy', 'Queen of the Skies'.[7]

She admitted that the celebrations were 'a good deal of an ordeal'—a mild understatement. A. E. Clouston, who later broke all records from England to New Zealand and back, 'took months before I recovered from the nervous tension' of the resultant publicity. Earlier, in 1937, he had with a girl broken the Cape record, and he made this frank comment, interesting in view of what is to be said of competition:

> . . . It seemed to me that they were turning us into seven-day wonder heroes, for the sake of basking in a somewhat question-able reflected glory. This was ballyhoo at its worst.
>
> Whenever I had raced before and lost, I had always been myself: a more jaded version at the end, perhaps, but still myself. Now I was becoming uncertain who or what I was. I had undertaken the flight because I wanted to do something a little better, a little faster than anyone else. I had succeeded, and that was that. It would be dishonest to pretend that I was not vain enough to get a kick out of the fact that my name with Betty's had gone down in the records. But that was all. Every-thing else seemed false and unreal, and I could not see what it had to do with the flight.
>
> I did not want to be an overnight hero. Maybe, deep down, I was doubtful about my strength of character; about my

[7] E. Garnett, *Heroines of Adventure*.

ability to take the hero worship in my stride without suffering
any adverse effects (*The Dangerous Skies*).

Those remarks bring me to the second point in the quotation
from Bombard. Publicity, with all that it involves, is bound
to get the motives of adventurers wrong. It is not even the
newspapers' fault—that part. It is quite simply impossible
to put into a column or a five minute Radio Newsreel all
that is going on in the man's mind, all that he does and why.
Therefore, there is nothing for it but to fall back on clichés
which will be understood: 'heroic', 'record-breaking', 'gallant company', 'daredevil feat' and the like. These are
agreeable simplifications and easy to digest. I do not think
that this point has been put better than by Eric Shipton, in
connection with the pre-war Everest expeditions.

It was quite natural that mountaineers should wish to climb
the highest peak in the world, or at least be interested in the project. But unfortunately Everest's supremacy among mountains
appealed to the popular imagination of a record-breaking age,
and gradually the expeditions began to receive a press publicity
out of all proportion to the value of the undertaking, and
certainly out of keeping with what used to be regarded as 'the
best traditions of mountaineering'. It was claimed that the
enterprise symbolised the spirit of modern youth, and that
success would represent a triumph of humanity over Nature.
[Shades of Sir Francis Younghusband!] In fact, of course, the
first part of the venture was an intensely interesting piece
of geographical exploration, and the second an absorbing
mountaineering problem—no more, no less; both were on the
same plane as any similar project.

I knew a man with a strong claim for a place on the
expedition (1933), who said that he wanted to climb Everest
so as to make a big name for himself, which would enable him
to use his influence in the cause of world peace. A worthy
ambition, no doubt, but surely it would have been more
profitable to devote his energies to the study of political
economy rather than proving himself a mountaineer with an
exceptionally large lung capacity, or whatever it is that

I

enables a man to climb to great altitudes. This is one example among many of an extraordinary distortion of values which has its roots in the opening of a short cut to fame.[8]

There you have it. What is sad is that, apart from these fame seekers, who are few, many others now who want to fare forth and do things have no option but to go along, cap in hand, to newspapers and ask them to accept articles, thus laying themselves open to the danger of having articles written about themselves—in fact the short cut to fame. I have done this myself and so speak in no spirit of lofty intolerance. Food firms and the givers of equipment must be allowed in return to use exploits for advertisement. The firms are extremely nice about it, indeed often give shining examples by presenting money or goods to causes which have nothing whatever to do with their particular commodity. It is just a pity that the two strands have had to interweave themselves so closely.

Of course, there are stalwarts at the other end of the scale who kick out against publicity and do things cheaply, thus getting by with very little fuss. But it will only be the sort of thing that can be done cheaply, or else under an aegis like a missionary society. The long flight or polar journey would be impossible. In 1934, however, Shipton and H. W. Tilman spent their five months in the mountains of the Central Himalaya, with three Sherpas, for £300. For three months in Nepal last year, with four Sherpas, we had to pay £3,000 between the five of us, and to advertise our wares. Prices have soared, admittedly, but even so theirs was a spartan effort. An earlier journey of Tilman's 'on the cheap' was his return by bicycle from East Africa, 3,000 miles across to the western sea. To him it was the cheapest and most reasonable way of getting home.

Had notoriety been sought, I might have ridden the bicycle backwards, or at least have done the thing properly and

[8] Eric Shipton, *Upon that Mountain.*

started from Mombasa, on the east coast, with the back wheel in the Indian Ocean under a battery of cameras.[9]

Putting the same thought more forcefully in the wider context of a plea for small, unpublicised Everest expeditions, he says elsewhere:

> Every genuine mountaineer must shudder involuntarily when he sees anything about mountains in newspapers ... Mountaineering is altogether a private affair between the man and his mountain; the lack of privacy is disagreeable and particularly so if, as usually happens, the newspaper gets hold of the wrong mountain wrongly spelt, adds or deducts several thousands of feet to or from its height, and describes what the wrong man with his name wrongly spelt did not do on it.[10]

The whole of this chapter is worth reading for its common-sense, wittily put view that publicity in connection with Everest expeditions (or similar ventures) may be a baneful necessity, but should be reduced to a minimum.

Both Shipton and Tilman, however, wrote books afterwards, and good ones. They have gone on writing good books since and become well known, whatever their attitude to publicity. Why does one write a book? For fame? With the altruistic object of giving pleasure to others? Or just to get the experience out of the system? Tilman's explanation, in the case of Everest, that books are written in the first place to defray expenses and then the series has to be kept up, comes near the mark. But what of his other books? A fascinating study, but not for these pages.

At one end of the scale, then, are the seekers of publicity. This is not necessarily an entirely selfish motive. We have had the Public Benefactor quoted by Shipton, and there was Maurice Wilson, who tried to climb Everest alone in 1934. He wanted publicity for his theory that if a man starved for three weeks 'his physical mind would establish direct communication with his soul' and he would be as if reborn with immense physical and spiritual strength. If he climbed

[9] *Snow on the Equator.*   [10] *Everest 1938.*

Everest alone the theory would receive a very favourable hearing. He died above Camp III. By and large it may be said that the fame seekers are using adventure as a means to their end.

A much larger class we have seen to consist of those who accept fame if it comes and are often surprised when it does. These may be called the stoics. Sir Ernest Shackleton once said, rather surprisingly: 'Except as an explorer I am no good at anything. . . . I think nothing of the world and the public. They cheer you one minute and howl you down the next. It is what one is oneself and what one makes of one's life that matters.' It is more usual nowadays for the public to forget than to howl, when a new 'hero' comes dazzling over the horizon. But Shackleton's point remains. What a person, a real person, gets from the adventurous life he gets from something inherent in himself and quite unaffected by outside considerations of fame and wealth. I know of no genuine explorer who would not have done what he did, granted that he could get the means, if not a soul was to know that he had done it.

That is not to say, of course, that he will not be affected afterwards, as Voss was, or be vain of his reputation like Sir Richard Burton, or jealous to guard it like Stanley or childishly pleased like Rebell. But in the main these men vary most in their willingness to use reputation to further their own projects or the causes they have at heart. On the whole it seems sensible to most, if fame comes unasked and if you have not had to go out of your way to collect her, to put the lady to good use but not allow her to run your life for you. And a sense of humour in all things.

Some, however, thrust her into the corner and prefer a complete anonymity even to the stoical attitude of Shackleton. They will have no truck with the public at all. These deserve the deepest respect; but they are impossible to track down since their very nature it is to be uncommunicative. Yet their collective name filters through, in the unknown

heroes of the great sail voyages, in the men of northern
Canada, in the missionaries who all over the world have
spent their life in a chosen anonymity.

Fame is seldom the spur. Much more often she seems to
be in the nature of a drag.

რ რ   რ რ   რ რ

It has been apparent already that the theme of money will
not long hold off from that of fame. It has firmly entangled
itself at the slightest provocation. One has got to live, therefore one has got to have money. With more money one can
live better, therefore do more of the adventurous things that
call to be done. And why not?

Complications arise at once. We have seen that fame
brings money, and it is an unfortunate fact that it brings
more than the learned societies which sponsor exploration.
Money from adventure is an old weakness of the human race.
In the early nineteenth century, for instance, we find Maria
Paradis, who kept a *crémerie* at Les Bossons near Chamonix,
already doing great ascents [11] because 'she used to tell the
story of her climbs and she got plenty of tips'. Nowadays it
is becoming customary to ring up a newspaper and ask how
much it will offer for your story before you start on the trip.
But there is one source of money that has been honoured
from antiquity: the source of trade or commerce. Columbus
certainly wanted to find his western passage for its own sake;
but he would never have done so if their Catholic Majesties
had not been persuaded that something substantial might
be got out of it.

Slaves, conquest, commerce—sordid interests perhaps,
but they called out strangely high qualities at times when
their emissaries arrived on the scene of action. Look at the
Spaniards in South America. The voyages of Captain Cook
were those of a very great man; but it was the hope of

[11] She was the first woman up Mont Blanc (1808).

material and imperial advantage rather than of disinterested discovery which inspired his first backers. A few years later we find Mungo Park recording in these terms his application for the post of explorer to the Africa Association:

> If I should succeed in rendering the geography of Africa more familiar to my countrymen, and in opening to their ambition and industry new sources of wealth, and new channels of commerce, I knew that I was in the hands of men of honour who would not fail to bestow that remuneration which my successful services should appear to them to merit.[12]

The second journey, which took him to his death down the Niger, was even more officially commercial in object, being 'for the extension of British commerce and the enlargement of our geographical knowledge'. Note the new order. Britain did indeed recognise the trade possibilities of having a river navigable right down to the coast. It is the more surprising that she did not jump at Stanley's propositions regarding the Congo seventy years later. In the wake of exploration came a complicated and sordid intrigue, which left Belgium with one of the fattest plums of Africa.

Thus commercial interest follows close upon the heels of colonising enthusiasm, nor can one be looked at apart from the other. In the Arctic and Antarctic regions we can see the same interests pursued, almost in a vacuum, with colonising zeal dropping disappointedly to the rear, as it was realised that the 'Great White Continent' was not for habitation by ordinary mortals. Then, gradually, as even the wealth hidden here proved to be not worth the candle, national prestige for its own sake took a spell to the fore, to be followed by disinterested science:

> The motive force of these (early) undertakings was—as has so often been the case—gain. Rulers greedy of power saw in their mind's eye an increase of their possessions. Men thirsting for gold dreamed of an unsuspected wealth of the alluring metal.

[12] *Travels.*

The scientifically trained world waited modestly in the background. But they have all had their share: politics, trade, religion, and science.[13]

At first there were private adventurers seeking their own profit. Then came the great merchant companies, such as the Muscovy and Hudson's Bay Companies, and private firms like Enderby Brothers, whose resourceful and energetic captains, Weddell, Biscoe and others, were filled with a true scientific zeal, in addition to their task of finding out new sources of commercial gain.[14]

By the end of the century the naval men were in control of exploration, to be succeeded very slowly (if they were succeeded at all: the commander of the 1952–3 Greenland Expedition was a naval officer) by the scientists.

The scientists, however, had still to be backed by the commercialists. As an instance, when the question of Arctic air routes came up, the whole commercial question sprang to the fore again. Watkins's 1930–1 Greenland expedition was projected, as others from other lands have been, to explore the possibilities of air travel; indeed it was called 'the British Arctic Air-Route Expedition'. In matters like these commerce and science must go hand in hand. Watkins himself argues: 'What good is going to come of it? Well, . . . it is certain that nearly all the great air routes of the future will lie across the Arctic . . . But before anything can be done these places must be scientifically explored.' [15]

How right he seems to have been! Often he was struck with the idea of science as the handmaiden of commerce, and jokingly deplored that Britain had ceded Alaska without having taken the opportunity scientifically to discover what it contained. In these days, when there is an air route passing straight over the North Pole and an American scientific base

---

[13] Roald Amundsen, *The South Pole.*
[14] Colin Bertram, *Arctic and Antarctic.*
[15] J. M. Scott, *Gino Watkins.*

air-dropped at the south, his dreams seem to have come
true indeed.

❧ ❦   ❧ ❦   ❧ ❦

Rather as Watkins went into the game for 'fun', then science,
then harnessed these to an honourable commercial interest,
so the underwater divers started their diving because it
seemed an amusing game, became interested in its science
and went on to justify it by its importance to human welfare.
True, the pearl divers, like Victor Berge, went in from the
first with their own individual profit in view. Berge was a
Swede who took to pearl diving because it excited him and
looked a quick road to fortune, as it was until he lost large
sums at it. Most divers, however, start at the end of pure
personal satisfaction and go on later to point out the commercial advantages of their art to the community, almost by
way of apologia and as if these justified it. Cousteau claims
in his summing up:

> Obviously man must enter the sea. There is no choice in the
> matter. The human population is increasing so rapidly and
> land resources are being depleted at such a rate that we must
> take sustenance from the great cornucopia. The flesh and
> vegetables of the sea are vital.

After referring to tidal oilfields, of which there is one already
off the coast of California, he goes on: 'When industrialists
apply themselves to the problem, we shall advance to the
6oo-foot "drop-off line".' [16]

Was that his hope when he played with his aqualung on
those mornings of 1943? But Diolé is equally emphatic. He
advocates commercial use of the underseas, and both of them
treat the poor aqualung as the puny beginning of great
things.

> We must now start moving downwards. For the portion of the
> world on which we live is small. The earth's surface is

[16] *The Silent World.*

124

196,940,000 square miles. We use only a quarter of it. It is time to remeasure the earth. In depth.[17]

Necessary as the commercial use of the sea or sky may be, I must confess that the marriage with adventure leaves me filled with no joy; nor does it, perhaps, leave many of the adventurers themselves happier than that similar notion of escaping one's worries and at the same time adding one's mite to scientific knowledge. Still, the marriage must be arranged. The adventurers need money, and are sometimes delighted to think that they are contributing to the material wealth of the world. The material world needs adventurers; the Press needs heroes. It is a *mariage de convenance*. Let us hope it does not end in tears.

[17] *The Undersea Adventure.*

9

Conquest and competition

Homme libre, toujours tu chériras la mer!
La mer est ton miroir; tu contemples ton âme
Dans le déroulement infini de sa lame,
Et ton esprit n'est pas un gouffre moins amer.

Et cependant voilà des siècles innombrables
Que vous vous combattez sans pitié ni remord,
Tellement vous aimez le carnage et la mort,
O lutteurs éternels, O frères implacables!

CHARLES BAUDELAIRE

However baby man may brag of his science and skill, and however much,
in a flattering future, that science and skill may augment; yet for ever
and for ever, to the crack of doom, the sea will insult and murder him,
and pulverise the stateliest, stiffest frigate he can make.

HERMAN MELVILLE

For the 'numberless centuries' of Baudelaire's poem man
has been trying to tame his environment. Sometimes he
seems to succeed; he discovers fire, he sails upon the sea, he
cultivates even the mountainside. But success is never complete, as he likes to believe. The fire burns him, the mountains strike at him with storm and avalanche, the sea drowns
his biggest ships. The air, which at last he supposes to himself that he has mastered, is a restive horse ready to throw its
rider. So the struggle goes on; and as it goes, he comes to
see in the elements and in the mountain moods a mirror to
himself, so that he loves them even as he fights.

In early days the fight was as often against neighbours as
against the obstacles of one's own environment. It is quite
wrong to think of war purely as the scourge of the Middle

Ages. Heaven knows, the life of wresting food from stubborn soil was grim enough. War was often a relaxation from that struggle, and a pastime. The historian Marcel Bloch, in an entertaining chapter on medieval warfare, tells us that 'in war . . . the noble loved first of all the purely physical sensation of exerting his animal strength, a strength maintained from childhood up by constant exercise'. Moreover, courage, being a virtue very highly prized, 'it was because this virtue had the chance to show itself that war was so gladly welcomed'. Finally, it was a relief from the monotony of peaceful existence. 'Accustomed not to fear danger, the warrior found one more charm in war: it was a remedy against boredom.'

These delights, of course, had their disadvantages to the rest of the populace. The roving knights became a menace; but it is worth remembering that not only the knights were enjoying themselves, but their henchmen too. These, the humble fiefs, welcomed war because their masters would provide extra largesse, not to mention the booty and ransom which might turn up by other paths. All in all, except for the wretched merchants and peasants who were 'not much good anyway', peace involved 'une crise économique et une crise de prestige' [1] and was to be avoided like the plague.

This happy state of affairs went on for some time. Good Queen Bess's days would not have been so golden but for the exploits of her warrior admirers. Even the battles of Marlborough smell faintly like Test cricket. And it seems to me that it was not until after some of the grimmer episodes of the Napoleonic struggle that war finally lost the glamour of early days. What was lost in one field was gained, in strength and enthusiasm, by the old desire to 'conquer Nature', whatever that meant; while another part of the weakness for subjugating people filtered itself off into competition of a more peaceful nature.

This does not mean that war had ceased to be an outlet, if an unfortunate one. In all fields also it continued and still

[1] *La Société Féodale.*

127

continues to give practical impulse, through the improvement of the means of travel, ships, aircraft and the like. But it had become unsightly, and not a thing on which a man readily fixed his adventuring eyes for its own sake; nor did the Indian Mutiny and the Crimea do anything to endear it. Those who could no longer indulge the warrior outlet found their adventure more and more in exploration and discovery the world over.

In any discussion of the 'conquest motif' in the field of exploration the issue tends to be clouded by two distinct uses of the word 'conquest'. By a phrase like 'The Conquest of Everest' most people mean standing fifteen minutes on top, or the film of that title. But by 'The Conquest of Peru' you are bound to mean something very different. This confusion was recognised by Sir John Hunt when he refused to allow his book to be called 'The Conquest' and made it 'The Ascent of Everest'. (He was not successful over the film.) But it is a confusion common even in many good writers. The yearning is towards conquest. But how many would dare, thinking deeply, to call the reality conquest—the tracing of a narrow line, one day when the elements are kind?

However that may be, exploration of land has been as often linked with real conquest as with commerce, the conquest being that of the inhabitants. The story of the British and other Empires needs none of my inexpert comment. Tremendous feats of courage and endurance were performed, in the sure belief that one's country would benefit from the acquisition to follow. The very first explorers, too, who were followed by the soldiers, the builders, the traders, and so forth, often believed also that the natives would benefit equally. Stanley's famous remark on examining enthusiastically an improved Maxim gun: 'It is a fine weapon and will be invaluable for civilising the heathen', was both sincere and representative of a belief not peculiar to Stanley, that *all* the 'benefits' of civilisation were also of benefit to the conquered races. 'The sincerity of his belief in himself and what he stood for was astonishing, admirable and yet sinister,' a biographer wrote, and has also described 'an admirable, almost unanswerable simplicity in this great traveller, who believed as tenaciously and fixedly in the civilisation he represented as the natives did in their fetishes and fates. . . . Stanley made a great impression on these simple yet sinister people (the cannibals). They respected the force of his character, his even-handed impassive justice, his air of pride and strength. To them he was Bula Matari, the breaker of rocks, as to his own followers he was the Great Master.' [2]

Stanley is only an extreme exponent of a general view and type. Exploration and Empire went hand in hand, and never more so than in the great acquisitive period of the latter nineteenth century. The 'lesser breeds without the law' were brought into it, to their own benefit and that of their masters, though the latter was not so openly talked about. It may be fanciful to see in the emphasis on domination of a people a tacit recognition of the truth that it is difficult to dominate, or even have much impression of dominating, really big country. (I do not mean *a* big country, like Peru, but country in which Nature is at her most grandiose.) I never heard of 'conquering the Nile', or the Sahara or Amazon, though the 'conquest of the Pole' slips out sometimes. Stanley may have felt, at one moment, that forests and cataracts acknowledged his sway. But when he came to the point, that of living with them, it was the luckless inhabitants who spoke the desired words of submission.

Flying over the earth and sea or standing on a mountain top gives a more positive, if equally illusory, impression of conquest. That is perhaps why, in these pursuits, conquest talk is more common than in, say, diving or caving. The conquest of the top of the sea is popularly talked about in

[2] A. J. A. Symons, *H. M. Stanley*. Even so modest a character as Mary Kingsley 'wanted power' over people, according to Cecil Howard. In Africa traders, ship's captains and primitive tribesmen acknowledged her mastery; for the first time she had tasted power and the taste was sweet in her mouth'. (*Mary Kingsley*.)

connection with big liners, but I cannot find the word used by those who sail the ocean in small boats, or large clippers for that matter.

The idea of flight, however, has from early times given men the feeling that they have or would have power to conquer if they flew. 'The makers of myth, religion and legend seized upon the power of flight to convey through space their heroes, gods and holy men.'[3] Jehovah and the gods of Olympus flew to the scenes of their activities, a winged Perseus slew the monster, the myth of Daedalus and Icarus has still a deep symbolic meaning in human consciousness. 'The idea of human flight . . . has always made a powerful appeal both to the longing for escape and to the desire for power and exhilaration.'[4] So they started to try, flapping their home-made wings, climbing to the tops of towers, flopping down to break their legs or necks. What concerns us here in the history of flight is that for centuries men tried to 'master' the air. Minds of the calibre of Leonardo da Vinci's absorbed themselves in this ambition. When the dream came true, when at last they flew indeed, they had a sense of sheer magic power, long sought, which we are beginning to lose now that the game is becoming as easy as driving a car. Even a writer as careful as Saint-Exupéry refers, in the early days, to the aeroplane as 'this instrument of conquest', though almost every page that he wrote helps to show how far that conquest is from being complete.

The illusion persisted. Winging his way through sunset the flier would contemplate the magic power which for these brief hours seemed to be his. Sometimes he even complained when it was too easy. 'The spirit of conquest is gone from the air,' has been said of a quiet night. Sometimes he surveyed the map upon which his course was plotted.

I stand looking at the completed chart . . . What freedom lies in flying! What god-like power it gives to man! I'm independent

[3] C. H. Gibbs-Smith, *A History of Flying*.   [4] Ibid.

of the seaman's coast lines or the landsman's roads; I could as well have drawn that line north to the Arctic or westward over the Pacific, or south-east to the jungles of the Amazon. I'm like a magician concocting magic formulae. The symbols I pluck from paper, applied to the card of a compass held straight by rudder and stick, will take me to any acre on the earth where I choose to go.[5]

The excitement of these words, the old gleam in them, is gone. For the process has continued, the thrill has been partly lost in a flood of technical detail, while phrases like 'The Conquest of the Air' have become clichés which it is not really worth the trouble of talking about. Smugly we watch Globemasters dropping whole encampments on the South Pole and congratulate ourselves that one more element is mastered. . . . And yet, as I write these lines, a newspaper is before me with an account of seventy-nine killed in a crash on the flight from London to Canada. The conquest is going to be a puzzle to the conquerors for some time to come.

So long as we realise that the conquest is unreal, that we are men and 'of the earth earthy', the illusion may perhaps do us no hurt and be a harmless escape from the very *un-heroic* sensations besetting our everyday life. Like the glider, we come down to land after a good flight and are refreshed:

As I stopped, and figures began running towards me, I had the illusion of victory. It was only an illusion, of course, like the cool lake which grows out of the sand before a lost traveller can die of thirst. But for the moment it was real. It was the thing for which every human being strives—a victory over the earthiness of our bodies and lordship over mortality.[6]

A temporary lordship, but a satisfying one. The writer of those words was killed in a gliding accident.

Undaunted, however, by reflections of impermanence, man turns his eyes, like Dante, only from rather a different

[5] C. A. Lindbergh, *The Spirit of St Louis*. The chart was that of his course across the Atlantic.
[6] Terence Horsley, *Soaring Flight*.

131

angle, towards the stars. Already in recent times phrases like 'Now that we have conquered . . . even the stratosphere' (Diolé) have been creeping into writers' heads. And, for the ambitious, realms beyond the stratosphere have loomed up, vast and alluring. Long before the Russian *Sputniks* arrived, the men of space flight had formed their plans, had engendered their literature. It is a literature, they assure us, even more extensive than that of flight, for 'the conquest of space [has] a fundamental appeal'.[7] And how near it seems to be! At the time of writing the two Russian satellites, one containing a dog, have put the moon once and for all within reach. And yet . . . How many disasters are in store! Even when the first rocket traces its thin line to the planets, space will be no more conquered than is the sea, or, for that matter, than the mind of man by the tyrant who subdues his body.

In works about mountaineering the idea of conquest often appears; partly, I think, because we are psychologically attuned to setting a foot on 'conquered' foes; partly because 'to conquer' is a useful alternative to 'to climb' if one is writing a long book. But besides this, conquest is thought of as the inevitable outcome of struggle, and struggle there certainly must be, with the mountain sides as really as with Baudelaire's sea.

In the last century it was Edward Whymper who underlined the struggle most forcibly; and that may be one reason why *Scrambles amongst the Alps* has brought more boys to mountains than any other book. The tragic 'conqueror' of the Matterhorn assumed the role, consciously and artistically, of fighter against the huge and rugged peak. David wins sympathy against Goliath, and the smaller fighter always appeals to boys. 'It is kept vividly before us, the flashlight representation of a flinty mountain and a steely Whymper

[7] J. N. Leonard, *Flight into Space*.

11: 'It was like drowning in a human sea.' Lindbergh's reception at Croydon.

12

13

in continuous concussion; all illuminated by the sparks of perilous incident they struck out of one another,' G. Winthrop Young puts it. Nobody can help admiring Whymper, journalist, egoist, trumpeting the great news of battle and conquest to the world.

But notice this. It is the struggle, unending and unresolved, which moves Whymper, not the finality of victory. 'Whymper hardly for a page lets us feel that getting to the top of the mountain is more than an incident in the great duel . . . All the time he is shouting at us: "These are mountains and this is me! And thus went the unending conflict between us." ' [8] If man really conquered the mountain there would be no more interest left in its ascent, no mirror to himself, no joy of uncertainty that gives life its zest.

But the idea of conquest went on developing in common thought. Shackleton, not a mountaineer, wrote of the 'Conquest' of Mount Erebus. And when Sir Francis Younghusband came to write the story of the first three Everest expeditions, he summed it in a way popular at the time and accordant with his own philosophy.

> The struggle with Everest is all part and parcel of the perpetual struggle of spirit to establish its supremacy over matter. Man, the spiritual, means to make himself supreme over even the mightiest of what is material. [9]

Mallory's references to conquest, in his letters from Everest, are in line with this thought. Everest the lodestone was also the adversary.

Mountaineers nowadays are less inclined to speak in these terms (though they are much in general use by public and press) because the feeling now is that, if conquest there be, it must be conquest or mastery of oneself. If you have a formidable rock face in front of you, split by cracks and glazed with ice, and if you climb it, you have not conquered

[8] Both quotations from 'Mountain Prophets.' *The Alpine Journal*, Vol. LIV, No. 267.

[9] *The Epic of Mount Everest.*

'*Great God! This is an awful place. . . .*' *Scott's party at the South Pole. January 18, 1912.*

The next visit. Admiral Dufek plants the U.S.A. flag. October 31, 1956.

it because it is quite unaffected by your passage. But you train and master your body so that it can make use of those cracks, scrape the ice off and find the footholds beneath. That, I think, was how the great rock climber Menlove Edwards, who was also a practising psychologist, set about his problems. And he added loose rock and vegetation to the other hazards, so that gymnastics of the nerves could be practised too. That also is partly why the emphasis in mountain writing has come to be on the 'how' rather than on the 'why'. Joe Brown has said that in order to do the excessively difficult rock climbs of today he has got to be thinking of them even between the times he is doing them, planning the moves. But as to *why* we do these things at all we no longer have so much leisure to ask.

So it is with a great snow mountain in the Himalaya or Andes. The route is 'there'—if you can find it, if the weather is kind and if you are skilful enough to get up. To do that, each should also be master of his whole self, conquering and repressing the unruly bits which, for instance, insist that he of all the party should be the one to reach the top. If you cannot do that, then the mountain is less likely to be climbed. If you can, then you, like the glider, have conquered mortality.

The motive of conquest, then: a little out of fashion now, partly because military conquest is also out of fashion, but still very popular in the press.[10] The word 'conquest' slips from the pen of the most unassuming, when they forget themselves as I like to think. We need surely to go deep and know ourselves long before we claim to conquer worlds of which as yet we know very little. If we do that we are likely to be afflicted with a healthy awe first. What Julius Kugy said of the mountains might equally have been said of sea or

[10] And among non-mountaineers! I read in an otherwise masterly book: '1953 (Everest climbed and Pierre Saint-Martin descended) will appear in future history books as the year in which the final conquest of the terrestrial world took place.' *Man and the Underwater World*, by P. de Latil and J. Rivoire.

sky, desert or jungle. 'I cannot imagine any place less suitable to choose than the high mountains, wherein to display the mastery of mankind.'

꙰ ꙰   ꙰ ꙰   ꙰ ꙰

Peaceful competition is perhaps a *pis aller*, but certainly another helpful outlet for the conquest complex. In sport its excellence is recognised and its practice encouraged. All agree that it is better for the Russians to come over and beat or be beaten in rowing contests than in H-Bomb battles. In adventure and exploration however the issue is a little more complicated.

It is complicated because the two things, adventure and sport, so greatly overlap and yet are not entirely the same. Suppose an air race is organised (not a feature nowadays as between the wars). That is pure sport: somebody wins and is acclaimed victor by his country, having beaten the other man. Then, say, two airmen from different countries try to fly helicopters over the Pole for the purpose of proving that stores can be dropped that way. If one of them fails, the successful other will certainly again be hailed as victorious and a national hero, neither of which he is. It is natural, and a point well illustrated by Lindbergh's Atlantic flight of 1927. Davis, Nungesser, Chamberlin and the rest all failed for one reason or another. Lindbergh therefore 'Smashed his Rivals', as the press put it.

The falsification slips through because it is not realised that in the case of big adventure a greater player has stepped in, one not to be so lightly disregarded as headwind by the yacht racer or heat by the tennis champion. The adventurer who has stepped beyond the boundaries of sport is wrestling with forces, with Nature for want of a better word, which make nonsense of competition. Not only nonsense but dangerous nonsense. If you are struggling, not to conquer but to impose yourself over one thin line of ocean or ice cap, and if you are seriously influenced by somebody else's effort to do the same and try to better that, then you are likely to be killed. The real serious adventurer is concerned with doing something new in the face of the elements around. Their opposition is quite enough for him. He is pitting himself against no human adversary but himself, what he has done and what he can do, whether he be climber or diver, speleologist or lone sailor. The problems posed by the elements are so great that there is little room to think of difficulties set by other human beings.[11] If other people do come along, they are more likely to be welcomed as allies than frowned upon as foes.

With flying the case is a little different. In the earliest days, certainly, the struggle lay between primitive plane and the forces that pulled it down. There was a wealth of new flights to be done. But even then it is noticeable what a part competition played in helping the struggle along. In Britain, which made a sluggish start, Lord Northcliffe of the *Daily Mail* offered monetary prizes for the first man across the Channel (won by Blériot from a very sporting rival, Latham), the first to fly London to Manchester, the first across the Atlantic. Alcock and Brown, who won the latter prize, were undoubtedly pleased with the money. But I submit that in their calculations money was a very secondary consideration to the idea of accomplishing a flight which proved as big an ordeal, and with that plane as big an achievement, as any since. Later on, flights became more openly sporting events, competitive either against an established record or directly against other entrants. And that is why, though the line like all others is absurdly impossible to draw, I would class *more*

[11] It is a little startling to find the Slocum Society organising a race for single-handed sailors across the Atlantic in 1960. It might be argued that, with the Atlantic now crossed many times by small boats, the feat is no longer quite the adventure it was. But it is still more startling to learn that a race took place as early as 1891, from Boston, between W. A. Andrews in a 15-footer, and J. Lawlor, followed by another the next year in which Lawlor was lost. (*Strand Magazine*, August, 1901.)

in the category of sporting or scientific competition than of adventure even such great flights as Wiley Post's and Gatty's round the world to beat the Graf Zeppelin record, Clouston's to beat Amy Johnson's record, Mollison's to beat somebody else's record, or all the modern record flights which pour breathlessly into our newspapers every month.

I italicise 'more', because clearly it *is* an adventure to fly faster than anybody else, just as it is to break water or land speed records. On the other side of the coin it might be argued that many accepted adventures, like mountaineering, have a sport side which very often has little to do with adventure at all (I am thinking of rock climbing in some of its forms). Might we not be allowed proportion in these things, and then everyone will be happy? Thus sailing round the world will be accepted as adventure, while sailing is also a sport. Motor racing is a sport, but he would be a bold man who did not allow it to be in its own way an adventure too. And so on. The line, if it can be drawn at all, may come somewhere at this point: the competitor is juggling with a number of 'knowns', the reliability of his machine, the competence of his rivals and so forth, which go to make an 'unknown'. When the unknown increases, as it does in adventure proper, it *becomes* the competitor, the 'greater player' as we called it above, and so the idea of a human competitor fades, or should fade, away. There is no room for him.

❧ ❦   ❧ ❦   ❧ ❦

So much for competition in the exploration world, one might say. But despite all my lofty sentiments, and owing to the natural frailty of us all, competition there is and always will be, to some degree, everywhere. It can be national, or private, or both. In all cases it seems to me a weakness, but usually harmless and sometimes stimulating. It is at least more honourable than some stimuli. Take the story of the Poles. 'Now the days of pole hunting are over . . . The impelling force then was largely national glory, a motive which, though not the highest of all, is far above the simple desire for power and wealth.[12]

That is true. In the last century it was fairly well known that there were no profitable North-West Passages or rich minerals to compensate explorers materially, but we now find Admiral James Ross, in 1838, setting out to discover new Antarctic seas and the great Barrier named after him, 'impressed with the feeling that England had ever *led* the way of discovery in the southern as well as in the northern region'.[13] Ross was a very great pioneer. His type of exploration, quite distinct from flag-planting followed by colonisation or empire, was founded on science and national prestige. It went on a long time, and culminated in the attainment of the two Poles themselves.

Similarly, in all the eight attempts, and through all the misery of storm and discomfort (his 1894 expedition must have been one of the most unpleasant on record, body lice being the nastiest suffering of all), I believe that Robert Peary was moved by a whole-hearted and indeed well founded belief that he was winning new glory for the United States. There is something very moving about the words in his journal on its attainment, out of date though they may seem to some.

> I tried to realise that, after twenty-three years of struggles and discouragement, I had at last succeeded in placing the flag of my country at the goal of the world's desire. It is not easy to write about such a thing, but I knew that we were going back to civilisation with the last of the great adventure stories—a story the world had been waiting to hear for more than four centuries, a story which was to be told at last under the folds of the Stars and Stripes, the flag that during a lonely and isolated life had come to be for me the symbol of home and everything I loved—and might never see again.

[12] Colin Bertram, *Arctic and Antarctic.*
[13] *Voyage of discovery and research in the Southern and Antarctic regions,* 1839–43.

In similar words he replied to the award of the Hubbard Gold Medal in 1907, before the Pole was reached.

> To me the final and complete solution of the Polar mystery . . . is the thing which should be done for the honour and credit of this country, the thing which it was intended that I should do and which I must do.[14]

This makes it the more bitter that the story should be followed by the sordid quarrel with Cook as to who reached it: a quarrel which influenced some against the innocent Peary and delayed his promotion.

The story of the other Pole is the best known story of national and personal competition in the history of exploration. When Shackleton made the route up the Beardmore Glacier and reached a point only ninety miles short of the Pole, his emphasis was both scientific and exploratory; though he does once take pride in the Polar region being 'British Territory'. He and Scott represent in a sense the beginning of the new, scientific approach, Amundsen the old: Amundsen all out for the Pole and very little beside (he had the resources to do good scientific work), Scott falling between the two stools of science and priority at the Pole. It redounds to Scott's glory that he made science so big a part of his programme that he lost the race; indeed he refused to race at all. But he dared not confess quite how big a part it was, to a British public more interested in flag planting than in physiology. On that public he depended for funds. In a letter preserved at the Royal Geographical Society he wrote:

> I believe that the main object, that of reaching the Pole, will appeal to all our countrymen as the one rightly to be pursued at this moment, but the plan which I present provides also for the scientific exploration of a considerable extent of the Antarctic continent. (September 16, 1909.)

Amundsen, on the other hand, intended to go north, but

[14] Quoted by W. H. Hobbs, in *Robert Peary*.

according to his own account changed his plan when the message 'The North Pole is reached' arrived. He admits [15] that nothing short of a Pole would keep his Norwegian contributors happy. In this he was in the same boat as Scott: it was a question of prestige and money, but in the Norwegian's case the prestige masked no science.

Amundsen disclaimed rivalry. In a passage perhaps not well enough known, but not convincing, he put it that:

> I foresaw, of course, that there would be some who would attack me and accuse me of 'shabby rivalry', etc., and they would perhaps have had some shadow of justification, if we had really thought of taking Captain Scott's route . . .
>
> Scott's plan and equipment were so entirely different from my own that I regarded the telegram I sent him later, with the information that we were bound for the Antarctic regions, rather as a mark of courtesy than as a communication which might cause him to alter his programme in the slightest degree. The British expedition was designed entirely for scientific research. The Pole was only a side-issue, whereas in my extended plan it was the main object. [16]

He would have been startled could he have seen the state of fury into which his arrival threw the British. Some wanted to go straight to the Bay of Whales and have it out. 'We had just paid the first instalment of the heartbreaking labour of making a path to the Pole; and we felt, however unreasonably, that we had earned the first right of way. Our sense of co-operation and solidarity had been wrought up to an extraordinary pitch; and we had so completely forgotten the spirit of competition that its sudden intrusion jarred frightfully.' [17] The mood passed, and Scott wrote in his journal: 'The proper, as well as the wiser, course for us is to proceed exactly as though this had not happened. To go forward and do our best for the honour of the country without fear or panic. There is no doubt that Amundsen's plan is a very

[15] In vol. I of *The South Pole.*　　　　[16] Ibid.
[17] A. Cherry-Garrard, *The Worst Journey in the World.*

serious menace to ours.'[18] Why—if patriotism was not a strong motive? Why—if the Pole was 'only a side-issue' to scientific work?

As everybody knows, Scott left later than Amundsen, partly because of his ponies, and arrived at the Pole more than a month behind his rival. We know also of his disappointment.

> The Norwegians have forestalled us and are first at the Pole. It is a terrible disappointment, and I am very sorry for my loyal companions. Many thoughts come and much discussion have we had.

That is very human, as is his little postscript: 'certainly the Norwegians found an easy way up'. They did not. Perhaps of all those men Wilson was the only one dispassionate enough not to be disappointed. 'I do not believe that it mattered to Wilson when he found that Amundsen had reached the Pole a few days before him—not much.'[19] He had a strength which puts even Scott in the shade.

'Great God! This is an awful place and terrible enough for us to have laboured to it without the reward of priority,' Scott wrote on the 17th of January. On the 18th, camped at the Pole itself, 'We built a cairn, put up our poor slighted Union Jack and photographed ourselves—mighty cold work all of it. We must face our 800 miles of solid dragging, and goodbye to most of the day dreams!' I sometimes wonder with what feelings Amundsen, who has described gleefully his first act, the planting of the Norwegian flag, read those lines. Certain it is that a lowering of morale was one contributory cause of the final disaster.

There is a restrained nationalism about these stories, and a personal pride which is of course impossible to disentangle from it. The man identifies himself with his country; and most men would be proud to think of themselves representing a country at the Pole. It was not till after World War One

---

[18] *Scott's Last Expedition*, vol. I.   [19] *The Worst Journey in the World.*

that 'total nationalism' had its spell—we hope a short one—
to the fore, and I can think of no better illustration than that
of mountaineering. In the earlier days rivalry was personal
and often between fellow countrymen.[20] The only time that
I can think of when international rivalry raised its head
among the mountaineers of last century was after the first
ascent of the Matterhorn, already referred to, in 1865. Even
so, small things have been magnified by small minds.
Edward Whymper had climbed with Jean-Antoine Carrel,
the Italian guide who was trying the mountain from the
Italian side. He would have made the ascent with him earlier
had circumstances allowed. As it was, Whymper's party
reached the top from the Swiss side, to see the Italians well
below on the southern ridge. It is a jarring thought that
Carrel was later reproached by his compatriots for having
previously helped the Englishman; and Whymper is not at
his best when he beseeches the guide Croz upon the summit
'in the name of friendship' to throw down rocks near the
Italians and make them realise their defeat.[21]

That is an isolated instance, and a small one. After 1918
an exaggerated nationalism did come to the fore, in countries particularly which had not done well in the war, the
totalitarian countries. All sport was affected, and as we have
seen earlier the idea of proving oneself linked itself with the
idea of proving one's country's worth. Amusing are the patriotic Italian newspaper extracts quoted by R. L. G. Irving.[22]

> A climber has fallen. Let a hundred others arise for the
> morrow. Let other youths strew edelweiss and alpenrose upon
> the body of the fallen comrade; and lay it with trembling
> devotion face upturned under the soft turf. Then up, once more
> to the assault of the rocks and of the summit, to commemorate
> the fallen one in the highest and most difficult of victories!

[20] Rather after the manner of the great exploration quarrel of Burton and
Speke as to whether the Nile rose in Victoria or Tanganyika—a quarrel only
ended by the news that Speke had accidentally shot himself, just when he
should have been disputing the point.

[21] *Scrambles amongst the Alps.*   [22] *The Romance of Mountaineering.*

The medal for valour in sport, the highest distinction accorded by the Duce to exceptional athletes who break world records or are victors in international contests, will be awarded to climbers who vanquish mountains by new ascents of the sixth standard.

All Italians ought to know how to live in mountainous country. All our wars will always take place in the mountains, and the cult of mountaineering passionately pursued, and spreading more and more among our young men, will contribute to the military preparedness of the young generation.

That tone set up a perhaps exaggerated outcry in Britain, against 'flags flying from the tent poles of Himalayan expeditions, pitiful and absurd symbols of nationalism', as Smythe called them. 'Nature is outraged when an atmosphere of feverish human competition is introduced into her sanctuaries.'[23] Whatever Nature may think of it, he is quite right in adding that the British had not helped by 'roping off' Everest; and Tilman pushed the point: 'The Indian Government has thrust on them the thankless task of deciding whether a party from one nation should be allowed to attempt a mountain which has already been visited by another . . . Probably the phase is a passing one, born of an age of advertisement.[24]

The advertisement persists; the competition, in many cases more apparent than real, seems to have settled down. After the Second World War there was another short burst of what might have been termed nationalism in the Himalaya. The British climbed Everest, the Swiss having broken through the 'rope' the year before. The French, who already claimed the first twenty-six thousander and who had booked Everest for next year, took vengeance on Makalu. The Austrians climbed Cho Oyu (Buhl having already got up Nanga Parbat), the Italians K2 and the British Kangchenjunga. The Americans felt disappointed, understandably,

[23] *The Spirit of the Hills.*   [24] *Everest 1938.*

about K2, for they had suffered heavily and come near to the top three times; I know that we would have felt equally disappointed had the Swiss climbed Everest in 1952. The Swiss have now crowned all these triumphs by climbing Everest and Lhotse at one sitting, if that is the right word. But now that the greatest giants have fallen, public interest has on the whole waned, and it needs public interest to fan competition. The climbers themselves sink back into a welcome obscurity. They are spreading comfortably and friendly fashion over the many remaining twenty-five and twenty-six thousanders, and I have heard nobody in these days objecting to the flags left on any of the peaks, from Everest down. They are also finding that the 'slightly stunted giants' of 24,000 and 23,000 feet often yield the hardest and most satisfying climbing of all. Finally, they are including the splendid peaks of the Andes in their programmes, and that evens the field out still more.

As in mountaineering, so in all land and most sea exploration, it seems to be no pious hope that nationalism is dying. All the really obvious points on the earth's surface having been reached, people either go out privately, in which case the lone sailor and explorer, caver and diver, hail each other as fellow lunatics in a sane world (or vice versa); or they form large bodies to partake scientific feasts like the Geophysical Year. It is perhaps of happy omen that the leader of the American party now wintering at the South Pole has written that he hopes to lay courtesy depots for the British Commonwealth party which will be crossing the continent this year.

Would it were the same story in the exploration of air and space! But here a curious dichotomy is observable. On the one side science has become more cold, more impersonal and austere, seeming to allow no competition save with her own results and by herself; no place for petty individualist rivalry. So on the earth all is, comparatively speaking, peaceable. But in the air—for when all is said it is from the air that future war will be won, if won it can be—in the air, their potential enemy, men's passions seethe and boil as merrily as they were wont to do below. The Russians launch satellites; President Eisenhower, the Americans, the British, are staggered. Think of the propaganda effect on the uncommitted countries! Scientists must be trained at once, money must be poured out to them, all must be given to science. And, incidentally, a scapegoat must be found for the present shocking state of things. At any cost, at all costs, this stolen lead must be obliterated. Oh merciful heavens! Give us a satellite too! Just one satellite, to beat theirs!

It looks childish on paper; but whatever their scientific glories, it is a truism that men have not grown up. If only we could spend some of the money on rectifying just that little omission! Satellites are not of their nature at all childish. In so far as they are a quest into the unknown for its own sake, they are an adventure (in my sense). In so far as they collect information about conditions above the stratosphere, they are a calculated experiment. But in so far as they are connected with the turning out of intercontinental missiles, they are just part of the great arms race which may, as all serious folk think, end our species. Moreover, out of this last race even the personal thrill has vanished. In Amy Johnson's time what excitement there was about it all! In the Hunter and its peers men enjoyed the exultation of speed competing with the speed of sound.[25] But in rockets and guided missiles! No, if science destroys us, because we have come too near to that conquest of which our fathers dreamed, it will be quite impersonally, for all our angry gesticulations. There she stands, waiting for us.

> Crowned with calm leaves, she stands
> Who gathers all things mortal
> With cold immortal hands.

[25] And other speeds. In 1953, for instance, Mike Lithgow was eagerly contemplating 'the possibility of winning back from America the much-coveted honour of holding the absolute World Speed Record', for England and for Supermarines. (*Mach One.*)

❧ ❧ ❧ ❧ ❧ ❧

10

The scientific man

Exploration is the physical expression of the Intellectual Passion.
A. CHERRY-GARRARD

What a field is science! The last chapter was drawing us slowly towards the conclusion that her shadow falls larger and ever larger over every adventure left open to us. Now we must look at her from closer range, a prospect before which the callow non-scientist trembles understandably. Down the library shelf he goes, pencil and note-book in hand. *Science and Religion, Science and Art, Science in the Modern World, Science in the Ancient World.* . . . He pauses, terrified, before even reaching *Science and Adventure* (if it exists), retires to one of those little stools placed conveniently at the shelf-ends for the exhausted seeker after learning, licks his pencil and begins to scribble nervously.

I must whittle down, and whittle down, and grasp an essence. First, we are not concerned with scientific results, which are legion and to me largely incomprehensible, but with motives, and those the motives only of the scientists who go out into the world surrounding to get their results. Laboratory adventure does not concern us. Fundamentally, it is a truism to say that the motive of it all is quite simple, being the human urge to know where things are, why they are, how they work, why they won't work, which was with us when we were born and needs no more explanation than a desire for food. But we shall have to whittle down a good deal more on that before we find the scientific explorer. It will make things easier, and I think be fair, to start with a broad division between *physical* exploration, in which the human body actively takes part, and *mechanical* adventuring in which, when all is said, a man puts 'kindling' into his machine and sits in it. If the kindling lasts and his machine lasts, he gets there. If not, that, for the adventure, is that. There will admittedly be plenty of overlaps. What if Ellsworth walked the last twenty miles of his flight across the Antarctic? When does an aqualung become a bathyscaphe? And where does the mesoscaphe come in? But these fences can be kept out of sight until they loom directly before us.

The great science of geography, with which this chapter is largely concerned, came in almost incidentally at first in the wake of explorations patriotic and commercial. The heirs of Sir Martin Frobisher were not usually disinterested enquirers, and the scientists of last century often felt called upon to justify the abstract pursuit of knowledge. Among the most fortunate were the naturalists. Men like Joseph Hooker in his Journals, Charles Darwin (I am thinking of *The Voyages of Adventure and Beagle III* particularly and H. W. Bates in his splendid and absorbing account of *The Naturalist on the River Amazons*) felt that their work was directly important to the world, as indeed it became; that it was related to current literary experience and even to common profit. The Victorians were enthusiastically botanical and naturalist, and these books, excellent reading even to the unscientific, feel no need to be on the defensive. Their reason at any rate is accepted.

The mountaineering scientists also were lucky, since science was from the first the respectable façade behind which their 'improperly dangerous' ascents shielded themselves. This was partly because it was science which had started the game. R. W. Clark says:

> It was natural that the scientists, the men who wanted physical questions answered in some detail, should be the first in the mountain field. [I query the 'naturalness', but let it pass for the moment] . . . The new enquirers began to ask why it was that one began to pant and gasp at a great height. Could birds and

insects live above the places where snow lasted throughout the year? How and why did the glaciers, those white dragons of the medieval prints, move just as they did? . . . To secure the answers to the questions they posed it was necessary for them to be out and about not only in fair weather but in the full blast of the mountain storm; it was necessary for them to camp, to train and hire guides who could carry their delicate instruments, to build up a technique of travel above the snowline and to produce a demand for better inns below it.[1]

Partly the reason for their acceptance lay in the comparative cheapness of these enquiries, only a few weeks each year being involved. Besides this there was some hope of material gain in the discovery of minerals; while the scientists involved were from the first of very high quality, being joined later by men of the calibre of Forbes, Tyndall, Bonney and T. H. Huxley. John Tyndall's science, according to Lord Schuster, even got in the way of his mountaineering prowess.

> Tyndall . . . was always too much absorbed by the claims of natural science or of physical beauty to give his whole mind to the business of pure mountaineering.[2]

It was only behind the mask, as we shall see, and ready to flash out at moments, that the smile of adventure was allowed to lurk.

In the wider field of exploration at that time science was allowed into its own because it combined well with other more obvious motives. The 'heroic phase' of African discovery, beginning with James Bruce, owed much to missionaries as well as to emissaries of governments. Thus the 1858 expedition of Burton and Speke to the Central African lakes was commissioned by the Foreign Office 'at the instance of the Royal Geographical Society'. The quest for the sources of

---

[1] 'Half of their Lives', *The Cornhill*, Summer 1952.
[2] A. S. Eve and C. H. Cready, *Life and Work of John Tyndall*. It may be objected that the first ascent of Mont Blanc had little to do with Science. This makes Paccard's achievement all the more remarkable, to my thinking.

148

14: '*Speleology is not only a sport; it is also a science.*' *Descent o ladder pitch, Lamb Lair, Somerset.*

15

16

the Nile, important to geographical science, was also of interest to the British Government. Livingstone was throughout a great geographical scientist, but he was also a missionary and a protagonist in the fight against slave traffic. When Stanley heard of his death he exclaimed:

> The effect which this news had upon me, after the first shock had passed away, was to fire me with a resolution to complete his work, to be, if God willed it, the next martyr to geographical science, or, if my life was to be spared, to clear up . . . the secrets of the Great River throughout its course.

As expressed in the *Daily Telegraph* his purpose was:

> . . . to complete the work left unfinished by the lamented death of David Livingstone; to solve, if possible, the remaining problems of the geography of Central Africa; and to investigate and report upon the haunts of the slave-traders.[3]

The last purpose has been added; but none of the others was inimical to the intention of the later Stanley—that of adding territory to an empire. The change which took place about the 1870's was from the inquisitive, which had been approved, to the acquisitive, which was warmly welcomed. In Stanley the two are inextricably entwined.

In Asia the strong personality of Sven Hedin, on his first great journey in 1893, did not feel bothered about defending his intention 'to traverse Asia from west to east, from the Caspian Sea to Peking, and in particular to explore the intermediate regions which are least known'—all for the sake of 'scientific labours, upon which the chief part of my time, energy and attention were constantly expended.'[4] What a masterful scientist he was! Everything, especially on the 1893-7 journey, had to be shown to have a scientific object; and it is something of an anticlimax to find him, still a veteran traveller in the 1930's, only allowed in Central Asia on the condition of testing motor vehicles for the Chinese

[3] *Through the Dark Continent.*　　　[4] From the Preface to *Through Asia.*

'Dr Livingstone, I presume?'
'Look out, you drop that box—I'll shoot you.' Stanley and his porters.

Government. But in these early, rapturous days even climbing Mustagh Ata (24,388 feet, near Kashgar) was a scientific excursion. 'It was my desire, as it was also my intention, to climb to the summit of the mountain, examine its geological structure, its coat of ice-mail, and the gigantic glaciers which plough their way down its rugged sides. But alas . . .'[5] He underestimated the mountain, as Freshfield did Kangchenjunga, but reached 20,600 feet on the back of a yak, and remarked very justly that what stops difficulty of breathing at high altitudes 'is the avoidance of bodily exertion.' Another grave problem resolved, and long before the physiologists attacked it!

When he crossed the great Takla Makan desert he had as objective the buried cities of an ancient civilisation, and also the location of the Masar-Tagh range of mountains. I have already hinted, however, that the sheer fascination of this desert may have had something to do with his three crossings; for the first time, in 1895, his experience was grim enough to keep any man away from the place for ever. Misled by the guide, the caravan wandered and died. Their leader struggled on with one servant, burying himself in the sand by day to keep cool. When he finally reached water, alone, after four days quite without it, he was still so much the scientist that he took his own pulse before drinking. It was forty-nine.

Sven Hedin may very properly represent the many geographical and archaeological scientists who were exploring in the same way—a way that might just be of use to their countries and was considered honourable by them. But the polar explorers were having a more difficult time. Science had made its *entrée*, certainly; as early as 1838 Charles Wilkes's southern expedition had taken twelve observers (not very effective ones). But in these regions the commercial and territorial baits were now appearing very slender indeed, and a note of self-defence creeps into the writings of the scientists.

[5] *Through Asia.*

People, perhaps, still exist who believe that it is of no importance to explore the unknown regions. This, of course, shows ignorance. It is hardly necessary to mention here of what scientific importance it is that these regions should be explored thoroughly. The history of the human race is a continual struggle from darkness towards light. It is, therefore, to no purpose to discuss the use of knowledge; man wants to know, and when he ceases to do so, he is no longer man.

That is Nansen. But at the beginning of the twentieth century these 'people' were still sufficiently numerous for it to be impossible to announce that one was taking a purely scientific expedition to Arctic or Antarctic. Amundsen, as we have seen, abandoned science and went for patriotic sentiment. Shackleton, in his approach to the Royal Geographical Society over the 1907 *Nimrod* expedition, went cautiously in both directions. 'I do not intend to sacrifice the scientific utility of the expedition to a mere record-breaking journey, but say frankly all the same, that one of my great efforts will be to reach the Southern Geographical Pole.' And Scott, in his letter to the same body already quoted (page 139) falls back on patriotic pride as an incentive to public generosity.

In his Journal, however, Scott states the case more frankly.

One cannot affect to be blind to the situation: the scientific public, as well as the more general public, will gauge the result of the scientific work of the expedition largely in accordance with the success or failure of the main object. With success all roads will be made easy, all work will receive its proper consideration. With failure even the most brilliant work may be neglected and forgotten, at least for a time.[6]

The scientific members of the party went further; and every word of Wilson and Griffith Taylor (*With Scott: The Silver Lining*) rings out the cardinal importance of the scientific work. Sometimes, even, like Cherry-Garrard, they go so far as to say: 'We were primarily a great scientific expedition, with the Pole as our bait for public support,

[6] *Scott's Last Expedition*, vol. I.

though it was not more important than any other acre of the plateau.'[7] And elaborating this theme:

> It is really not desirable for men who do not believe that knowledge is of value for its own sake to take up this kind of life. The question constantly put to us in civilisation was and still is: 'What is the use? Is there gold? Or is there coal?' The commercial spirit of the present day can see no good in pure science.
>
> Now unless a man believes that such a view is wrong, he has no business 'down South'. [He goes on to say that the meteorological and magnetic work are the only sources of immediate practical benefit.]
>
> The members of the expedition believed that it was worth while to discover new land and life, to reach the Southern Pole of the earth, to make elaborate meteorological and magnetic observations and extended geographical surveys . . . They were prepared to suffer great hardship, and some of them died for their beliefs . . . Without such ideals the spirit which certainly existed in our small community would have been impossible.[8]

That is an extreme, if admirable, position, taken up perhaps because of suspected opposition. Before we reach modern times, in which science has become more firmly entrenched, I want for a moment to challenge it in the case of the Pole, and not just on the grounds that the Pole in the passage quoted has got mixed up with the scientific motives, or that it is not necessary to have *esprit de science* in order to have *esprit de corps* in a community.

I can do this perhaps by the analogy of mountaineering. There we left science firmly in the seat, but chinks soon began to appear in her armour. In the middle of the century John Tyndall was pouring forth learned papers on glaciology and kindred subjects. But look at Tyndall himself more closely, with G. Winthrop Young:

> How I used to try and peer into that tantalising background, which he left uncoloured and unfilled-in lest it might disturb

---

[7] *The Worst Journey in the World.*   [8] Ibid. From 'We travelled for Science'.

the balance of a scientific presentment. And yet, the first conqueror of Pic Tyndall on the Matterhorn, the first man to ascend the incomparable Weisshorn, who built the chalet above Belalp so as to be able to look for the rest of his life upon the mountain he considered to be the most beautiful, and who built the chalet at Hindhead as the first settler to profit by the contrast of that near wild scenery throughout the London working year—surely behind the professorial façade was hidden a romantic of the first order![9]

And if he was a romantic, equally or more were his contemporaries, men like A. W. Moore. Soon the detectors of Emperor's Clothes began to raise their voices more boldly. Leslie Stephen offended Tyndall bitterly in an after-dinner speech, part of which may reappear in his famous account of the summit of the Rothorn:

'And what philosophical observations did you make?' will be the inquiry of one of those fanatics who, by a reasoning process to me utterly inscrutable, have somehow irrevocably associated alpine travelling with science. To them I answer that the temperature was approximately (I had no thermometer) 212° (Fahrenheit) below freezing point. As for ozone, if any existed in the atmosphere, it was a greater fool than I take it for. As we had, unluckily, no barometer, I am unable to give the usual information as to the extent of our deviation from the correct altitude; but the Federal map fixes the height at 13,855 feet.[10]

Although, even after this, Whymper was to have fun with a mercury barometer in the Andes, by and large, with the appearance of Mummery and many others, the real motives to mountaineering had by the end of the century been so laid bare, that very few spent their time on the summits reading thermometers or boiling them. By the 1920's it was the scientists who started their mountain books with an apologetic preface. It was only later that the pendulum started to swing towards science once more.

Now go back to the Poles. Are there any chinks in the

[9] *Alpine Journal*, Vol. LIV, No. 267.   [10] *The Playground of Europe*.

armour here? I believe there are, both in the journals of the scientific explorers themselves and in other records. Amundsen we have classed with the non-scientists already. And what of Bowers, a tough naval lieutenant serving in the tropics? I cannot accept that he applied to join the expedition simply because he believed 'that knowledge is of value for its own sake'. He applied, primarily, in the hope of making a great journey to the South Pole—and he made it. And Edward Evans, another fine naval officer? And the seamen? I even find it hard to accept that Cherry-Garrard himself and Bowers joined Wilson on that 'Worst Journey' wholly because they believed in the objective importance of an Emperor penguin's embryo. Cherry-Garrard's own amusing account of his reception with his eggs at the Natural History Museum (he had great difficulty in getting a receipt) and the subsequent inconclusive report hint to me that the result was less important than the inspiring journey. Only to Wilson, I believe, did these eggs have a real and crucial value, which made them worth even the responsibility of asking two others to risk their lives in the search.

I submit, then, that it was the Poles, just as it is the summit of a mountain, that fired the imagination of these men, and that the scientific consideration came later, lending added and weighty arguments; also that for this reason the 'Polar period' was the period of purest adventure in the history of Arctic and Antarctic exploration. Scott was not a scientist, though he interested himself in every branch and acquired remarkable knowledge. There is something very moving in the number of rock specimens which his party, with only one pure scientist among the five of them, dragged back, and which must by its weight have contributed to their weakness and death. But another contributory cause, there is no doubt at all, was that 'terrible disappointment' of finding the Norwegians there before them. If the South Pole had been 'not more important than any other acre of the plateau', they could never have been so distressed.

Shackleton also was not a scientist; indeed his biographer, H. R. Mill, says that the Discovery (1900) was 'an opportunity and nothing more. He would have tried to join just as eagerly a ship bound to seek buried treasure on the Spanish Main.' Nobody who reads *South* can believe that his plan in 1914 was 'scientific', in the sense of having science as its main object. He wanted to do a great thing which had not been done, to cross the Antarctic Continent, to achieve with slender resources and pitifully fragile ships exactly what the British Commonwealth Expedition is attempting now. Only in its broadest terms could science be described as such a probing of the unknown. In the narrower sense the Australian, Sir Douglas Mawson, was more a father of the modern scientific expedition than either of the two better known men.

What I think Cherry-Garrard's words may be taken as meaning is that at the Poles the urge to exploration *by itself* is not enough. With that interpretation few would quarrel. A man should have a good deal beside if he is to survive the boredom of Polar night, to regard even a spring blizzard as worth while. With science his incentive will be the assured hope that something will come out of it all, that he can 'look forward to a harvest, however distant it may be, when some fruit will be reaped, some good effected'. Those words are Charles Darwin's, and his advice to travellers is relevant:

> If a person should ask my advice, before undertaking a long voyage, my answer would depend upon his possessing a decided taste for some branch of knowledge, which could by such means be improved. No doubt it is a high satisfaction to behold various countries and the many races of mankind, but the pleasures gained at the time do not counterbalance the evils.[11]

This applies forcibly to polar travel. If science offers the satisfaction of results in the foreseeable future, then it is doubly worth the pain and discomfort. And besides, an

[11] *The Voyages of Adventure and Beagle, III.*

interest is engendered, if it is not already there, which can carry a man even through misery. It is remarkable how, on the *Terra Nova* party, the hard core of initially fine scientists, Griffith Taylor, Wilson, Debenham, Priestley and others, was augmented by the naval men who came into the game as it were by chance and stayed fascinated, to produce their valuable contributions.

᷾ ᷾   ᷾ ᷾   ᷾ ᷾

The years passed. Men like Mawson had intensified the scientific emphasis of exploration. The members of Watkins' and Lindsay's expeditions, questioned as to why they were being uncomfortable in Greenland, answered in a loud voice 'For Science!' with something under the breath about the Arctic Air-Route. In the same tone Byrd, having flown over the North Pole, justified himself for resisting attractive business offers and turning to the South. 'It has always seemed to me that science is the loser so long as there remains a large unexplored area left in the world. To quote Sir Douglas Mawson: "Science is a homogeneous whole."' [12] Those who had not the scientific sympathy, would not acquire it or were not interested, branded themselves in the eyes of the serious as dilettantes, and usually tried to get fixed up with a newspaper. The uneducated public still had a soft spot for levity.

The attitudes of the non-scientific to the recent advances of science have been many and various. Sometimes, like Lindsay in Greenland, they keep step, more or less. Sometimes, particularly impenitent mountaineers like Tilman after Everest 1938, they protest:

I merely ask that mountaineering and science should be kept distinct, in particular that the problem of climbing Mount Everest, like any other mountain, should be left to mountaineers to solve, and that those actively engaged in solving it should not

[12] *Skyward.*

be expected to enter what Goethe calls the charnel house of science.[13]

And it is almost comical to find Tilman, like many another and many years after the emancipation of mountaineering from science, being compelled later not only to uphold but to practise the latter, in order to be allowed to go on climbing at all. In 1949 the Nepalese Government insisted that his climbing party of two must be supplemented by two scientists.

> This condition meant . . . a change, almost a volte-face, on the part of a leader who had hitherto refused to mingle art with science. To be too stiff in opinions is a grave fault; a man should be sure of more than his principles before deciding never to break them. Benedick, when he swore he would die a bachelor, did not expect to live until he was married; and just as the great Henry once deemed Paris worth a Mass, so I thought a glimpse of the Nepal Himalaya worth the swallowing of a strong prejudice.[14]

Tilman took to collecting beetles, and later flowers. It is curious evidence of today's trend that mountaineers like myself will come back from an expedition full of apology. 'Of course we did some survey work as well, took angles on peaks and rounds of photographs. That was the most important part really.' Times change, and the Everest Foundation can only give grants where scientific work is involved. In the same way, nowadays, a business man off on holiday to Italy will confide that 'Of course I shall be doing a bit of business there as well.' And it is bad form not to be seen 'dashing back to town' after a country weekend, whereas fifty years ago you

[13] H. W. Tilman, *Everest 1938*. In an appendix to the same book Dr Raymond Greene is found arguing: 'I think that future expeditions to Mount Everest should be planned primarily on a scientific basis . . . The expedition should go out primarily as a scientific expedition accompanied by a small climbing party which, if opportunity arises, will undoubtedly reach the top.' The dispute continues. In 1953 we had one physiologist, but no one could say that we were a scientific expedition.

[14] *Nepal Himalaya*.

would go off by another station to avoid revealing the dismal fact that you had to.

❧ ☙   ❧ ☙   ❧ ☙

So compellingly does science come back into her own! In the undersea adventure, the explorers seem to have yielded from the first to Professor Piccard's dictum that 'throughout this field of exploration it is oceanography which will guide humanity'. In this spirit Cousteau says: 'We are obsessed by the incredible realm of ocean life which is still waiting to be known.' But the picture which he goes on to paint of the process of knowing it is not, to many aqualung enthusiasts, attractive. Writing of the 'shelf', the undersea land mass round our coasts where the sea is not more than 600 feet deep:

> Our best independent diving range is only half-way down to the border of this shelf, so we cannot yet occupy the ground to which governments lay claim. But when research centres and industrialists apply themselves to the problem, we shall advance to the six-hundred-foot 'drop-off' line. It will require better equipment than the aqualung. The lung is primitive and unworthy of contemporary levels of science.[15]

Here there is a mingling of motives, commercial with scientific, and an unwelcome late entry of politics into the fray.

The exploration of caves has something of the same story. It began as pure sport, and much has been written in climbing journals of the delights of 'pot-holing' by those who like immersing themselves in cold water at the bottom of dank dark pits. A sport it still is, to most. But here is the citation of Chevalier of the Légion d'Honneur awarded posthumously to Marcel Loubens, who died in the 2,389-foot Pierre Saint-Martin.

> Moved by his unselfish devotion to speleology, in which self-love played no part, he brought thereto from early youth the finest qualities of mind and heart . . . He embarked with his

[15] *The Silent World.*

valiant comrades, in August 1952, upon the most perilous of them all—the descent of Pierre Saint-Martin; and there he met death bravely in the cause of Science.

After the 1953 expedition, which succeeded in reaching the bottom, its leader concluded that 'speleology is not only a sport; it is also a science, a many-sided and exacting science'.[16] Now, with the deepest caves explored, the scientific aspect of their many recesses is likely to come more than ever to the fore. We must turn elsewhere.

Turn to the sea surface. There will always be adventure there, for sea and mountains are too big for us ever to lose awe of them. But the surface of the sea, like its depths, has plenty for the scientist too, especially if he be one to put his theories into practice. Two of the most adventurous voyages of modern times were made with a scientific object: to prove a theory about the migration of peoples from South America hundreds of years ago, and to prove that it is possible for the human body to nourish itself from plankton. For such objects the men of the *Kon-Tiki* and Dr Bombard underwent hardship and risked their lives.

To men like these it seems to me that there is the brightest path through a scientific future. It is denied to us amateur travellers, who will continue to alternate between shaking our metaphorical fists at science and rendering thanks to her for our down clothing and microcellular boots, for the lowering gear of the caver and the raising gear of the glider, or for the aqualung, by means of which the diver escapes into his dream world, whatever he may think of Cousteau's Utopia. But for those explorers who have even a touch of science in their make-up, what opportunities! Not only is their science itself an adventure, as has been said too often for me to dare to add my mite, but it can be physical adventure with two distinct spices of excitement to it. It is worth pausing to ask what these are.

[16] Just how much a science, in Britain too, can be seen from the remarkable book *British Caving* by members of the Cave Research Group (1953).

The two are closely connected. When Thor Heyerdahl wrote about the possible migration of the tribes driven out of South America by the Incas, across the Pacific Ocean on balsa rafts, he could get no hearing for his views. There was nothing for it but to build a raft himself and do what they did. He said:

> 'It's easier to interest people in an expedition than in an unread manuscript.'
>
> 'But what can you gain by it?'
>
> 'Destroy one of the weightiest arguments against the theory, quite apart from the fact that science will pay some attention to the affair.' [17]

The building of the raft and the sailing of it, against the advice of all the experts, right across the Pacific to the Polynesian Islands, was a defiantly exciting adventure which needs no elaboration. But it was also, and here is one important point, enjoyable. The crew forgot sometimes exactly why they had come.

> 'Bengt,' I said, 'can you tell me how the hell we come to be doing this?'
>
> 'The devil I do. You know best yourself. It was your damned idea, but I think it was grand.' [18]

In the same way, though he did not enjoy the voyage, Bombard reaped a fierce and exciting satisfaction out of proving wrong those who said that he would die if he tried to live off the sea. The only way of proving that he would not, was to do it. In similar straits, during the 1914–18 war, Sir Joseph Barcroft proved that a certain gas was not poisonous to humans by shutting himself up in it with a goat. The goat died. In Bombard's case the experiment was longer, involving not only a diet of unappetising, indeed revolting food from the sea, but also life under the conditions of a shipwrecked sailor, that is, on a small inflatable raft aptly named *L'Hérétique*. The passage from the Canaries to the West Indies

---

[17] *The Kon-Tiki Expedition.*   [18] Ibid.

alone took sixty-five days; and he lost in all 55 lbs weight. But he had proved the theory; and the reader of *Naufragé Volontaire* (*The Bombard Story*) is struck repeatedly by places where, faced with disaster, he appears more concerned with the demise of the theory than of himself.

Enjoyment and the disproving of a theory, or proving of another in the face of accepted belief: there are plenty of holes which the naughty boys of science can amuse themselves by widening. It has sometimes seemed to me that a fascinating study could be made of those who have successfully defied the pundits, from the days, and earlier, when everyone said that Nansen's *Fram* would be crushed by the ice—and she wasn't, nor was his bold theory of Arctic drift currents confounded, as Greely and Nares expected. Then it was said that human life could not survive above 23,000 feet —and it very successfully did, as proved by Kellas and Longstaff. In more modern times Byrd was told that his Fokker would ice up hopelessly over the North Pole; Martin Lindsay crossed Greenland west to east with two others, 'an expedition which had been condemned as unsound by all the best authorities'[19]—and was eminently successful. Professor Piccard met opposition before his first ascent into the stratosphere. 'The specialists of those days considered my suggestion as unrealisable . . . But the single objection that they were able to make to me was that up till then nobody had done it. How often have I heard reasoning of this sort!'[20] And *Kon-Tiki* and Bombard . . . How many pioneers have had the experience of Columbus with his egg! And how much fun is still to be had proving learned opinion wrong! It seems to me that for the scientific lone wolf there are a mass of pieces still to be fitted, even without vast cost and apparatus, into the cosmic jig-saw, which will never be finished. And let him take comfort that, even if he can never get to the bottom of anything, there will always be happiness in the quest.

[19] *Three got Through.*   [20] *In Balloon and Bathyscaphe.*

It is nothing new to suffer from the fact that our knowledge can be but fragmentary, that we can never fathom what lies behind. But suppose, now, that we could reckon it out, that the inmost secret of it lay as clear and plain to us as a rule-of-three sum, should we be any the happier? Possibly just the reverse. Is it not in the struggle to attain knowledge that happiness consists? I am very ignorant, consequently the conditions of happiness are mine.

Let me fill a soothing pipe and be happy.[21]

If, however, a man still wants to do the biggest things remaining in exploration, he must unite with others, and that is where Geophysical Years come in. 'Experts are quietly consolidating the gains of spectacular amateurs' (Peter Fleming). On the South Polar continent alone nine nations are said to have established forty bases,[22] at a cost of millions of pounds, in the attempt to solve a few of the enormous problems there remaining. Nearly forty-five years after Scott and his companions stood shivering upon it, the first of the American South Pole party dropped from Globemasters and started to erect a base at the Pole itself (October 31, 1956). That base is now established, an enormous and (comparatively) comfortable station equipped with radio, 40-foot radar masts, heating, laboratories, good food and drink. This is only one of the American bases, but it is experiencing the severest conditions. Dr Paul Siple, the leader, wrote: 'Here at the Polar Station my calculations show we may have to endure the frightening unknown of 120 degrees below zero or even lower! But the weather after all is one of the reasons we volunteered to come here.' Low temperatures in difficult country, eased but not obviated by modern aids, will also be endured by the Commonwealth party (have been endured, by the time this book appears). Motor transport cannot overcome all the difficulties; but the thought of hot hamburgers at the Pole itself with the Americans must have been an encouragement.

[21] Nansen, *Farthest North*.   [22] *Geographical Journal*, Vol. XXIII, Part 1.

These two expeditions, and the many others at present operating and co-operating over the problems of the Geophysical Year, show to my thinking how the big problems are now increasingly scientific, and how Peter Fleming has hit the truth in his remark; for nobody, in the privately run, ill-clad days, could have faced such temperatures, or entrenched themselves so prosaically in the most mysterious quarters of the earth. Even crevasses, those awful symbols of danger, can now be detected by electronic devices; while the American equipment landed at McMurdo Sound last year included pianos and refrigerators. What is good about this formidable set-up is that, so far as one can see, the I.G.Y. seems to be passing as amicably as was its intention. In the words of an American,[23] 'Antarctic exploration hitherto has often been marred by international rivalry . . . The future of polar exploration [indeed all large scale exploration?] and polar science lies in international co-operation and exchange and it is hoped that the pattern of the International Geophysical Year will be the pattern for future polar work.'

The really big explorations remaining on our planet involve, therefore, vast resources of money and equipment, as well as the scientific turn of approach. In their moving to and fro they rely less and less on human bodies, more and more on machines. If one can gain access to these resources, if one follows the Cherry-Garrard line and joins wholeheartedly in the give and take of this international year, then there are wonders of discovery in store. Meanwhile those who watch enviously or scornfully from a distance can comfort themselves that in the total sum of human wisdom even the greatest discovery is very small beer. In what way are we wiser than the Greeks? And what do we truly *know*? Gleefully, perhaps, they may echo the scientist de Saussure: 'Placed on this planet since yesterday, and then only for one day, we can but desire knowledge to which, seemingly, we shall never attain.'

[23] Captain L. H. McAlpine, *Geographical Journal*, March 1957.

❧ ❧ ❧ ❧ ❧ ❧

11

The machine-loving man

Each clown may rise
And climb the skies
When he hath found a stair.
But joy to him
That dares to climb
And hath no help but air.

GEORGE WITHER

A machine is like a desert. Either it fascinates or appals you.
It may be that you overcome an initial panic and do great
things with 'the crouching beast'. But to many like myself
adventure will always remain the act of running away from,
rather than towards machinery. As I contemplate this
chapter my thoughts return to the Motor Battalions of the
60th Rifles in wartime, and I hope devoutly that no sergeant
of mine ever reads it. The mysteries of the working of an
internal combustion engine can be explained convincingly
with the aid of blackboard and paper at O.C.T.U.s. That
was about as far as I got. But it is one thing to know how the
spark leaps, how the petrol flows, what the dynamo is for.
When a fifteen-hundredweight truck, captious creature, stops
dead in its tracks for no reason at all, the prudent subaltern,
knowing that his N.C.O.s were all garage proprietors in
peacetime anyway, will have no hesitation in saying: 'Carry
on please, sergeant.' And the dozen anxious faces in the
truck brighten no doubt at the prospect.

That sense of inferiority is still with me. But I must face
the truth that many who go adventuring start that way
because they are interested in the machine. This is a comparatively recent development, unless you count ships as

164

18

19

machines. They are, of course, and so was the cumbersome diving apparatus in use since early last century. This was a means to an end, for the pearl divers and searchers of wreckage. It served its purpose in drawing them to the undersea jungle; while on the obverse side, it was the sight of a man being crushed to death in a diving suit that inspired the Swede, Victor Berge, to invent his diving mask (1941), and so lead to the aqualung.

Diving apparatus, however, is hardly in the main line of development; while the adventure of big ships was coming into line with that of other mechanical devices. In those early days of machinery as we know it, the machine itself was the adventure. And the question of how to do something nobody else had done posed itself quite simply as: How to get steam working an engine, and then get the engine running along rails? How to get the internal combustion engine on to a road? Last and most imposing of questions: How to get a heavier-than-air machine into the air?

Out of all the early history of flying I am going to take one point only: that the reward of flight went to an almost miraculous patience, doggedness in research and the kind of courage that takes obstacles as they come and does not worry about the one after next; also that those who have these qualities do best in present-day flying. I think myself that they are not the most imaginative qualities, since they lie chiefly in carrying on along a charted path, and that therefore flying is not the most imaginative, or greatest, adventure —except in special cases. To make up for this it has other virtues, service to the community, service to ground exploration, and the like. It is perhaps a better handmaiden than mistress.

The story of the Wright brothers, still to my mind the great men of flying with others like Blériot in support, demonstrates this virtue of patience. The Wrights began at the very beginning by reading all the books. They read of Leonardo and his preoccupation with the idea of the bird; of

The first powered heavier-than-air flight, December 17, 1903.
'*The Hunter lives and is obedient to your slightest wish.*' *A Hawker Hunter in flight.*

The springs of adventure

Roger Bacon, who had the first inkling of the use of gas. They studied the Montgolfier balloon, the first to fly, in 1783, with a fire burning under the envelope, and soon succeeded by the more efficient hydrogen balloon. They then began on the heavier-than-air attempts, at that time becoming numerous. The German, Otto Lilienthal, had constructed an experimental mound for gliders and studied bird gliding; but he was killed in 1896. Another important pioneer, P. Pilcher, lost his life in 1899. The Wrights remained undeterred; and the Frenchman, Octave Chanute, encouraged them.

> Now faced with the truth that the pioneers, for all their near successes, had as yet failed to make the decisive conquest [the motive of conquest again!] the brothers felt themselves burning with a resolve to be the first to achieve where so many brilliant, painstaking, imaginative others had—so far—failed.[1]

On they went, coming upon the idea of ailerons to give rise and drop instead of the previous arrangement whereby the human body shifted its weight. Then came the wind tunnels, constructed with unbelievable patience and skill so that they could study the set of wings at various wind speeds. Sometimes they despaired. At last, on a windy day of December, 1903,—they flew. Here the courage came in. Years after (as published in *Flying*) Orville Wright said:

> With all the knowledge and skill acquired in thousands of flights in the last ten years, I would hardly today think of making my first flight in a strange aircraft in a twenty-seven-mile wind, even if I knew that the machine had already been flown and was safe. After these years of experience I look with amazement upon our audacity in attempting flights with a new and untried machine under such circumstances. Yet faith in our calculations and the design of the first machine, based upon our table of air pressures . . . had convinced us that the machine was capable of lifting and maintaining itself in the air, and that, with a little practice, it could be safely flown.

[1] M. Harrison, *Airborne at Kittyhawk*.

This courage and faith in the gruelling experimental work that precedes seems to me the mark of the aeronautical genius. And equally true to the ideal was the Wrights' dignity in the face of jealousy and mud-slinging, which seem the inevitable gloomy accompaniment of brilliant pathfinding. *Magna est veritas et praevalebit*—fortunately.

A little story is told of Amy Johnson, on her flight to Australia. The Turks at Istanbul wheeled her plane into the hangar, not realising how heavily loaded it was in front; and it tipped over on to the propeller. Having done her servicing (usually five to six hours, a single-handed job) she had taken the precaution of leaving the propeller in the horizontal position, so that little damage was done. The attention to detail was in as direct a line with the Wrights' thoroughness as the persistence with which she did her own servicing.

The twenty years from 1919 to 1939 were the golden age of adventurous aviation. They were the years of my boyhood heroes and heroines. The Atlantic was flown, Parer and Macintosh made their great flight to Australia (1920). Then New York to Paris, the Atlantic both ways, the Pacific, London to New Zealand and back. The Poles were flown over in turn, and in 1933 the Houston Expedition flew above Mount Everest. Post and Gatty circled the world in brisk time, then Post by himself in brisker. The adventure of the airships ended in glory and tragedy. What all these people had in common it is difficult to see, unless it were the negative quality of not being out for fame or money; not more than a handful got either, except of the overnight variety. Post and Gatty could hardly have been more different, the one a tough and hearty doer of deeds, the other a scientific, almost academic researcher. They were not, even, men and women who dreamed great dreams. What linked them was the quality allowed by a puzzled journalist to Amy Johnson: 'Until you know her she seems quite ordinary—nothing striking about her—there are dozens like her, working in the

City. The only thing that really impressed me was her dashed doggedness.'

Doggedness, patience and courage—for the machine was at the temperamental stage (as it still is) and could not carry much fuel. A missed ground meant death. John Alcock, Bert Hinkler, Charles Kingsford-Smith, Wiley Post and Amelia Earhart, all met their death flying; to be joined later, in the war, by a legion which included Saint-Exupéry, Amy Johnson and Hillary. More than a spark of imagination too, one must allow that: the ability to see that where the hazardous route now went, one day an air line would be. Not the least remarkable achievement of the adventuring era was the establishment of the air services, rickety as yet and irregular, but spreading in embryo as the direct result of untold heroic feats. Only read *Night Flight* to see what I mean.

It was about this time that the controversy as to whether the machine was destroying natural adventure waxed with a particularly lurid brightness. The argument is moribund now, but its important premises remain. The Old School maintained that we were much better off before the arrival of these abominations overhead. The New School claimed with equal fervour that not only was progress inevitable, so that there was no point in arguing the toss anyway, but that a new *kind* of adventure was now possible, complementing rather than cancelling the others. If you can see Nature from the air, you are penetrating her in a new dimension. You have gained something infinitely precious thereby; and the story of her revelation is at the same time one stage nearer complete.

It is worth at this stage quoting two or three expressions of the latter view, because what was said then of the machinery of flight applies even now to all machinery used in exploration. I should add that the whole argument seems to me to come up against a dead wall. Machinery, like reality, depends for its value upon the beholder. Things can be real or unreal, machines helpful or unhelpful, depending on how the person concerned makes use of them. And that is another human imponderable. Here, anyway, is Saint-Exupéry, for the new view:

> The realities of nature resume their pride of place. It is not with metal that the pilot is in contact. Contrary to the vulgar illusion, it is thanks to the metal, and by virtue of it, that the pilot rediscovers nature. As I have already said, the machine does not isolate man from the great problems of nature but plunges him more deeply into them.
>
> Numerous, nevertheless, are the moralists who have attacked the machine as the source of all the ills we bear, who, creating a fictitious dichotomy, have denounced the mechanical civilisation as the enemy of the spiritual civilisation.
>
> If what they think were really so, then indeed we should have to despair of man, for it would be futile to struggle against this new advancing chaos. The machine is certainly as irresistible in its advance as those virgin forests that encroach upon equatorial domains. A congeries of motives prevents us from blowing up our spinning mills and reviving the distaff. Gandhi had a try at this sort of revolution: he was as simple-minded as a child trying to empty the sea on to sand with the aid of a tea-cup.
>
> It is hard for me to understand the language of these pseudo-dreamers. What is it makes them think that the ploughshare torn from the bowels of the earth by perforating machines, forged, tempered, and sharpened in the roar of modern industry, is nearer to men than any other tool of steel? By what sign do they recognise the inhumanity of the machine?
>
> Have they ever really asked themselves this question? The central struggle of man has ever been to understand one another, to join together for the common weal. And it is this very thing that the machine helps them to do! It begins by annihilating time and space.[2]

There is a crusading spirit about that, to be noted by nations supposedly united. The answer to the querulous, he goes on in modern tone to say, lies not in the *fact* of the machine, but in the *use* of it. Admittedly we do not yet use it properly.

[2] *Wind, Sand and Stars.*

The springs of adventure

We have perhaps driven men into the service of the machine, instead of building machinery for the service of men . . . Young barbarians still marvelling at our new toys—that is what we are. Why else should we race our planes, give prizes to those who fly highest, or fastest? We take no heed to ask ourselves, why we race: the race itself is more important than the object.[3]

An important verdict, and perhaps notice has been taken of it. In the air, at any rate, much of the old *individual* competition is gone: the Schneider Trophy, the Cape Air Race, the Paris to Damascus Race—these are things of the past. In 1931 the world's high altitude record was broken by Professor Piccard's FNRS. Piccard, another prophet of things to come, gave the line by contradicting a patriotic congratulator with the words: 'It will be a fine day for me when other stratospheric balloons follow me and reach altitudes greater than mine. My aim is not to beat, and above all not to maintain records, but to open a new domain to scientific research and to aerial navigation.'[4]

He was well ahead of his time, heralding a modern view. A little later, his attitude arrested what might have been unpleasant rivalry between the Piccard bathyscaphe *Trieste* and the FNRS3.

In the air individual competition is on its way out; partly owing to technical difficulties, perhaps, but still—on its way out. National competition for military purposes goes on, alas, and presumably will go on until we have either learned sense or blown ourselves up. Fighter speeds and then intercontinental missiles will continue to occupy us for some time. I have before me an account of the new Saunders-Roe 53 mixed-power-plant fighter, capable of flying at 2,000 miles an hour, or 'under operational conditions' at Mach 2, that is to say twice the speed of sound. And Mr Kruschev says already that fighters are obsolete! However, a silver lining there is, even to such terrifying clouds. The tests which go to make possible these high figures are for strength and stability as

[3] *Wind, Sand and Stars.*   [4] *In Balloon and Bathyscaphe.*

well as for speed. Other aircraft emerge from them, such as those now helping the Commonwealth party in its crossing of the South Polar Continent. Planes are being used for reconnaissance there in a way that would have delighted Saint-Exupéry. 'Thanks to the metal, and by virtue of it' Nature is being explored with a vengeance.

I suspect that he would have recognised that you cannot explore *only* from the air. It is a mistake sometimes made by aviators to think that you can. You can drop bases, as the Americans have succeeded in doing at the Pole, but by this means you only get to know particular points. On the ground, mechanisation has raced ahead almost as fast as in the air—very far from the days when Scott gallantly but fruitlessly took motors with him to McMurdo Sound. Cars have crossed the Sahara a number of times, some of them almost casually, bearing people on their way back from leave in England to Rhodesia. The journey across country to India or Burma or Malaya, in Dormobile or Land Rover, is becoming a prerogative of enterprising undergraduates. Those more limited in resources ride scooters up Snowdon or land helicopters on Striding Edge. Truly the mechanised age is with us. The results of the more serious experiments are reaped and threshed, and the Commonwealth expedition, to get back to more solid ground, enjoys the benefit. It uses Snocats, developed from the 'obsolescent' Weasels, to get it across the continent—in co-operation with aircraft.

Admiral Richard Byrd went for the ideal of 'rediscovering'—and indeed discovering—Nature as whole-heartedly as Saint-Exupéry. His purpose in trying to fly over the Pole is stated as follows:

> There were two fairly good reasons for our wanting to fly to the North Pole; first, by travelling at high altitudes over unexplored regions we might discover some new land or unexpected phenomena; second, a successful flight would, like the first crossing of the Atlantic, be sure to accelerate public interest in aviation.[5]

> [5] *Skyward.*

The first reason we have already noted in Saint-Exupéry.
The 'interest in aviation' Byrd thought, and thought right up
to his death last year, to be important because flying is part
of the inevitable human adventure. Sooner or later men will
have explored this planet and the space around it. 'The
sooner the better,' say the airmen. Approaching the theme
of civilisation from a different angle, Byrd holds aviation to
be an inseparable part of that civilising process. 'Civilisation is
just as much a product of the cosmical processes as is the bee-
hive or the ant-hill'—not a struggle, but a development into
which the part of aviation, not clear now, is bound to fit.

> Some can't see this; but aren't they like men looking at a
> great painting, too near to see more than the blobs that make
> the picture, not the picture itself? . . .
> So it is with hazardous pioneer flights. May we not suppose
> that they are happenings, however small, that assist the great
> procession of the race towards its goal—though the meaning of
> these movements may be inscrutable. They would have their
> place in a painting of that procession—a small place that would
> none the less be a necessary part of the picture.[6]

That view of the pioneers has become so generally held now
that it has passed into common speech and thought. Rather
like mountain beauty, which was first fought over and then
accepted until it started to be forgotten, the science of the
aeroplane has become respectable. Men forget that it has not
been there always. Even a world record flight is a matter of
routine, as an extract from *Life Magazine* 1957 will show. An
American Squadron had just circled the world in forty-five
hours. 'The men were not particularly impressed by their
job's historic significance, even though the ground crews
wished them luck with more than the usual fervour. B52
crews had been doing similar jobs for years. Flying around the
world . . . was not very different from flying jets around the
North Pole or around the U.S. It just took longer.' Now they
look forward to developments from there with the eagerness

[6] Ibid.

of their ancestors thinking up improvements on the bow and arrow. It can almost be said that, the argument being over and the way of thought set, the literature of conventional flight as *literature* is ended—though tales of heroic or interesting deeds in the air will go on being interesting. The future of mechanical adventure, with its corresponding imaginative literature, looks like continuing above the stratosphere or at the bottom of the sea.

Moreover, as this process goes on, as experiment is added to experiment and discovery to discovery, the pieces of the puzzle, or to use Byrd's metaphor the parts of the picture, will continue increasingly to fit together. Already when he set out to make high ascents in a balloon Professor Piccard found the problem to be directly connected with undersea research; and when he went back to the bathyscaphe, it was with a sense of fortification from the knowledge won in the stratosphere. Continuing through the realm of mechanical science, he found, as many have, that all his work was connected part to part. Because of this it was no longer necessary to announce defiantly that abstract experiment is 'of value for its own sake'—the Cherry-Garrard note you will remember. As each part fits with others, it will or may *become* useful. So runs the argument now.

Of what use is oceanographic research? This question has been asked me more than once. It is pointless. Two kinds of research exist. To begin with, the scientist works out of a love of research, without a determinate object, without always perceiving direct, practical applications of his work. He discovers new facts, unknown relations. Even if this appears insignificant, a day will come when the results obtained will prove useful. It is then, but only then, that research turns towards the practical. Industry with its great resources then takes a hand. The most disparate pieces are adjusted like pieces of a Meccano set, and what is missing is discovered in new researches. Then a new scientific edifice is built, something from which humanity will benefit.

We can make the following statement without risk of being

contradicted by future events: each discovery, even the most apparently insignificant, will end by being of use to man.[7]

Seen in this light science is a great pattern in which everything, everything in this world and then beyond, may finally be found to have place. And seen in this light the aeroplane, or for that matter the balloon, satellite, bathyscaphe and now Piccard's mesoscaphe, are tools towards the end, an end to which man aspires but which he will, perhaps, never reach.

We are at present still in the happy stage of development, though getting perilously near to leaving it, when the tool itself is fun. The aviator uses his machine as the sailor his dinghy, until under his fingers it seems to spring into a life of its own. In it he moves at will, an almost centaur-like creation, the machine one with the man, answering his every touch. The pilot who really knows his plane, what it is doing and why it does it, tastes (as I believe, for I am not expert enough to know) the purest delight of mechanical travel. Even the proud inventor of the 'Flying Flea', that self-made oddity of the 1930's, got it thus. 'My machine is no longer something which has been made and glued and sold . . . The Man and the Thing have become one, a single whole; the wings are animated by the hand'.[8] And the modern test pilot gets it. 'It [the Hunter],' Duke writes, 'lives and is obedient to your slightest wish.' That is a mechanical partnership which may be the more poignantly blissful for being—as the history of the world goes—short-lived.

For in the recent work of the scientists who make and handle the machine there is the same turning of hope into reality by patience along a set path which we saw earlier. Sheer dogged effort increases the range of the problems even

---

[7] *In Balloon and Bathyscaphe.* This conclusion may be questioned. For instance, on pages 79 to 83 of *A Mathematician's Apology*, G. H. Hardy points out the harm which 'trivial' mathematics, in the guise of ballistics and aerodynamics, can do in war. Piccard's answer, I suppose, would be that he is concerned with the findings of 'real' mathematics, or science of any sort, which are of lasting value to humanity.

[8] H. Mignet, *The Flying Flea.*

as it overcomes the obstacles, and the obstacles are never-ending. An unending complexity of mishaps can turn up in the best organised world. All this leads to a greater complexity of arrangement, less for the human being to do and more for him to think about. When the first interplanetary flights are successful one thing is sure: that the human body, as opposed to brain, will have very little to do with them. Even when a man is allowed into one of the rockets, it will be as observer and director rather than active performer.

'A goose I cackle among swans'—so feels the man who dares to say something about space travel. Fortunately all that concerns me is the impulse to that adventure; and it seems to me that the *motives* (but certainly not the resultant complexities) are the same here as elsewhere, an extension rather than a different species. There is the idea of proving man's worth. There is the lodestone: have we not been hankering after the moon for centuries? There is the economic motive:

> . . . The physical resources of our planet are limited. Sooner or later sheer necessity would have forced men to travel to the other planets. It may well be a very long time before it is easier —to take an obvious example—to obtain uranium from the moon than from the earth, but eventually that time is bound to come.[9]

Added to these inducements there is even the idea that expansion beyond our planet will precede a great creative and aesthetic revival. 'With the expansion of the world's mental horizons,' Clarke writes, 'may come one of the greatest outbursts of creative activity ever known.' Evidence is not lacking from the anthropologists, J. D. Unwin pronouncing that 'In human records there is no trace of any display of productive energy which is not preceded by a display of expansive energy'. Even the awesome name of Sir James Frazer is

[9] A. C. Clarke, *The Exploration of Space*.

invoked, with his remark that 'Intellectual progress . . . receives an immense impetus from conquest and empire' (the parallel being the Renaissance).

On the aesthetic side, it is claimed that a rocket flying off into space is itself a lovely object. The German makers of V2 are said to have cheered at the splendid sight of their creation disappearing as a tiny flame above dark earth into the higher sunlight. The beauties come incidentally, and beauties there certainly are. The present holder of the world height record, Major Simons, who in August 1957 reached 102,000 feet in a balloon, was moved so far as to say over the radio: 'I have a "ringside view" of the heavens and it is indescribable.' But nobody went so far as to claim that he made his ascent for the view.

Patriotism comes into the picture, of course, and unfortunately military expediency with it. Russia having won the 'space-race' with a satellite (at the time of writing two satellites), Britain's first reaction was of amazement at the victory, coupled with characteristic and irrelevant horror at the fate of the dog Laika. Now, throughout the western world, military import is slowly sinking in. The race for the moon has become also a race for the solution of a big problem: how to make a warhead descend again into the atmosphere and still be sure of its target, the target being another continent. What opportunities there are here for the conquest motive! The earth, 'this little piece of mud about which we wax so warm', had seemed to be parcelled out, more or less, apart from chunks of still unexplored Antarctica. And the hydrogen bomb had seemed a fair deterrent, as well as preserver of the *status quo*. But now! The 'adventure' of space takes on a grim significance which has nothing venturesome about it at all.

For most of us, I suppose, the motive of our interest in things as distant as that is one of plain, if extremely vague, curiosity. This can be collective as well as personal. We can feel, still in a very vague way and jogged by spectacular happenings, that Britain 'ought to do something about it'. Apart from that we ask ourselves: What is it like up there? What life is there, if any? What does the earth look like from there? And we dive into our space fiction. Only the scientists can sharpen and direct this curiosity, by pointing to the exact problems, and so we come back to the scientific motive. Already, long before the Russian bombshell of October 1957, the leading figure in the American field, Dr Wernher von Braun, had stated, and others had agreed, that 'it is possible to build a rocket, probably of three stages and not very large, which will land a small payload on the moon.' This will be the beginning of good things, to be followed by a missile circumventing the moon and an unmanned observatory. Finally, after quite a number of years more, a team of human beings. Science will have triumphed indeed.

Here the religious motive enters; and I do not mean only in characters like the priest who is said already to have sited his optimistic moon-church. (He must be greatly preferable as company to those who sell plots at a dollar a plot.) But I mean it in the sense of a mission. In America this has been the most observable. The hotel bedrooms of El Paso, gateway to the rocket station of White Sands, contain each a Gideon Bible. The story is told of the rocket man who read his Old Testament and then, reflecting, seemed to find in that history a confirmation of the purpose behind space flight. From the bare skies and parched rocks of Palestine the tale passed to the cloudy horizons of Europe, first home of steam and power. Thence back to other parched rocks and sands, in a new world where the next logical developments were to take place. 'The people of the Old Testament, the rocket man thought to himself, would see nothing ridiculous in a project to fly into space. They would write psalms about it and honour those men who made progress towards such an ideal.'[10] What he would have thought of the Marxist psalm-writers on the steppes of Russia is hard to see; but there is still time, I suppose, for the Americans to justify their new world.

[10] J. N. Leonard, *Flight into Space*.

Nor are the Marxist psalm-writers so much out of place as might seem. There is about most space pronouncements, the Russian included, an air of the prophetic, even of the monkishly devoted. I do not on the present evidence believe that the Russians stinted themselves and sated their scientists for no other reason than to provide warheads against the foe. Rather they might, with a smile of partly conscious irony, echo the westerner, who says of space flight that 'a deep technological faith, which can be strong as religious faith, is wanted—and is not lacking'.[11]

In Russia technological faith has taken the place of doctrinal religious faith. Perhaps that is why, along this road, they have got so far. In the western world minds remain 'clouded with a doubt'; and a defensive note creeps in.

If the religionists, say the space advocates, claim that God gave to man dominion only over the earth and sea, then it can be argued that He gave him also his faculties, his 'talents', to use these to the best and fullest. And if so, how can He object to one form of travel devised by those talents more than to another? And if life *is* found on other planets, how can a comparison be feared, by a religion solidly founded, with any other beings that exist? For is not 'a better understanding of Man's place in nature' (Gatland and Kunesch) an argument advanced by the space men which no religionist would dare to call in question?

So the discussion goes on, endless and futile, leaving most with the slightly embarrassed feeling that one has when two people argue loudly about the sermon in church. To the Russians it must be as unintelligible as the protests about Laika. But the fundamental case is simple, if we go back and accept Nansen's dictum that without the exploring urge

[11] J. N. Leonard, *Flight into Space*. I find this faith very frightening. Recently reading *Man into Space* by Hermann Oberth, a rocket king, I was suddenly appalled by the confidence of his assertion, not only of interplanetary flight, but of flights to the planets of other suns and corresponding lengthening of human life to hundreds of years (as speed reaches that of light). ' . . . As strong as religious faith. . . .' Or a substitute?

'man would not be man'. People are going on with these experiments, as they did with flight, whether the rest of us would or no. Some day in the far future, if we are still here, it looks as if they will succeed, to what degree nobody can say. The earth satellites at present revolving round us are a finger pointing to the stars. When all this happens, one more segment will have been fitted into the puzzle, one more step taken along the path prophesied by Byrd and Saint-Exupéry. It will be a mistake to think that life's 'dome of many-coloured glass' is thereby all that much nearer completion. The heart of man will probably be very much where it was. For the progressive in other directions there will be plenty to fit into the pattern, for a very long time to come.

12

The curious traveller

Ah, who shall soothe these feverish children?
Who justify these restless explorations?
WALT WHITMAN

It may be claimed that the curious traveller is essentially indistinguishable from the scientist, since the motive behind each, the desire to have one's queries satisfied, is the same. I would allow many overlaps, but essentially I would not agree. Straight human curiosity is a personal thing, the satisfying of a private need. It is a factor in general education. The real scientist, the man who supplies the answers, is impersonal; since the work in which he loses himself takes on a detached importance, a greatness and a personality of its own. For it he would sacrifice his all, because of it he can do things normally reckoned impossible. The curious traveller is not likely to go quite so far as that, though he may take risks. If he shares the fate of the cat, it is generally because his own curiosity carried him too far; whereas the scientist's tragedy is that he can be used and then discarded by men less disinterested than himself.

The arbitrary drawing of a line somewhere at the end of the eighteenth century seems unsatisfactory when I face up to this motive which is as old as man. What of the Greeks, Venetians, Elizabethans? It is all very well to say, as say I must, that in the early explorations there was a strong admixture of the commercial and political in the motive; that Marco Polo was a merchant, Columbus and Vasco da Gama in the pay of expansive Empires, Vitus Bering an emissary of Imperial Russia, Cook the officer of an acquisitive Britain.

180

20: *'The desert is a very wonderful thing to see.'* Desert uplan
the Yemen.

(observation of the transit of Venus being all my eye) and Anson engaged on military missions; that the sixteenth-century seekers after North-East and North-West Passages had their pockets firmly attached to the patriotic flags which they carried. It remains true, both that these men were also motivated by genuine curiosity, which they must needs put into somebody's pay in order to raise money and ships, and that there were others, like the little known Venetian, Ludovico di Varthema, who did make their journeys armed with no more than 'a desire to behold the kingdoms of the world'. This great sixteenth-century explorer of the East desired to see specially those countries 'which had been the least frequented by the Venetians'. And I must admit that there were others like him.

No, we are inquisitive creatures, that is all there is to it. The most that can be said is that perhaps during the eighteenth century a certain consciousness of curiosity as a separate force developed, along with self-consciousness in other directions. In eighteenth-century France, for instance, the gates of the world were now flung open with a quite startling suddenness, barriers lifted, *objets d'art* from distant Turkey or Persia cooed over as if they were babies. Even, and this is an important leaning of the curious travellers, one's own country and civilisation were compared with those of other peoples. Hence the *Lettres Persanes*.

In England, where most things find themselves tied up with Education in the end, the Grand Tour was extended, a system whereby young men about to start their careers put their curiosity to use by sharpening it on the study of other nations. And in England there began that remarkable line of women which stretches from Lady Mary Wortley Montagu to Freya Stark. Whether it is because they are more observant, more inquisitive or simply more sensitive to impressions and interested in people I cannot say; but the most hardened mysogynist must admit that in this field of curious travel the women come into their own.

N   181

'An animated top of the mountain.'

The springs of adventure

Had Lady Mary been alive in these days her curiosity might have taken her far along many roads. She might, for instance, have made the ideal foreign correspondent, though she would certainly not have stopped at that. As it was, she counts as a pioneer. In the early eighteenth century it would have been unthinkable for a woman to go off exploring on her own; what she achieved as the wife of the Ambassador to the Ottoman Empire was as remarkable as the more distant journeys of her posterity. To mix with Turkish women, to visit their baths and on occasion take the yashmak herself (she favoured it for women), to see their towns and even, most daring of all, to have her own son vaccinated after their custom—this was a mixture of curiosity and common sense which set a model to all who travelled after.

It was in the nineteenth century, along with the gradual segregation of adventure as such, that curiosity became generally admitted as a worthy motive on its own account, without the educative bias of the Grand Tour type of travel, the practical and political researches of a Lady Mary, or science declared as an end in itself. It is significantly in the middle of the century (1854) that Francis Galton produced the first of many editions of the *Art of Travel*. What could better encourage the curious traveller than his opening words?

> If you have health, a great craving for adventure, at least a moderate fortune, and can set your heart on a definite object, which old travellers do not think impracticable, then—travel by all means . . . If you have not independent means, you may still turn travelling to excellent account; for experience shows it often leads to promotion, nay, some men support themselves by travel.

Galton's classic manual (it contains what should be a classic sentence: 'Savages rarely murder newcomers') was not written for the scientist, though it imparts some fairly abstruse information on how to make anything, from catgut to carriages. It was written for the general traveller, a breed now coming into its own, and with its own prestige.

It is one of the most grateful results of a journey to the young
traveller to find himself admitted, on the ground of his having
so much of special interest to relate, into the society of men
with whose names he had long been familiar, and whom he had
reverenced as his heroes.[1]

That is the earliest version of the great band of those who go
out, 'for the fun of the thing', and who in the intervals write
or lecture or talk before learned societies about what they
have done, not to mention what they are shortly going to do.

At this point there confronts me grimly a distinction
which must, and yet which cannot, be drawn. At what point
does this curious traveller of the nineteenth century shade off
into the scientific traveller? Take the case of African exploration. We have drawn a distinction, as Dorothy Middleton
does in *Baker of the Nile*, between the 'geographers and
naturalists . . . urged on by a burning desire to know, to
map, to classify' of the heroic phase begun by James Bruce,
and the political explorers who followed Stanley's Congo
journey of 1874. But among the geographers how are we
to divide the real scientists from the simply adventurous?
Samuel White Baker himself, who was 'consumed with
curiosity about the sources of the Nile' and who did great
service to geographical science in his efforts to locate them,
ranks as a hunter and explorer, and later as a fighter of the
slave-trade, rather than as a scientist. Livingstone was a
scientist, but started as a missionary with an impulse towards
the unknown. Stanley was a seeker after the new, but also a
political exploiter. Mary Kingsley was certainly a scientist,
but if ever anyone was inquisitive of things for pure
curiosity's sake as well, it was she. And so on.

While leaving the line undrawn, as I must, I define as the
curious those who are drawn to distant places primarily by a
general and unscientific interest in what is new, as well as by
a desire for personal adventure. If you take more pleasure in
meeting new people than in observing the shapes of their

[1] *Art of Travel.*

heads, I would call you a curious traveller rather than an anthropologist. If you write poems about the butterflies of the Amazon but have no idea how many species you have seen, you are no entomologist for me. At the same time you may be a scientist in one direction and a curious traveller in another. Mary Kingsley, when she climbed the Great Cameroon by an arduous and probably new route, was moved by impulses foreign to those of a seeker after beetles, fish, or even fetishes.

In exploratory curiosity, if there is such a thing, there are to my mind two main ingredients. The first is the plain desire for what is new, mysterious, unknown. This takes many forms. Sir Richard Burton states as his object in going to Mecca 'the purpose of removing that opprobrium to modern adventure, the huge white blot which in our maps still notes the Eastern and Central regions of Arabia.' This would seem also a simple geographical objective, but the second page of his book shows that his curiosity extended further:

> Being liberally supplied with the means of travel by the Royal Geographical Society; thoroughly tired of 'progress' and 'civilisation'; curious to see with my eyes what others are content to 'hear with ears', namely, Moslem life in a really Mohammedan country; and longing, if truth be told, to set foot on that mysterious spot which no vacation tourist has yet described, measured, sketched and photographed, I resolved to resume my old character of a Persian wanderer, a 'Darwaysh', and to make the attempt.[2]

He was, in fact, interested in going where few had been, speaking to those to whom none had spoken, seeing if he could act a new part. He was intensely curious.

His next expedition, with Speke in search of the Nile sources, was more geographical in nature and sponsored by the Foreign Office. Yet the preparations and attitude were so curiously off-hand that it could by no stretch be classed as 'scientific' in the modern sense. When the great quarrel as to

[2] *Pilgrimage to Al-Madinah and Meccah.*

whether the Nile rose from Tanganyika or Victoria blew up, Speke had to return to verify his findings; and here Baker again comes in, since he and his wife came down to meet Speke and Grant from the North.

> In March 1861, I commenced an expedition to discover the sources of the Nile, with the hope of meeting the East African expedition of Captains Speke and Grant, that had been sent by the English Government from the south, via Zanzibar, for that object.[3]

So simple does it sound! And however fine the journey, the conclusions drawn from it were those of a brilliant guesser rather than of a scientific analyser of facts. It took Stanley much energy, years later, to put the finishing touches.

However, by guess and by God the work was done, slowly, and the nineteenth century can be called justly the great epoch for filling in the major 'Blanks on the Map'. While Africa was being traversed in length and breadth Burton and his successors penetrated Arabia. Asia, the largest continent, came on more slowly, with the journeys of the Russian Prejevalsky, Sven Hedin, Younghusband and many more. Australia was explored by Sturt, Burke and Wills.[4] Canada proceeded more anonymously, explored by the Mountain Men, 'a breed of men who made it possible for others to come to the farthest frontier'.[5] South America also was proceeding with hesitation, after the great initial impulse of the Jesuits.

About much of this bigger exploration there was a national as well as a scientific character, which tended to harness curiosity to utilitarian ends. Russia, after all, wanted to define her eastern borders—so sent Prejevalsky. All countries had an interest in the riches of Africa and America. Australia wanted to know more about the inside of her own continent. All very important and prestigeful, whatever the

[3] Quoted by Dorothy Middleton, *Baker of the Nile*.

[4] Also see, for the explorations from the *Beagle*, J. L. Stokes, *Discoveries in Australia*.

[5] From *The Farthest Frontier*, by L. Paine.

basic instincts of the explorers. But away from these major fillings-in there was also growing up, as I have indicated, a great body of purely curious travellers who worked on a small scale and for whom Galton's book was written. Pre-eminent among them was Charles Doughty; and it is notable that this great traveller was so far removed from officialdom that he found himself refused protection for his Arabian journey by the British consul at Damascus, and ran severe dangers from that refusal.

Doughty's initial purpose in Arabia was archaeological. He heard of inscriptions at Medain Salih and wanted to copy them. But unlike, for instance, the Central Asian archaeologist Aurel Stein, he found that purpose changing. When he set out in 1876 'he had left Damascus as an archaeologist; he struck out into the open desert as a searcher into life. He had come to Arabia with a scholar's curiosity; he abandoned himself to it in obedience to an impulse that was obscure, but above all irresistible and vital to his whole nature.'[6] That impulse, I submit, was curiosity in a deeper sense even than that of the scholar; the curiosity of a great writer, a great person.

As Fairley points out, a book of his scientific findings could have been turned out in a year or two. *Arabia Deserta* took ten. Both the journey and the book are a monument to effort, a monument built from 'the seeing of an hungry man and the telling of a most weary man'. The effort was deliberate and willed. For two years he lived with the Arabs, not disguised as was Burton but unprotected and often in danger up and down the length of the country; trying without cease to learn about Arabs, to understand Arabs if not in the true sense to be friends with them; to enquire, always to enquire. Certainly the Arabs did not understand him, nor the purpose of such enquiry. 'Though thou shouldst know, O Khalîl (Doughty's name in the desert), the name of all our

---

[6] Barker Fairley, *Charles M. Doughty*. This book is a fascinating study of Doughty's motives and achievement.

camping grounds and of every jebel (hill), what were all this
worth when thou art at home, in a far country?' Again:

> I passed for a seeker of treasure with some who had seen me
> sitting under the great acacia . . . now they said to me, 'Didst
> thou take up anything, Khalîl, tell us boldly?' [7]

Unanswerable questions! The only reasonable solution
seemed to many that he was a spy; hence the dangers that he
ran without British protection, the escapes that he often
made.

Doughty was a greater writer than Burton. His book
mirrors the monotony as well as the mystery of Arabia and
its people. But essentially their task (or pleasure) is the same,
'doing odd jobs and trying to understand things, pursuing
knowledge with unbroken devotion', in Mary Kingsley's
phrase. 'Trying to understand things'. She, more than most,
might have added: 'and trying to understand people'. For
one hall-mark of the curious traveller is an absorbed interest
in those among whom he travels. Doughty's Arabs live, as he
himself lives, in his book. So do Mary Kingsley's Africans in
her writing. Indeed she, like Daisy Bates later among the
aborigines of Australia,[8] found the pull of the people so strong
that her original work gave place to the work of championing
the 'natives' whom she had come to love. And in a different
way the same identification of interest took place in one upon
whom the mantle of Doughty fell in Arabia—Gertrude Bell.

Gertrude Bell had the misfortune to do her greatest
journey, to Hayil, in Central Arabia, just before the First
World War. The book that she had intended was never
written. But her letters reveal, as few books could, a way of
travel in which the people encountered form an integral part

---

[7] *Wanderings in Arabia,* vol. I.

[8] 'As the years had passed I had been more and more convinced that it was
impossible to leave these people. So savage and so simple, so much astray
and so utterly helpless were they, that somehow they became my responsibility. I went to them to learn and in the end I could not leave them.' From
The Passing of the Aborigines.

of a total way of life. Knowing their languages, customs, even mannerisms, she could be of them when she was among them. That was the fun of it—as can be seen, for instance, in the beginning of her journey through Syria and Asia Minor in 1905:

> I'm deep in the gossip of the East! It's so enjoyable. I thought today when I was strolling through the bazaars buying various odds and ends what a pleasure it was to be in the East almost as part of it, to know it all as I know Syria now, to be able to tell from the accent and dress of the people where they come from and exchange the proper greeting as one passes.[9]

A little later: 'What a country this is! I fear I shall spend the rest of my life travelling in it. Race after race, one on top of the other, the whole land strewn with the mighty relics of them.'[10]

To report on those 'relics' was the official purpose of most of her journeying, and it was effectively done. To be in the East, to absorb herself into its life far more thoroughly than could a Lady Hester, for all her dressing up, this was the undeclared intention. In the letters quoted she hits upon a deep impulse, common to not all of those who travel for curiosity. For in a far wider sense than that treated of in Chapter 5, which discussed only the aesthetic effect of certain scenes, we are facing now a kind of magnetism from a whole environment, places, people, objects, and of course scenes too, which demands imperatively that a person shall find out about and even lose himself in it. There is a sense of inevitability about the quest, a feeling of homecoming when the travellers return to chosen lands. Gertrude Bell, now on her journey to Hayil in 1913, put it that 'Already I dropped back into the desert as if it were my own place. Silence and solitude fall round you like an impenetrable veil'.[11] Like Rosita Forbes, who penetrated the Senussi tribes of the Sahara to

[9] *Letters*, Vol. I.   [10] Ibid.

[11] Ibid. 'Happiness, pure and immaterial,' Freya Stark was to call the feeling.

Kufra, she confessed herself homesick when she left the desert
to return home, instead of the other way round.

Gertrude Bell's way of helping came with the First World
War, in the service she gave to the Arab nation, and to T. E.
Lawrence.

The desire to help, however, is by no means indispensable
to the curious traveller's equipment. Some, indeed, consider
it a positive hindrance to the important business of disinterested observation. The traveller, say these, should maintain a discreet equilibrium and not take sides. Let us admit
simply that there is an infinity of ways, all with basic
similarities, in which the idea of being in 'The Right Place',
as well as of wanting to find out more about that place, can
transport a person through difficulty and hardship. The urge
to help was vigorous enough in Mary Slessor of Calabar.
But when she wrote (at about the same time as the Hayil
journey): 'I feel drawn on and on by the magnetism of this
land of dense darkness and mysterious forest,' that feeling had
nothing to do with her missionary work. She was about to go
up country and inspect the dreaded Ju-Ju society of witch-
doctors, and was fascinated both by them and their home.

Something of the same process worked, in a rather
different direction, through my last chosen traveller of the
pre-1914 period—Sir Francis Younghusband. His curiosity
takes a deep enough tone in all conscience, but it is a tone not
directly philanthropic, since for him curiosity deepened in
other directions than those for which a single prescribed code
is the answer. The process in his case involved a change of
focus. When he set out on the long journey from Peking to
India in 1887, it was in the role of curious traveller *par
excellence*.

We should be able to see these secluded people of Central
Asia, dim figures of whom I had pictures in my mind from
reading the accounts of the few travellers who had been among
them. Then, too, there was the fascination of seeing the very
heart of the Himalayas, as we should have to cross their entire

breadth on the way to India. And all combined was one grand project—this idea of striking boldly out from Peking to penetrate to India—that of itself inspired enthusiasm and roused every spark of exploring ardour in me.[12]

The journey was carried out with military thoroughness, and brilliantly successful. So thorough was he that after the true finale, the famous crossing of the Mustagh Pass in the Karakoram, he must needs defy exhaustion and turn back, to have a look at the New Mustagh Pass as well and make quite sure there was not a feasible route there. Yet while all this was going on he succeeded in exercising not only the practical curiosity about people which later made his mission to Tibet successful, but already, at the age of twenty-three, the bigger curiosity which comes to a man under the stars and makes him wonder what is the purpose of doing all this at all.

> I would watch them in their courses over the Heavens and think on what they are and what they represent, and try to realise the place which we men hold in the universe stretched out before me.[13]

That greater curiosity was only satisfied, if satisfied it was, by his religious experiences.

ๅ ๕   ๅ ๕   ๅ ๕

After the First World War the emphasis of the curious traveller shifted. The interiors of every continent (except the Antarctic, which is not explored to this day) were now known at least in outline. Africa, the Dark Continent of Stanley, had been so well traversed even by 1900 that the authors of *From the Cape to Cairo* pleaded as motive for their walk, not exploration but the prosaic plan of proving the possibility of 'transcontinental communication by electricity and steam'. This was to be, as E. S. Grogan claimed in his Introduction, 'the

---

[12] *The Heart of a Continent.*
[13] Quoted by George Seaver in *Francis Younghusband.*

realisation of a great Imperial idea'. Clearly some readjustment was needed, in the ranks of the purely curious.

It came in a number of ways. There remained, and still remain, an ever-diminishing number of blank spaces to be filled, especially (apart from the Antarctic) in South America and Central Asia. These continued to be explored and written up. Then, as they began prosaically to fill the geography books with details now considered trite, other excitements were demanded by a realistic age which still wanted its mysteries. Gradually in the Himalaya, for instance, there appears the *yeti*, or Abominable Snowman, a superb blend of reality and legend who built himself so firmly between the wars that he has become, at the time of writing, the possible prey of two full-scale American expeditions. (To hunt him costs even more on the Nepalese tariff than to climb Everest.) Britain had to spring a Loch Ness Monster. And on the other side of the world, in the far Matto Grosso, a rather different mystery has equally exercised the faculties of the curious: the mystery of Colonel Fawcett.

Of Fawcett the man, and the magnet of his lost Atlantis, we have seen something already. Fawcett the mystery is different. He is—or was—one of the powerful enigmas of our time. What happened to the explorer who set off with two companions to find an unknown city in the middle of impenetrable jungle? Was he murdered? A prisoner, as the Swiss, Stephan Rattin, alleged, claiming to have found and spoken with him? A chieftain in the hidden realm, and his son Jack married to an Indian woman who bore him a fair-haired child? The tug of mystery unadorned must have been powerful if it produced funds for a full-scale relief expedition (Dyott's) and moved a Hollywood film actor, the luckless Albert de Winton, to spend months in discomfort and danger, with a revolver over his stomach and boots on at night, before he was poisoned by Indians and dragged up-river to be finished off. The emphasis had shifted indeed.

By far the most entertaining Fawcett expedition was that

joined by Peter Fleming, answering an advertisement in the agony column of *The Times*, in 1932. As far as finding anything went it was a failure, even a fiasco. Its so-called leader failed completely when it came anywhere near the only place where there was a chance of finding traces. Fleming and two others, ill equipped, pushed up along an unknown part of the Tapirapé River, then turned back. They had reached Fawcett country, but that was about all. More important, however, the journey gave him a first opportunity of airing the new view of 'the Unknown' and 'Adventure'. His writing provides as witty an example as any of the modern attitude to orthodox exploration.

Fleming admits that there is still 'plenty of adventure of a sort to be had'. Hence the Fawcett expedition. But throughout it he is at pains to debunk words hallowed with a faintly phoney prestige. The Unknown, for instance. At their farthest point he writes:

> You know perfectly well that there is for practical purposes no difference between a place to which no one has been and a place to which hardly anyone has been. Moreover it is quite clear that your visit is going to be entirely valueless; for all the useful data you are capable of bringing back the Great Unknown will be the Great Unknown still. You will have made a negligible reduction in that area of the earth's surface which may be said to be Untrodden; that is all.[14]

As for Adventure itself with a capital A, it comes in for short shrift:

> . . . adventure is really a soft option. Adventure has always been a selfish business. Men who set out to find it may—like men who go and get married—feel reasonably confident that a successful issue to their project will be of service to the world. But the desire to benefit the community is never their principal motive, any more than it is the principal motive of people who marry each other. They do it because they want to. It suits them, it is their cup of tea.[15]

[14] *Brazilian Adventure.*   [15] Ibid.

In this frank view, at any rate in the view that far too much fuss is made about the far corners of the world just because they are far, he received stout support from Ella Maillart, on their journey of 1935. Embarrassed to be travelling together, when both preferred to be alone, on this point they did agree.

> We were united by an abhorrence of the false values placed— whether by its exponents or the world at large—on what can most conveniently be referred to by its trade-name of Adventure. From an aesthetic rather than an ethical point of view, we were repelled by the modern tendency to exaggerate, romanticise, and at last cheapen out of recognition the ends of the earth and the deeds done in their vicinity. It was almost the only thing we ever agreed about.[16]

When they had agreed in debunking alligators, man-eating fish, trackless deserts and other trappings of the Adventurous, what they had in common may be taken as a basic qualification for the modern version of the curious traveller.

> We had certain fundamental things in common. The most important of these was a liking for the kind of life we were leading. We neither of us particularly minded discomfort and doing without most of the things which civilised people consider, or imagine that they consider, essential to a rational life; and we both liked fresh air and exercise, of which we got plenty. We were both adaptable and fairly phlegmatic; and we were both fatalists, as all travellers, and especially travellers in Asia, ought to be.[17]

That seems to sum up the new situation. The curious traveller goes on liking being curious and (usually) recording his curiosity. But he is a more sober individual than he was. He may be a *Times* correspondent like Fleming or a steady contributor to a publishing house like Freya Stark. In all cases he goes phlegmatically on, filling in gaps and enjoying himself doing so, crossing Takla Makan deserts, for instance, without the discomfort of Sven Hedin ('We were sure of finding

[16] *News from Tartary.*   [17] Ibid.

more and more comforts at each oasis we came to,' Ella Maillart wrote) but appreciating no less. He asks questions and jots down the answers in little note-books. Sometimes, when put to it, he performs great feats of endurance. But he is careful not to dramatise these, knowing that nothing he does can be compared with the endurance of those who face the rush hour in London five days a week. Above all he (or she, for as I have said the female is if anything more curious and observant than the male) remains to the end interested deeply in the people among whom he moves. If you think of Freya Stark, you think inevitably of the characters that jostle and swarm upon her pages. You think of their faces, their ways and customs, their legends and their valleys of historical assassins. You think of these and you see yourself, strangely enlarged and enriched by the knowledge of how others live. And if you feel that, you have given the curious traveller his greatest triumph; far greater, to my mind, than any service he may incidentally render to science. Being an ordinary person, an extension of themselves, so to say, he enlarges the field of sympathetic vision of his fellows.

In time, I suppose, as the earth's surface becomes docketed to the last acre, the curious traveller may degenerate into the foreign correspondent. But I doubt it. He may well be finding new spheres for his activities. There is still, after all, the sea, in breadth and depth. I am struck, in the pioneer book of Hans Hass, by the sheer curiosity of the early explorations. Science may harness the faculties, but the impulse, the desire for new and wonderful experience, for meetings with strange fishes as one might meet strange people—this is largely, if not wholly, curious.

No matter where we swim, the great unknown [note Fleming's word] is always ahead of us; we never know beforehand what we shall encounter . . . Where on dry land could there be such adventures as here in the ocean? Today, in the twentieth century, where are there regions still so virginal and untouched, places whose magic has never been profaned by man, where everything still remains as it was when no man lived on earth? [18]

And if the sea fails, why, there will always be the planets. A persuasive advocate (A. C. Clarke) has told us:

The desire to reach the planets is only the extension of the desire to see what is over the next hill or

Beyond that last blue mountain barred with snow,
Across that angry or that glittering sea . . .

If there were not a single good 'scientific' reason for going to the planets, man would still want to go there, just the same.[19]

And that man would be the curious traveller, of whom we have been speaking.

[18] *Diving to Adventure*. Written after seven months' diving off Curaçao shortly before the Second World War. Similarly Ann Davison, writing of the urge to sail over the Atlantic, put it: 'If I was honest I would admit it was largely curiosity, the urge to find out the why, the what, and the how at first hand, without simply taking someone else's word for it.'

[19] *The Exploration of Space*. At the point where curiosity merges into the discovery that life is bearable after all, nationalism rises once more to complicate, as it may do in Antarctica, now that Dr Vivian Fuchs's and other journeys have removed the veil of inaccessibility.

13

❧ ❧ ❧ ❧ ❧ ❧

The doers of good

When one travels with the specific object of ameliorating the condition of the natives any act becomes ennobled.

DAVID LIVINGSTONE

Religion in adventure divides itself very sharply into two. There are the missionaries, or in a broader sense the philanthropists, who go to distant places with the object of bringing benefit to somebody. Besides these, and often mingled with them, are those myriads who to a greater or lesser degree regard their explorations as part of some divine intention, however odd at the moment may seem the connection between purpose and poles, or deserts and divinity.

The object of the doers of good deeds for their own sake is largely self-explanatory. The deeds are done because they are beneficial, whether under the aegis of a revealed religion or out of simple pity; whether by an Anna Harriet Leonowens masking her faith because she would have greater opportunities of educating the nineteenth-century Siamese court if she did so, or by a Mary Kingsley who felt she had nothing to mask, since all she asked was common sense and justice, all she was doing was 'odd jobs' for the West Africans. It is on their fruits that we shall judge the doers of plain good, on their deeds that we know them. When Bombard, of his raft-riding voyage over the Atlantic, declared that 'my object was to give these unfortunates (the shipwrecked) a better chance of reaching land. Several thousand widows less a year seemed to me an objective fully justifying the risk of one's life',[1] there is little we can add except 'Well done'. No dogmatic doubt

[1] *The Bombard Story.*

96

disturbs us, no dispute. Conscience and pity we recognise, certainly; or perhaps sympathy is the word, 'the greatest power in human life' as it has been called. In no name but its own, following no creed but that of common humanity, it can make the most ordinary of us achieve the strangest journeys.

But for many the position is more complicated. The doers of doctrinal missionary work are a clearly defined—and enormous—body with their own great literature. They are Christians normally; for as Marco Pallis has remarked, it would be difficult to imagine the fate of a band of 'Evangelical' missionaries from the East who arrived and planted themselves opposite a Catholic church in Ireland. Into the corners of the earth these men and women go, following hard upon the heels of the explorers and often outpacing them; sometimes combining in one person the role of breaker of new ground with that of emissary of God.

In two respects these missionaries concern us. In the name of their faith and reliant upon a power deemed greater than their own, the men of religion have from the first been able to perform feats quite out of the question by ordinary standards. Not to go too far back in time, I have only to think of the exploratory journeys made by the Jesuits through the South American jungle, in their unsuitable clothes and with primitive equipment; journeys which modern explorers, armed with all the latest devices, have found great difficulty in equalling. If you read, say, of the years between 1600 and 1750 in Brazil, it is almost impossible to overpaint the heroism of the priests and their converts, in the face of barbarous (but understandable) onslaughts from the Indians. Father Antonio Roiz de Montoya, as an instance, explored and founded eleven colonies. But to offset that he had the pain of being met with fanatical hatred and saddened by the atrocities of the Bandeirantes, who 'practised the most terrible cruelty, killing women and children by cutting them through the stomach; they destroyed the churches and whipped priests'.[2] Probably no one has ever faced greater obstacles than these Fathers, or explored more ground with less help.

However, the very hardships and the very act of travelling have a spiritual value when they are combined with a spiritual experience which few can share but all must envy. To take a later instance, the finest nineteenth-century missionary that I have read of, Mary Slessor of Calabar, faced the dangers of starting a mission in the interior of Nigeria, in Okoyong, fortified only by the faith that not she but another was in charge. How else could she have written home, as she was canoed upstream to certain danger, 'I am going to a new tribe up country, a fierce, cruel people, and everyone tells me that they will kill me. But I don't fear any hurt—only to combat their savage customs will require courage and firmness on my part?' Courage and firmness, yes; though small and frail she had these, and a lively temper too at times. But to do what she did, in her old-fashioned dress and with equally old-fashioned instruments, she needed also a degree of physical endurance far beyond what could humanly be suspected of her. Whether it was the star above, always guiding, or the 'common pool' of subconscious human strength below upon which she drew, her sureness remains the more wonderful from her physical weakness.

Small women, for Isabella Bird is another, seem to have a priority in that sort of courage. A later Mary Slessor, Gladys Aylward of China, was barely five feet high and a parlourmaid in London. She made the journey to China because 'she had to', with a few shillings, some tins of food and a stove. Her missionary ventures in Yang Cheng became legendary and culminated in a grim flight over the mountains to escape the invading Japanese. At the head of a hundred children she reached the Yellow River; but for asylum they

[2] J. R. de Sá Carvalho, *Brazilian El Dorado*.

198

had to wander much further. Most moving is her prayer, on an occasion when she was in doubt which path would save her from approaching troops, 'D'you hear me, Lord? Whichever path I face when I stop turning, I shall go along.'[3] In her extreme of fatigue she took the right path, and had the strength to follow it.

If this rather stern path is to be followed, the weaker self which loves luxury and fears pain must be subdued. The subjection has a different object, though its operation may be the same, from that practised by the self-mortifiers of Chapter 2. There, it was the attainment of some great objective which usually made discipline worth while and indeed necessary. Here it is missionary service in the cause and under the aegis of revealed religion. I need take one example only, a modern one from the Arctic: that of Archibald Lang Fleming, its first bishop. His was a bleak diocese, and he has described his first winter in an Eskimo village as 'always cold, incessantly hungry and permanently uncomfortable'—with temperatures down to minus 50° and no privacy anywhere.

> I wrestled with myself . . . In a marvellous way once I had conquered my weakness and become freed from the complexities of civilisation, I was able to enjoy primal peace.[4]

That conquest of self which had served a mundane purpose with our other explorers here fits neatly into Christian doctrine and is therefore, in theory at least, quite simple. Link it with the idea of mission, and for my purpose it gives the cleanest cut of all motives for doing bold and even dangerous things.

The second point about missionary faith, incidental as it may seem to our main run of adventure, is that it also presupposes a conviction that what is done is good for those to whom it is done. Some of the men of last century were a little naïve on this point, and, it may be, engendered their own

[3] Alan Burgess, *The Small Woman*.   [4] *Archibald the Arctic*.

opposition. So it was that in Africa the Bakers 'disliked missionaries', while Mary Kingsley disliked their work. 'The African . . . has both a fair sense of justice and honour, not much worn by daily use, and very easily eliminated by a course of Christian teaching.' She blamed them for the 'contempt and horror' in which the African was held in England, because of the complacent way in which his religion was written off as paganism and himself dismissed as a barbarian. But she 'became deeply attached to many of the missionaries whom she met', and admired particularly Mary Slessor, with her uncanny understanding of the real desires and needs of the Africans.[5] This admiration in no way weakened her stand against the missionaries' incursions.

Such voices, however, tended to be drowned in the general voice, whose sentiments came nearer to those of the young Darwin, after his voyage on the *Beagle*. 'The march of improvement consequent on the introduction of Christianity throughout the South Sea, probably stands by itself on the records of history.'[6] That march was, of course, closely connected with material prosperity, for 'to hoist the British flag, seems to draw with it as a certain consequence, wealth, prosperity, and civilisation'. A little later Stanley of Africa, admittedly no missionary in his methods, was probably also voicing popular sentiment when he exclaimed, on meeting the ruler of Uganda, 'O for the hour when a band of philanthropic capitalists shall vow to rescue these beautiful lands!' There was no hypocrisy in the wish, a very reasonable one at that time. Commerce, thought Stanley, brought benefit (as we have seen); Christianity too, and there was no reason why the two should not be very happily married. The great majority of his countrymen nodded their heads in approval.

The certainty of spiritual benefit conferred was strongly shared by Livingstone. Not concerned with the commercial openings, he still seems to have had no qualms about his

[5] See Cecil Howard, *Mary Kingsley*.
[6] *The Voyages of Adventure and Beagle*, III.

exploratory work outstripping the missionary, and was highly indignant at the suggestion of that possibility. 'I view the end of the geographical feat as the beginning of the missionary enterprise,' he replied to the London Missionary Society's insinuation that he had neglected missions in order to make the great journey from Loanda to Quilimane. And when it was put to him, by Sir Richard Murchison, that his third journey ought to be 'purely geographical', he said 'I could only feel in the way of duty by working as a missionary.' And doubtless said it very gruffly.

Along these lines of faith which can remove mountains Christian missions have penetrated all corners of the world which to the home-stayers seem most fraught with mystery and danger. But while the faith may remain the same, the voices of woe raised by the earlier doubters seem to have begotten offspring. The grandchildren of the Victorian age missionaries have reaped the whirlwind. Many go on in the old way; many have thought deeply about readjustment. It would be easy, and could be unfair, to multiply instances of travellers, generally the curious, making adverse comment on the fruits of proselytising zeal. I must remember Gladys Aylward and avoid quoting more chunks of the all-too-quotable Fleming—on 'evangelical claim-jumping', for instance. But I shall take just two modern travellers, from very different parts of the world, as specimens.

In 1947 André Migot, in the course of his Chinese and Tibetan journeys, stayed with Father Leroux of the Kangting Mission. 'We had a long talk, and I could not help being sadly aware of the deep melancholy which his air of dauntless optimism strove in vain to conceal.' Again:

> Our Missions in Tibet, like our Missions in Cambodia, have been a failure; their original object—the preaching of Christianity to the natives—has been for practical purposes abandoned, the missionaries having realised that it is a hopeless task to convert sincere Buddhists in either country.[7]

[7] *Tibetan Marches.*

Migot is himself a Buddhist, and he goes on a little later: 'It would really make more sense if India and Tibet sent missionaries to Europe, to try and lift her out of the materialistic rut in which she is bogged down, and to reawaken the capacity for religious feeling which she lost several centuries ago. But Buddhists do not go in for missionary work; they are too tolerant, they have too much respect for other people's convictions to want to superimpose their own upon them.'

That is a point of view. In 1956 Ross Salmon, a fairly open type of traveller, met with hostile Ijka Indians on his way to make touch with the Motilon Indians of South America. One of them, explaining briefly his hostility, said: ' "The boy told us what you want. You are"—and I have never known such contempt and loathing put into a word which has so much Godliness, love and service surrounding it—"missionaries".'[8] Salmon's comment is: 'I feel that good would be appreciated more if the missionaries would try to have a deeper understanding of deep-rooted tribal customs and beliefs which go far back in time.' That is another thought. The Mary Slessor touch seemed lost.

It begins to look as if proselytising zeal by itself is not enough. The most successful missions of these days are perhaps those concerned with understanding (Salmon speaks of Alexander Clark, friend of the Yuko, in this connection) and healing. Wonderful things are being done in far places by bodies like the British women at Pokhara, in Nepal. Albert Schweitzer, 'believing it to be my life's task to fight on behalf of the sick under far-off stars', can devote himself to that task in the confident certainty that what he does is *good*; much as the Friends solved the problem of conscience in war, by devoting themselves to ambulance work which nobody could deny to be valuable and worthy.

This approach I hold to be a fair one, despite the natural indignation which it sometimes rouses in Evangelicals bursting to spread the good news. The Quaker line, they would

[8] *Forbidden Jungle.*

say, is an avoidance of real issues by burying the head in a sand of good deeds. And they would find unexpected support in Marco Pallis, a modern Buddhist (as I think he now is), when he discussed twenty years ago the failure of missions in Sikkim and elsewhere.

> The professional missionary stands at a disadvantage. It is unavoidable that he should be much concerned with the counting of heads of converts, for these are required for the statistics of the societies who collect subscriptions. The less scrupulous make use of disguised bribery, such as the distribution of medicine or the offering of free tuition. Few, nowadays, are ready to trust frankly to the doctrine of Christ as their only weapon. Ostensibly charitable deeds, operations in hospitals, gifts to the poor, and the care of orphans, can become, for the doers, so many deceitful crimes in masquerade—in spite of the undeniable gain to the beneficiaries—if they are designed, even in part, to be used as a stalking-horse.
>
> Those who feel a Christian call to the service of the needy can do wonderful work; but then, in my opinion, they would do better to leave the proselytising to others.[9]

This view would draw a sharp line between religious and medical missionaries, and perhaps that is what is happening —but to the detriment of the specifically religious. Pallis, like Migot, notes that religious missions are not banned in Tibet, or rather were not before the war; on the contrary they are welcomed. But answer is given to them in the words of Asoka in the third century B.C.: 'Do not decry other sects, do not run them down, but on the contrary, pay honour to all in them that is worthy of honour.'

Follow this line of thought very far in one direction, and you arrive at 'Unity of religion', a pudding in which, to my mind, the savour of the ingredients risks losing itself in an insipid mixture. If you go the other way, towards practical works prompted by sympathy and understanding, you may come back to the plain philanthropic motive from which we

[9] *Peaks and Lamas.*

started. And it is a very good starting point. As the previously unknown peoples of the world make contact with other men and associate pride in their nationality with consciousness of their religious heritage, it is in the role of healer and sympathiser that the missionaries from the western world look their best. They may not have the same great rosy opportunities of opening heathen gates to Christ as once they dreamed of; but they have compensations, and a debt to pay. I know of no greater contrast than that between Stanley's confident assertion of the automatic benefits of advancing Christian civilisation, and Albert Schweitzer's view of his mission at Lambarene:

> We and our civilisation are burdened, really, with a great debt. We are not free to confer benefits on these men, or not as we please. Anything we give them is no benevolence but atonement. For everyone who scattered injury someone ought to go out to take help, and when we have done all that is in our power, we shall not have atoned for the thousandth part of our guilt.[10]

[10] *On the Edge of the Primeval Forest.*

❦ ❦ ❦ ❧ ❧ ❧

14

The greater mystery

Power dwells apart in its tranquillity,
Remote, serene, and inaccessible:
And this, *the naked countenance of earth,*
On which I gaze, even these primaeval mountains
Teach the adverting mind.

PERCY BYSSHE SHELLEY

There are many persons in each man. The complicated creature does everything that he does from a mixture of motives, and this fact becomes nowhere more obvious than in what may be called, for want of better, the religious motive behind adventure. Whether a traveller's stated aim in going out be science, or pleasure, or just plain curiosity, he is likely to find, at certain reflective moments upon the journey, that there was something else beside. He may be an atheist, an agnostic, a priest. He may be able to express himself, he may not. He may be one of those people who 'prefer not to talk about these things'. He may even have no conscious recollection of anything afterwards at all, only a vague sense of wonder at times. But the feeling is there, and it involves something strangely outside himself. It is a feeling of 'greater' purpose, and of reverence.

Some people crystallise this feeling of purpose. They see their own small exploits and explorations as somehow intended for them, as if they were part of a divine pattern. An outstanding and sufficient example of this type is that of Edward Wilson of the Antarctic. Here was a man of many parts. A medical student, then a doctor, he almost killed himself with tuberculosis brought on by overwork added to religious teaching at the Caius Mission in Battersea. He was also a skilled naturalist and an artist of astonishing quality. He might have become a missionary, medical or religious, an ornithologist, a painter or priest. Instead, though married, he went twice to the Antarctic and died there.

In the winter of 1902, on the *Discovery* expedition, he himself seemed to realise the oddity of the situation, in a letter to his wife:

> This work of Antarctic exploration is very different from the work I had planned for myself some years ago. And yet I do honestly believe that God's will is being worked out for us in what we are doing, and though it may seem more 'worldly' and 'scientific' than 'spiritual', yet there *is* a spiritual work to be done here. And as for its main object, the acquisition of knowledge pure and simple, surely God means us to find out all we can of His works, and to work out our own salvation, realising that all things that have to do with our spiritual development 'are understood and clearly seen in things created', and if it is right to search out His works in one corner of His Creation, it is right for some of us to go to the ends of the earth to search out others.[1]

Thus the purpose of discovery was linked with the purpose of praise. In another letter he puts it:

> Shackleton, Ferrar and I were actually the first men who ever saw that red glow on the southern side of Erebus and Terror . . . 'The works of the Lord *are* great, and very worthy to be praised and had in honour;' I don't think you and I will ever get tired of praising them, but I do wish that you could see them here.

He came back from the *Discovery* and lived happily in marriage, working on grouse disease for the Grouse Commission. When he accepted Scott's second invitation, to join the *Terra Nova* expedition, he wrote two oddly different

[1] *C. J. W. Simpson*, in *North Ice*, says: 'If a man is an explorer, the greatest quest of all is his search for the Creator. In this all lesser expeditions are contained. . . .'

letters. The first, to his parents just before departure, contains this:

> . . . even the disappointments and apparent checks are all in their proper place and have been first-rate schooling.
>
> Well, it only means that free-will in the eyes of God means the willingness to do one's best at whatever comes in our way, however difficult it may seem; but though He does not like us to look back after putting our hands to the plough, He often takes the plough away as soon as He knows we mean to carry through.

The second is to his wife:

> I always feel so certain that I shall be given time to write and publish some of the things that are in my head, and also paint some others, not in a hurry as I have to now, but my best possible. This conviction makes me absolutely fearless as to another journey South, for whatever happened I know I should come back to you . . .

The first I think contains the truer feeling; the second was written to calm a natural anxiety. In either case, these letters help to show how firmly Wilson was possessed of the idea that there was some divine purpose in his work, guiding and directing his explorations, even stopping them short, if so it seemed good.

He was a scientist to his finger tips, that must be remembered. But however ardent his pursuit of the truth about Emperor penguins, I doubt if he would have asked Bowers and Cherry-Garrard to join the Cape Crozier journey without this greater conviction beside. Nor, for that matter, would he have become father-confessor to the whole party; and there is no need to repeat here the tributes of those who wrote of him, as the finest spirit of them all. He seemed to have an inner certainty before which even Scott felt awe.

When Scott, dying himself, looked across the little tent at the dying Wilson, he wrote: 'His eyes have a comfortable blue look of hope and his mind is peaceful with the satisfaction of his faith in regarding himself as part of the great scheme of the Almighty.'

🦌 🦌 🦌 🦌 🦌 🦌

Wilson's feeling of something guiding and directing ran through his whole life. But in the moments of difficulty or effort themselves there is a rather similar sensation which takes more concrete form. The first stage, and it comes to many of us, is that we seem to become two people. It has been said that 'it doesn't matter talking to yourself; it's when you start answering yourself back that you should get worried.' But in fact the interesting sense of detachment and of 'another person' begins to come just then. Lawrence found it in Arabia:

> . . . Such detachment came at times to a man exhausted by prolonged physical effort and isolation. His body plodded on mechanically, while his reasonable mind left him, and from without looked critically on him, wondering what that futile lumber did and why. Sometimes these selves would converse in the void; and then madness was very near.[2]

It is not always near, however. Lone seamen make a practice of conversing with themselves, asking when breakfast will be, what the time is and so on. I remember the sensation as very clear, almost expected, on Everest in 1953. I was trying to speed my pace a little, with a load of over 40 lbs, over the Geneva Spur without oxygen. I had one Sherpa with me. A week before, with oxygen to help, the thing had seemed a fairly Alpine climb. But now, at the stopping places every three steps, a regular conversation took place, the top half expressing itself scornfully about the panting body below. And there seemed nothing odd about it.

Carried one stage further, this state produces a feeling that there is *someone else there*. This too is not uncommon, in times of loneliness and exhaustion. Shackleton experienced

[2] *The Seven Pillars of Wisdom.*

it; particularly when, as climax to his miraculous journey from the crushed *Endurance*, he found himself crossing the uncharted mountains of South Georgia.

> I know that during that long and racking march of thirty-six hours over the unnamed mountains and glaciers of South Georgia it seemed to me often that we were four, not three. I said nothing to my companions on the point, but afterwards Worsley said to me, 'Boss, I had a curious feeling on the march that there was another person with us'. Crean confessed to the same idea.[3]

Frank Smythe experienced it too, on Everest alone at 28,100 feet.

> All the time that I was climbing alone I had the strong feeling that I was accompanied by a second person. This feeling was so strong that it completely eliminated all loneliness that I might otherwise have felt. It even seemed that I was tied to my 'companion' by a rope and that if I slipped 'he' would hold me. I remember constantly glancing back over my shoulder, and once, when after reaching my highest point I stopped to try and eat some mint cake, I carefully divided it and turned round with one half in my hand. It was almost a shock to find no one to whom to give it. It seemed to me that this 'presence' was a strong, helpful and friendly one.[4]

Smythe's other illusion, that of seeing kite-balloons floating over Tibet, has been shared by no one that I know of. But the feeling of 'another person' was experienced by Buhl in rather similar circumstances, near the top of Nanga Parbat.

In the last stage the feeling becomes so strong that the 'other person' actually helps. Slocum on his lone voyage had his boat steered for him one night by a mysterious pilot. Ann Davison, on her 1953 voyage, arrived at Gibraltar exhausted after nights of watching. Two people came aboard and said: 'You kip down. We'll keep watch.' She obediently went below and next morning, coming out, said a sleepy 'Thank you'. No one was there to answer.[5]

[3] *South.*　　　　[4] *Everest 1933.*　　　　[5] *My Ship is so Small.*

Many exhausted and bewildered persons have had experiences of intervention, of this and other sorts. My brother, sunk by shell fire during the war, told me that after six days in an open boat he and his companions were convinced that the Spanish ship which picked them up had appeared in direct answer to their prayers. Gladys Aylward was equally convinced that the power which directed her along the path that avoided the Japanese was one quite outside herself. And among all the instances I cannot omit one which, if it reads the most oddly, is certainly as striking as any on record. About its veracity each may form his own opinion.

Fred Rebell was a man of little education in the conventional sense, but a vigorous reader and, in 1931, a strong sceptic. After his failure to commit suicide at Sydney, he had defied the American consul's refusal to give him an immigration permit. The boat in which he set out to cross 9,000 miles of Pacific was an open 18-footer, and the instruments were home-made. Rebell got into not unnatural difficulties, at first owing to heavy clouds which hid the sun and thus obstructed navigation. Prayer seemed the only solution, so he tried it out and prayed. The sun obediently came out. Some time later, when in doubt about some apparently unmarked Fijian Islands, he heard 'a kindly but authoritative male voice say distinctly in English close to my ear, "Trust your instruments" . . .' He trusted them and all was well, as it was after a second prayer, that he should 'see the peaks of Fiji by sunrise tomorrow'.

The thing was becoming too easy. Once more he tried it, 'in danger of my life', on the notoriously rough winter seas between Honolulu and Los Angeles. 'In the name of Jesus Christ please moderate this gale before sunset'—and the gale moderated. Then he posed the Deity a more testing case, one in which he was not in real danger, only uncomfortable.

This case was different from the other two. There was no pressing need: I was not in mortal danger. In fact it looked as if I was becoming a regular cadger with the Almighty—and deserved to be treated as a cadger. But had not Christ said, '*Whatsoever* you ask of the Father . . . you shall have it'? I just wanted to test that statement.

Besides, why *should* I be battling with gales, when for all the harm it could do anybody else I might as well have fair sailing weather?

So once more I prayed in Christ's name for a moderating of the gale, and for fair sailing weather. Let me have it by noon, I asked: and then I settled down contentedly expecting it to happen.

That afternoon the gale went down . . .[6]

Joshua Slocum waxes sarcastic about people who pray for the right winds and then get them. He observes that it usually happens in areas where the winds are changing round every hour or so, not among the constant trades. Another apparently inexplicable experience which befell Rebell, that of dreaming that he was running against a rock and then waking to find one just in front of him, seems to stem from an instinct which many sailors have. It is quite possible, as he himself suggests, that human beings, like birds in their migrations, have a 'seventh sense' which comes into play, strangely but naturally, in cases of this sort. Even so hard-bitten a traveller as Tilman came on deck at two in the morning, 'perhaps by chance, perhaps because of that instinct which is supposed to rouse the sleeping mariner when his ship is in danger, but probably because Mike had called me to report the Amelia light abeam. Abeam with a vengeance. The thing was virtually above us.'[7] You can take whichever explanation you please.

The habit of finding prayers satisfactorily answered, however, did not lead Rebell straight to spiritual peace as one might have expected. Even after God had presented him with a motor car within his means (in America) almost before being asked, he was still seeking. At last he found a measure

[6] *Escape to the Sea.*   [7] '*Mischief*' *in Patagonia.*

of happiness, and certainly religious conviction, among the 'Holy Rollers' of California. But he was then deported back to Latvia, and of the end I know nothing.

I think myself that Rebell was as sincere as Gladys Aylward, to the point of reading, in all sincerity, more into his experiences than there may have been. Coincidence and exhaustion are other unexplored factors in human affairs. At the same time I do not go quite so far as the practical-minded Slocum; it is very possible to apply here the suggestion originated (so far as I know) by William James. There is a great common personality submerged below and far more powerful than our conscious individual personalities. By drawing upon this, even unwittingly, people can do things which to their conscious selves and to others seem quite impossible. Of this process one can have some conception without necessarily having recourse to any 'supernatural' at all. The laws which govern it may in time be defined, just as those which govern telepathy, for instance, are beginning to be clearer. How that greater personality of ours, and not only of the saints among us, seems able to influence even inanimate objects, must take a lot of explaining. But it looks as if men of certain temperaments, in certain moods and at certain stressful junctures of their lives, may stand in a certain relation to Nature which allows very odd things to be possible.

❧ ❧ ❧

Not many go to sea or into the wilderness *in order to* get into those conditions of exhaustion or loneliness which induce the sense of duality. But many, without admitting Wilson's 'purpose', have an undefined or half-defined feeling that they are going forth to 'get in touch' with Nature and so with the biggest things beyond. 'For the hills speak to us of what is behind them, and beyond the grasp of our mind,' as Charles Evans has it, and so do the seas and plains, the jungles and deserts. Slocum put the feeling, in religious context, when he was having a good spell of sailing across the Pacific: 'I was *en rapport* now with my surroundings, and was carried on a vast stream where I felt the buoyancy of His hand who made the worlds'.[8] And Shipton put it, on a level more readily appreciable, when discussing why people mountaineer.

> Above all, in my view, the attraction lies in the memory of those rare moments of intellectual ecstasy which occur perhaps on a mountain summit, perhaps on a glacier at dawn or in a lonely moonlit bivouac, and which appear to be the result of a happy coincidence in the rhythm of mind and scene. These moments are not, of course, peculiar to mountaineering; they may be realised in deserts, on the sea and elsewhere. Such exaltation of feeling is achieved more often, I imagine, and in more normal circumstances by the mind of the creative artist, but for ordinary folk it would seem that it is more readily found in close contact with nature.[9]

That is a sensation which most have had, at some time or another, in motion or at rest, and which when it comes is very precious.

One reason for this apparent harmony with nature, which is common to all forms of travel except, I think, the mechanical, lies in the sense of returning to the primitive. Everyone knows the delight of tearing off a best suit and digging fingers into the good earth, of feeling wind through the hair or looking, with eyes that seem new but on second thoughts are those of our forefathers, into moonrise from a small boat. To illustrate this urge or feeling, I offer first three short quotations from three very different people, then a comment.

Charles Darwin wrote, after his voyage round the world on the *Beagle*:

It has been said that the love of the chase is an inherent delight in man—a relic of an instinctive passion. If so, I am

---

[8] *Sailing alone around the World.*   [9] *Upon that Mountain.*

sure the pleasure of living in the open air, with the sky for a roof, and the ground for a table, is part of the same feeling: it is the savage returning to his wild and native habits.[10]

The later Darwin, if anyone, had a feel for this 'instinctive passion'. Next comes Hilaire Belloc, speaking of the amateur sailor:

In venturing to sail upon strange coasts we are seeking those first experiences and trying to feel as felt the earlier men in a happier time, to see the world as they saw it.

And now Freya Stark, travelling with bedouin through the South Arabian deserts.

The routine of our journey had begun, unexpected in its small incidents, immutable in its unchanging lines: this interplay of accident and law, the surprises of every day worked into a constant pattern by physical necessities, compelling people along the same paths for one century after the other—this surely is the charm of travel in the open.[11]

The impulse to return to the primitive confessed by these three is, to my mind, an important force in the lives of men. In a fascinating book, *Experiment in Depth*, P. W. Martin argues that only by looking *inward*, rather than outward at the contemporary scene, men are likely to solve the contemporary world's problems. Burrowing into themselves, trying to bring to their aid some of that massive subconscious which is at the root of their actions,—all this involves going back also to the early man and trying to feel, as well as to understand, his myths and mysteries. The reader will remember William James's night on Mt Marcey and the 'boulder of impression' from earlier times with which it left him. Commenting on this Martin says, in a passage impossible to cut:

The Mt Marcey method brings to a focus some three or four pre-disposing factors. The unusual effort called for lowers the

[10] *The Voyages of Adventure and Beagle, III.*
[11] *The Southern Gates of Arabia.*

threshold between consciousness and the unconscious, there is an *abaissement du niveau mental.* For a while we step out of the artificiality of urban existence and come a degree nearer to the natural man, the state of being where wind and weather, heat and cold, hunger and thirst, earth and sky are closer to us. At the same time, we are less distracted by irrelevancies. Normally our attention is diverted, our libido dispersed, by the thousand-and-one things about us. Let these thousand-and-one things be withdrawn and the inner world has a chance of coming into its own. Especially is this so when, in some fashion, 'the dark backward and abysm of time' is visibly and invisibly around us: as on a mountain, in the woods, at night. But the essence of the Mt Marcey method is that it takes a man out of the intellectual or sentimental miasma in which most of our seeking is other-wise done. It is a first earnest of the direct approach to the other side of consciousness. It is a tentative, partial, tacit recognition that the world invisible may be real.[12]

If that is so, as I believe it is, then those who enjoy returning to the primitive have a start along the road to 'depth'; and correspondingly, the desire to get back, to live as early man lived, becomes explicable in scientific terms. This means not at all that we necessarily make use of the start. Most will go on enjoying the simple sensations, the things that have always given pleasure to men, because—well, just because they enjoy them. And why not? Yet it is possible that if we make the effort to understand *why* we have the urge, if we experiment on the lines suggested by James, then we have a chance of living out our part more fully when we come back; and we may be led on along some of the other intriguing lines that Martin's book suggests.

❦ ❦   ❦ ❦   ❦ ❦

All the impulses so far have been in some way connected with the self of the person who has them. Yet there is, I believe, another attraction that has nothing at all to do with

[12] *Experiment in Depth.*

our own 'rhythm'. I mean the feeling that one occasionally has, and certainly seeks, of reverence or awe for majesty quite outside and beyond oneself. It was the feeling which prompted the Humpback of Breuil, after climbing the Matterhorn, to kneel on the ground and thank God for having created such a marvellous universe.

I said advisedly that this feeling had nothing directly to do with our own activity or even consciousness. Some think that activity even hinders receptivity (Buddhists for instance). Ruskin's chief objection to mountaineers was that they would always be *doing* things, not letting beauty come to them. 'To recover our awe for hills, to return to the monkish outlook, we must first of all rid ourselves of the habit of regarding mountains chiefly as places for gymnastic exercise.' There follows the famous diatribe against the enthusiasts for 'soaped poles'. For these poles, however, he substituted a complicated aesthetic which can require as much mental agility as mountaineering requires physical.

The state of awe is difficult to come upon. On the one hand, as seemed from Chapter 2, it is *through* hardship and exertion that we get our 'new vision of the world'. On the other, it now looks as if these allies can be a positive hindrance. The kind of awe that I mean, the awe in which self is for the time lost and consciousness absorbed in a greater consciousness normally incomprehensible to it, this awe would come probably to a Tibetan anchorite finding Nirvana after years of fasting in a rocky cave. But the western mind, as Leslie Stephen justly observes, is less apt for such abstractions. 'Thoughts of dinner begin to obtrude.' With us therefore the exertion often (but far from always) does what the fasting could do: through it we reach the physical state needed for the spiritual experience. The moments are fleeting and tenuous; but the memory of them remains all the more wonderful for that.

The temporary quality of our awe is partly due, no doubt, to the sad fact that we do not live on the wide uplands of Tibet, where mystery and mysticism are not only possible but natural. In our more crowded world we need to move, or stand, outside, and that cannot normally be done for long stretches at a time. Therefore we must look for other ways, and there are many, of reaching the same central experience. Some find it in creative activity, some in the doctrinal religion of their choice, some in brief moments spent upon the lonely places of the earth, to which they escape.

These last, with whom we are concerned, may be religious in the conventional sense, they may not. Shackleton, for instance, was a deeply religious man: when he had to abandon his crushed ship, the 'luxury' that he took with him was a fly-leaf of the Bible and a page of the Book of Job. Reaching safety he wrote reflectively that he had at last 'seen God in his splendours'. And in the same conventional group we may place the many clergymen among the Victorians who became mountaineers, though in their case a curious paradox is observable. R. W. Clark watches them being 'supremely confident of their position on God's right hand, able to give the answers so easily that in many cases religion had become more a matter of good cross-indexing than a basic belief'. They were masters of their jobs with a slightly disappointing sense that the mystery had gone out of them. And so, 'after the physical circumstances of the age had persuaded them into mountains, they found on them some hint of this mystic and needed link between themselves and the unexplained and inexplicable'. In other words, they recovered their capacity for awe.

But of all the priestly explorers I have read (there is a whole bookful of them in a new Italian work, *La strade è questa*), Achille Ratti, later Pope Pius XI, demonstrates that sense of receptive reverence the best. Mountains are, I think, more conducive to it than any feature of earth's surface except the sea, but a night out at 15,000 feet in the Alps would for most be conducive to little beyond thoughts of hot breakfast. Two nights out even more so. Yet this is what Ratti experienced, on his new traverse of Monte Rosa from the southern side in 1889. Far from complaining, he wrote: 'Who would have slept in that pure air? . . . We felt ourselves to be in the presence of a novel and most inspiring revelation of the omnipotence and majesty of God. How could we even think of the fatigue we had endured, much less complain of it?' The second night he spent on the glacier not far from comfort; but there was still no complaint. And when he was again benighted, on the Matterhorn shortly afterwards (the pioneers made more of a habit of benightment than we do), he wrote of the 'indescribable beauty of the surroundings and the assured possibility of priceless experiences, which can only be enjoyed during a somewhat lengthy sojourn on the highest peaks, and then only at hours when one is least wont to be there'.[13] If a man can be forgetful of discomfort during these hours, he will not lose the sense of awe.

But it is far from necessary to be a Christian in order to enjoy the experience. As I have said, a Buddhist can get it without moving a muscle, and over long periods. In the words of the sage: 'Whoso looketh on Himachal (the Himalaya) his sin shall be cleansed from him.' Or it can be just plain physical, coming in through the pores, so to speak. The diver Robert Gruss, said: 'The moment the sea closes over me I feel some great thing is happening. I am filled with a kind of awe, without really knowing why.' Or it can be the result of a direct, mystical, non-Christian 'revelation', like that which came to Younghusband in the same year in which Achille Ratti was benighted on Monte Rosa. Younghusband has interested us already as a 'curious traveller'. 'When I started travelling, it was the outward aspect that interested me: now, it is the inner motive.' After the experience, which came to him at a camp in the Karakoram, he gave himself to work for the idea of world religion, which

[13] Both passages from *Scritti Alpinistici*, translated by J. E. C. Eaton as *Climbs on Alpine Peaks*.

to his mind expressed human awe in spiritual terms. In Tibet he had a spiritual adventure which confirmed him in his view and purpose. He wrote and lectured. In a curious way, reverence for Everest and the mountains as 'the natural cathedral of the world' led to reverence for the act of climbing Everest as symbolic of the flights of united faith. Even acclimatisation had its symbolic significance. Religion becomes unified, a spirit burning across the sects. And if the result seems to lose itself in the mystic wrappings which surround it, none will deny the awe with which he invested his belief. 'The world is a temple: the spirit is all, is everywhere.'

This conclusion, of course, can be equally arrived at by a professed atheist like Shelley; or a priest turned agnostic, like Leslie Stephen, can have the profound experience lying full length on a summit and trying to make of himself 'an animated top of the mountain'—to lose himself for a while *in* the mountain.[14] Stephen's case was a queer one; for the feeling of awe with which Matterhorn, Jungfrau or Wetterhorn filled him was so strong as to be quite worrying to one who had renounced Christian tenets. 'At Stonehenge we ask what human beings could have erected these strange grey monuments, and in the mountains we instinctively ask what force can have carved out the Matterhorn, and placed the Wetterhorn on its gigantic pedestal.' It seemed that he had found his cathedral, as had Younghusband, but no god to put inside and worship. Nor could he explain, and I like him the better for that, just *why* sunset on Mont Blanc should move him to an awe which by its nature is indescribable.

By what strange threads of association the reds and blues of a gorgeous sunset, the fantastic shapes of clouds and shadows at that dizzy height, should stir you like mysterious music, or, indeed, why music itself should have such power, I leave to philosophers to explain. This only I know, that even the

[14] Like Mary Kingsley, who before an African scene seemed to lose all sense of human individuality, all memory of human life, with its grief and worry and doubt, and become part of the atmosphere.

memory of that summer evening on the top of Mont Blanc has power to plunge me into strange reveries not to be analysed by any capacity, and still less capable of expression by the help of a few black remarks on white paper.[15]

Not being a philosopher, and having no instrument but black marks on white paper, I must leave it at that; or rather leave it to the poets, past or yet unborn, to express.

> The wilderness has a mysterious tongue
> Which teaches awful doubt, or faith so mild,
> So solemn, so serene, that man may be,
> But for such faith, with nature reconciled.[16]

When all is said, the mystery behind remains a mystery. It remains something leagues outside ourselves, towards which, if you like to think of it that way, these greater things of sea and hills and deserts are a sort of half-way house, 'moods of larger rhythm and line, moving between the eternal mode and mine'.[17] The feeling of humility before such majesty is a salutary one, and the most apt, of all that I know, to release us for a while from the prison of our little selves.

[15] *The Playground of Europe.*   [16] From *Mont Blanc,* by P. B. Shelley.
[17] G. Winthrop Young.

❧ ❧ ❧ ❧ ❧ ❧

An end to it all?

And far away the future grew
faint as the very distant past,
for rank on rank the mountains rose
toward the horizon, where at last
the same untroubled flood of blue
covered those shining domes of snow.

WILLIAM BELL

Dr Johnson is said to have had a weakness for trailing his stick along the railings as he walked. If he chanced to miss one, he would go back to make quite sure of hitting it. I have the feeling, as I look back over this book, that I have been running to and fro tapping railings for quite a time; and that as each is tapped, behold another springs mysteriously into its place, just waiting for the stick.

It all comes, you may justly observe, from having railings at all. If I had not so artificially divided the categories, I would now have no worry about missing one out. As it is, there are hundreds. What of curiosity, for instance? Have I plumbed its real depths, its deepest spring from which, in a sense, all the other motives flow? We would have got on somehow, I suppose, without it, on the lines of the immortal eaters of Charles Lamb's roast pig. But we would not have got very far. From our survey it looks as if an adventurous sense of possibilities assisted his other faculties in pushing man through the centuries. Normally it was harnessed to these, speeding the process of 'civilisation'. Sometimes, even then, it broke loose. Did not Ulysses symbolise our curiosity by voyaging to Teneriffe (or Purgatory, as you will) just to see what was there? More usually, however, it remained subordinate to a desire to bypass burnt fingers and acquire more pigs; also to the spread of gospels and the discovery of good trade routes.

Historically, if our survey can be said to have verged on the historical, it was in the last century that adventure—or curiosity in the bigger sense—began seriously to shake its wings free of the commonsense shackles. We have seen Park and Ross, Livingstone and Burton, setting out on official missions; but we have seen also the truth becoming plainer, that it was the imp of curiosity, a being quite independent of missions, which stimulated them. Towards the end of the century we have found Doughty and Nansen, Younghusband and Mary Kingsley, casting aside the cloak of missions and going because the thing was 'there', because they were curious to try it, even against official frownings. The wings were spreading.

In our sense of adventure they have spread still further during the present century; further, perhaps, than the pioneers of the eighteen-hundreds would have liked. Amundsen's South Polar journey might have shocked them; since the conception of going out with just one object, that of treading untrodden ground, was original in a way in which even Scott's scientific programme was not. Through many subsequent feats it was a direct forerunner of, say, the ascent of Everest. In that exploit the resources of science were mustered to produce a feat so useless in itself that it must have made Chesterton chuckle in his grave. Here was a 'modern' adventure, and there are many like it; adventure for its own sake, and no other.

That might be the last word, but for science. She is not so easily defeated. Indeed she has started to swing the pendulum back in so big a way that not only does she gather the findings of the playboys to herself (oxygen observations on Everest, for instance), but she creates her own adventures, in which none but her own children can share. Where they will lead, none can say. But it will be a long way from where we started.

I have been afraid to follow the future where thoughts would lead me. I have only hinted at general directions, to the moon and elsewhere. As for this earth, it is sobering to reflect that the adventure of today becomes the commonplace of tomorrow. William Beebe (in *Half Mile Down*) describes the underwater game of the future, when boys will be playing among wrecks three fathoms down, and undersea artists complaining that clouded skies spoil their effects. 'Hosts and hostesses will be summoning their house-parties to . . . dive and inspect with them at leisure the new coral plantings and beds which a seascape gardener has lately arranged.' And Joseph Conrad ponders on the ease of travel by liner. 'A marvellous achievement is not necessarily interesting. It may render life more tame than perhaps it should be. I do not mean that any marvel of applied science can tame the wild spirit that lurks in all men, and of which the proofs are not far to seek. It only makes the conditions of our pilgrimage less exciting.' [1] Now we fly over the North Pole; soon we shall drive over it. But already we have lost the thrill that was Peary's; already we look feverishly round for fresh worlds. Perhaps the future is best dreamed of only in its most general outlines.

But to return to the railings: what have I said of love? That came in, perhaps, among the whims of the travellers. But what of *real* love, a passion that a man can develop for a mountain as strongly as for a human being, so strongly that men have been known to go through a marriage ceremony with the peak of their choice? The ecstasy of loving, and the pleasure of it? ' "I love you," I whispered into the ear of the ocean. "Ever since I've known you I've loved you. I must

[1] In *Last Essays*; 'Ocean Travel'.

see all your marvels, know all your beauty." And the ocean listened, and snuggled still closer to me.' A diver wrote that[1], and many have felt it; but I allowed their feeling a bare page or two, pressing on to the next in line. And the sheer working off of spleen as a motive? I quoted *Moby Dick*; but why did its hero go to sea at all? 'Whenever I find myself growing grim about the mouth; whenever it is a damp, drizzly November in my soul . . . then I account it high time to get to sea as soon as I can.' I left that out; but strange remedies can be chosen just to work the liver into a better condition.

An omission that I do not regret is the poetic impulse. If there is poetry in adventure, says the accusing voice, then surely the poets should occupy a far larger place when adventure is written about? I think not, despite those ages, like the Athenian and Elizabethan, when the active and the contemplative fused for a few happy generations together.

If Wordsworth had ventured more often above the 2,000-foot line, or if he had taken seriously to climbing rocks, I cannot think that his poetry would have been better. Keats just managed to get up Skiddaw and Ben Nevis, with 'much fag', but he wrote:

> Crag jutting forth to crag, and rocks that seemed
> Ever as if just rising from a sleep—

lines which every rock climber will envy, but none can emulate. As for Byron, the most venturesome physically of that period, he was some way from being its finest poet. And Shelley, the most receptive among the Romantics of natural moods, died because he could not bring a small boat through a storm.

No, the two do not mix, at any rate on the highest levels. Petrarch might be an exception; after all he made the ascent of Mont Ventoux for the delight of it, and will always be remembered for that. And there was Goethe, an exception to this as to most rules. Yes, and sometimes one is lucky, with

[1] Hans Hass, *Diving to Adventure*.

a Valéry or Bell (if he had only lived longer), or Masefield at his best and Winthrop Young, when the poet comes to the surface, as it were, in the active man. In general, however, it must be said the doers of deeds are best hymned by others than themselves.

I must clearly stop, or there will be no end to the procession. The other railings must stand there still, for ever untapped by me. 'Nothing is more strange than man', Sophocles said, and he will never be trapped, even one part of him, in a few casual marks on 'white paper'. Language fails; and even that splendid word ποικιλὸς, 'many-coloured', which was at Sophocles' command, is denied to me. When I think with what a bludgeoning brush I have taken those colours and tried to shatter the infinite rainbow into a dozen or so neat hues—I feel like a schoolboy found doing Certificate Mathematics with no knowledge of fractions.

The tints are many, perhaps more even than the wise Greek realised, but the force that joins them all, as I peer across my pages, seems now almost at my finger tips, tantalisingly simple. After all this ink, all this effort, there it is—if only I could define it. The nearest that I can get is the word 'expansion', and miserably inadequate it is. In pride of our humanity, and because we are made that way (I am not now asking why) we go for the new and so add, or endeavour to add, cubits to our stature. It is an old story, this proud instinct that brought man above the other competitors; this urge to expand into the world along the paths of power and pleasure and curiosity. It is not always pleasant, but it is very human. Mankind has never been modest.

ﻌ ﻌ   ﻌ ﻌ   ﻌ ﻌ

I must have been thinking about this instinct of expansion, or wondering whether after all I ought not to say more about the future, when I went to sleep.

I dreamed that I saw a man, very small, rather like the

225

frog in La Fontaine's fable, and above him there towered a mountain. This man, again like the frog, seemed determined to equal or overpass that soaring height. He swelled himself out as hard as he could go, and at first seemed successful. To my amazement he grew, until he had topped easily the trees and rocks at the mountain's foot. But at last the inevitable happened, and he burst.

The sequel was unexpected. Inside that man, as it seemed, was another man, unless he were the soul of the first. He was larger than the original; as if that experience of growing remained with him and allowed him to keep something of his added stature. Moreover his eyes were curiously bright, and I thought that from over those first little ridges and shrubs he must have been able to see new country, which it was a delight to remember even now. For the moment, however, he seemed more concerned with digging. In his hand was a spade, and stepping quite naturally from the fragments around he began to work with it. *Il faut cultiver son jardin*, his industrious air seemed to say, for he looked as if he had quite given up the idea of expanding again. With those bright eyes wonderfully full of love he watched the growing pile of potatoes, onions, leeks, cabbages and the rest—like a gardening advertisement—which soon surrounded him. Then he began to count them. Meanwhile the displaced earth grew in a heap that towered above, like a mountain.

At last he looked at the heap, he could hardly help looking since it had grown so big, and put down his spade. He started once more to throw out his chest, and 'I *must* beat it', I heard him say.

What happened next I do not know, for I woke up, and it was high time to finish this book. But I knew somehow that, after the next explosion, my man would be just that much bigger again. And again.

Bibliography

❦ ❦ ❦ ❧ ❧ ❧

I give here a list of books which have been helpful to me. It is far from complete, and nobody will be more conscious of that fact than I. I have not even included every single book referred to in the text. No list could be complete, and my aim has been to give information about books which may have struck a chord of interest, as well as to indicate those to which I personally have been specially indebted. Many of them are directly responsible for my venturing on my own book at all.

It will be seen that these are largely the books of the adventurers themselves, only occasionally of the biographers. This does not mean that I am not indebted to the latter (as I am to general books on exploration), but that I have only given their names when the new light they threw is of direct concern to my present purpose.

In the case of some nineteenth-century books I have not given the publisher; often his name has disappeared or changed, and a publishing history is beyond my scope and powers.

I would like to record the great debt I owe to those publishers and authors in this list who have been asked, and have given, permission to quote. In many cases they have gone to considerable trouble to find out about and help me over copyright. Without them the book could not have appeared, and I am very grateful.

In addition to these I must thank the following for special permissions: The Society of Authors and Dr John Masefield, o.m., for the lines from *Collected Poems*; Chatto and Windus (Publishers) for poems by C. Day Lewis; Messrs Christy and Moore for *Everest 1933* and *The Fight of the*

Bibliography

Firecrest; Messrs Curtis Brown for *K2 The Savage Mountain*; Mlle C. Eliane-Engel for an article in the *Alpine Journal*; Messrs Pearn, Pollinger and Higham for *Forbidden Journey*; Neville Spearman (Publishers), for *Alone*; Messrs A. P. Watt for *Gino Watkins* and *Forbidden Jungle*; the Trustees of the Lawrence Estate for *The Seven Pillars of Wisdom*; Viscountess Malden for *The Spirit of the Hills*; Routledge and Kegan Paul for *La Société Féodale*, by M. Bloch.

Where a book has been translated, details of the English edition are given.

❧ ❧   ❧ ❧   ❧ ❧

AMUNDSEN, R. *The South Pole*. John Murray, 1912.

BATES, DAISY. *The Passing of the Aborigines*. John Murray, 1938.

BATES, H. W. *The Naturalist on the River Amazons*. John Murray, 1892.

BAUER, P. *Himalayan Quest*. Nicholson and Watson, 1938.

DE BEER, G. *Escape to Switzerland*. Penguin, 1945.

BELL, G. *The Letters of Gertrude Bell*. Benn, 1927.

BELL, WILLIAM. *Mountains beneath the Horizon*. Faber and Faber, 1950.

BENUZZI, FELICE. *No Picnic on Mount Kenya*. Kimber, 1952.

BERGE, VICTOR. *Danger is my Life*. Hutchinson, 1954.

BERTRAM, C. *Arctic and Antarctic*. Heffer, 1939.

BOMBARD, A. *The Bombard Story*. Deutsch, 1953.

BUHL, H. *Nanga Parbat Pilgrimage*. Hodder and Stoughton, 1956.

BURTON, RICHARD. *Pilgrimage to Al-Madinah and Meccah*, 1855.

BYRD, RICHARD. *Skyward*. Putnam, 1928. *Alone*. Putnam, 1938.

CALDWELL, JOHN. *Desperate Voyage*. Gollancz, 1950.

CASTERET, N. *The Descent of Pierre Saint-Martin*. Dent, 1955.

CAVE RESEARCH GROUP. *British Caving*. Routledge and Kegan Paul, 1953.

CHAPMAN, F. S. *Watkins' Last Expedition*. Chatto and Windus, 1934. (Also other books, particularly *Living Dangerously*.)

CHERRY-GARRARD, A. *The Worst Journey in the World*. Constable, 1922.

CHEVALIER, P. *Subterranean Climbers*. Faber and Faber, 1951.

CLARK, R. W. 'Half of their lives', *Cornhill*, Summer 1952. (Also *The Victorian Mountaineers*.)

CLARKE, A. C. *The Exploration of Space*. Temple Press, 1951.

CLOUSTON, A. E. *The Dangerous Skies*. Cassell, 1954.

CONRAD, JOSEPH. *Youth*. (And the other stories.) Blackwood, 1902. *Last Essays*, Dent, Collected edition, 1955.

COUPLAND, R. *Livingstone's Last Journey*. Collins, 1954.

COUSTEAU, J. Y. *The Silent World*. Hamish Hamilton, 1953.

DARWIN, CHARLES. *The Voyages of Adventure and Beagle*. Vol. III, 1839.

DAVISON, ANN. *Last Voyage*. Peter Davies, 1951. *My Ship is so Small*. Peter Davies, 1956.

DIOLÉ, PHILIPPE. *The Undersea Adventure*. Sidgwick and Jackson, 1953. *4,000 Years under the Sea*. Sidgwick and Jackson, 1954.

DOUGHTY, C. M. *Travels in Arabia Deserta*. Cambridge University Press, 1888. (Abridged as *Wanderings in Arabia*. Duckworth, 1908.)

DUGUID, J. *Green Hell*. Jonathan Cape, 1931.

DUKE, N. *Test Pilot*. Wingate, 1953.

ELLSWORTH, LINCOLN. *Beyond Horizons*. Heinemann, 1938.

FAIRLEY, BARKER. *Charles M. Doughty*. Jonathan Cape, 1927.

FAWCETT, P. H. and B. *Exploration Fawcett*. Hutchinson, 1953.

Bibliography

FLEMING, A. LANG. *Archibald the Arctic*. Hodder and Stoughton, 1957.

FLEMING, P. *Brazilian Adventure*. Jonathan Cape, 1933. *One's Company*. Jonathan Cape, 1934. *News from Tartary*. Jonathan Cape, 1936.

FRASER, JOHN FOSTER. *Round the World on a Wheel*. 1899.

GALTON, FRANCIS. *The Art of Travel*. John Murray, 1854.

GARNETT, DAVID. *A Rabbit in the Air*. Chatto and Windus, 1932.

GERBAULT, A. *The Fight of the Firecrest*. Hodder and Stoughton, 1926. *In Quest of the Sun*. Hodder and Stoughton, 1929.

GIBBS-SMITH, C. H. *A History of Flying*. Batsford, 1953.

HARRER, H. *Seven Years in Tibet*. Hart-Davis, 1953.

HARRISON, M. *Airborne at Kittyhawk*. Cassell, 1953.

HASLIP, JOAN. *Lady Hester Stanhope*. Cobden-Sanderson, 1934.

HASS, HANS. *Diving to Adventure*. Jarrold, 1952. *Under the Red Sea*. Jarrold, 1952.

HEDIN, SVEN. *Through Asia*. Methuen, 1898.

HEYERDAHL, THOR. *The Kon-Tiki Expedition*. Allen and Unwin, 1950.

HILLARY, EDMUND. *High Adventure*. Hodder and Stoughton, 1955.

HILLARY, RICHARD. *The Last Enemy*. Macmillan and Co., 1942.

HOBBS, W. H. *Robert Peary*. Macmillan Co. New York, 1936.

HORSLEY, TERENCE. *Soaring Flight*. Eyre and Spottiswoode, 1944.

HOUSTON, C. AND BATES, R. *K2 The Savage Mountain*. Collins, 1954.

HOWARD, C. *Mary Kingsley*. Hutchinson, 1957.

HUNT, JOHN. *The Ascent of Everest*. Hodder and Stoughton, 1953.

IRVING, R. L. G. *The Romance of Mountaineering*. Dent, 1935.

KELLY, F. C. *The Wright Brothers*. Harrap, 1944.

KINGSLEY, MARY. *Travels in West Africa*. 1897.

KNIGHT, E. F. *The Cruise of the Falcon*. Sampson Low, 1884.

LAWRENCE, T. E. *The Seven Pillars of Wisdom*. Jonathan Cape, 1935.

LEONARD, J. N. *Flight into Space*. Sidgwick and Jackson, 1953.

LEWIS, C. DAY. *Collected Poems*. Hogarth Press, 1948.

LINDBERGH, C. A. *The Spirit of St Louis*. John Murray, 1953.

LINDSAY, MARTIN. *Three got Through*. Falcon Press, 1946.

LITHGOW, M. *Mach One*. Wingate, 1954.

LIVINGSTONE, DAVID. *Letters*. Several editions.

LUNN, ARNOLD. *A Century of Mountaineering*. Allen and Unwin, 1957.

MAILLART, ELLA. *Turkestan Solo*. Putnam, 1934. *Forbidden Journey*. Heinemann, 1937.

MARTIN, P. W. *Experiment in Depth*. Routledge and Kegan Paul, 1955.

MASEFIELD, JOHN. *Collected Poems*. Heinemann, 1923.

MEADE, C. F. *Approach to the Hills*. John Murray, 1940.

MIDDLETON, D. *Baker of the Nile*. Falcon Press, 1949. 'A Lady's Life in the Rocky Mountains', *Cornhill*, Winter 1952/3.

MIGOT, A. *Tibetan Marches*. Hart-Davis, 1955. *The Lonely South*. Hart-Davis, 1956.

MILL, H. R. *Sir Ernest Shackleton*. Heinemann, 1923.

NANSEN, F. *Farthest North*. Constable, 1897.

NORTON, E. F. *The Fight for Everest 1924*. Arnold, 1927.

OMMANNEY, F. D. *South Latitude*. Longmans, Green, 1938.

PALLIS, MARCO. *Peaks and Lamas*. Cassell, 1939.

PARK, MUNGO. *Travels*. Everyman Edition, 1940.

PEARY, R. E. *The North Pole*. Frederick A. Stokes, New York, 1910.

Bibliography

PICCARD, A. *In Balloon and Bathyscaphe*. Cassell, 1956.

PILLEY, D. *Climbing Days*. Bell, 1935.

PYE, D. *George Leigh Mallory*. Oxford University Press, 1927.

REBELL, F. *Escape to the Sea*. John Murray, 1939.

RÉBUFFAT, G. *Starlight and Storm*. Dent, 1956.

ROSS, JAMES. *Voyage of discovery and research in the Southern and Antarctic regions, 1839–43*. 1847.

RUTTLEDGE, H. *Everest 1933*. Hodder and Stoughton, 1934.

SAINT-EXUPÉRY, A. DE. *Night Flight*. Appleton, 1935. *Wind, Sand and Stars*. Heinemann, 1939.

SALMON, ROSS. *Forbidden Jungle*. Hodder and Stoughton, 1957.

SCHWEITZER, A. *On the Edge of the Primeval Forest*. A. and C. Black, 1922.

SCOTT, J. M. *Gino Watkins*. Hodder and Stoughton, 1935. *Portrait of an Ice-Cap*. Chatto and Windus, 1953.

SCOTT, R. F. *The Voyage of the Discovery*. Smith, Elder, 1905. *Scott's Last Expedition*. Smith, Elder, 1912.

SEAVER, G. *Edward Wilson of the Antarctic*. John Murray, 1933.

SHACKLETON, E. H. *The Heart of the Antarctic*. Heinemann, 1909. *South*. Heinemann, 1919.

SHELLEY, P. B. *Mont Blanc* (1816) and other poems.

SHIPTON, E. E. *Upon that Mountain*. Hodder and Stoughton, 1943. And *Narda Devi*, etc.

SIMMONS, J. *Livingstone and Africa*. English Universities Press, 1955.

SIMPSON, C. J. W. *North Ice*. Hodder and Stoughton, 1957.

SLOCUM, J. *Sailing alone around the World*. Sampson Low, 1900.

SMYTHE, F. S. *Climbs and Ski Runs*. Blackwood, 1929. *The Spirit of the Hills*. Hodder and Stoughton, 1935.

STANLEY, H. M. *How I found Livingstone*. Sampson Low, 1872. *Through the Dark Continent*. Sampson Low, 1878.

STARK, FREYA. *The Southern Gates of Arabia*. John Murray, 1936. (Also the other books, particularly *Traveller's Prelude* and *The Valley of the Assassins*.)

STEPHEN, LESLIE. *The Playground of Europe*. 1871.

SYMONS, A. J. A. *H. M. Stanley*. Duckworth, 1933.

TILMAN, H. W. *Snow on the Equator*. Bell, 1937. *Everest 1938*. Cambridge University Press, 1948. *Two Mountains and a River*. Cambridge University Press, 1949. *Nepal Himalaya*. Cambridge University Press, 1952. *'Mischief' in Patagonia*. Cambridge University Press, 1957.

VILLIERS, A. *The Cruise of the Conrad*. Hodder and Stoughton, 1937. *The Set of the Sails*. Hodder and Stoughton, 1949. *The Cutty Sark*. Hodder and Stoughton, 1953.

VOSS, J. C. *The Venturesome Voyages of Captain Voss*. Hopkinson, 1913. (Now The Bodley Head.)

WHALLEY, G. 'In the Land of Feast and Famine,' *Cornhill*, Spring 1957.

WHYMPER, E. *Scrambles amongst the Alps*. 1871.

YOUNG. G. WINTHROP. *Mountain Craft*. Methuen, 1920. *On High Hills*. Methuen, 1927. *Collected Poems*. Methuen, 1936.

YOUNGHUSBAND, F. *The Heart of a Continent*. John Murray, 1896. *The Epic of Mount Everest*. Arnold, 1926.

Index

❧ ❧ ❧ ❧ ❧ ❧

The letter 'q' refers to extracts quoted in the text

Index

Index

Index